ROBERTSON'S PRACTICAL

THAI DICTIONARY

Robertson's
PRACTICAL
ENGLISH-THAI
DICTIONARY

compiled by

Richard G. Robertson, B.S., M.S.

ASIA BOOKS

This edition is published and distributed by
ASIA BOOKS CO., LTD.
5 Sukhumvit Road, Soi 61
P. O. Box 40
Bangkok 10110, Thailand
Tel: (662) 714-0740-2, ext. 259, 225
Fax: (662) 381-1621, 391-2277

by arrangement with Charles E. Tuttle Co., Inc.

International Standard Book No. 974-8236-38-2

Printed in Singapore

CONTENTS

INTRODUCTION

This English-Thai dictionary is written for Americans and other English-speaking people in Thailand wanting a handy quick-reference guide to speaking and pronouncing many useful Thai words. Nearly 2,500 English entries, consisting of the most common and practical words needed to make simple conversations with Thai people concerning most any subject, are translated into approximately 5,000 Thai words and phrases that are written in hopefully clear and easily pronounced phonetics. Tones, which are very important when speaking Thai, are also indicated in the phonetics.

The phonetic system used in this dictionary is a compromise between precision and practicality. The system is precise in that it distinctly represents each of the different consonant and vowel sounds of the Thai language. Yet the phonetic spellings are kept as simple as possible with a minimum loss of accuracy. The primary intent behind the choosing of this phonetic system is that the pronunciation which seems most natural to an English reader should give the correct Thai sound. Some Thai sounds can be represented exactly, especially those sounds already familiar in English. However, some Thai sounds are unknown in English, and their pronunciation will require practice. It must be remembered that this dictionary is intended to be only a guide to the pronunciation of Thai words. To be sure, one must repeatedly hear how Thai people pronounce each word.

Those who wish to study more about the Thai language will benefit from learning to read Thai. In a few weeks under guidance, one can learn to read and pronounce all the Thai letters and syllables and thereby begin using larger English-Thai and Thai-English dictionaries. Also, knowledge of the Thai letters and vowel sounds will help to explain exactly how Thai words should be pronounced, and one then no longer needs to rely on a phonetic system. Tone rules, however, are complicated and very difficult to learn; consequently, this Practical Thai Dictionary can still be of use to those who can read Thai but are unable to determine the proper tones.

USING THIS DICTIONARY

1. **The phonetic system** used in this dictionary is defined inside the front and back covers.

2. **The tones,** indicated by a letter in parentheses, are defined as follows:

> (l) -low tone
> (h) -high tone
> (r) -rising tone
> (f) -falling tone

no indication -normal tone

3. **Syllables** within a Thai word are separated by a hyphen (-). The tone symbols are placed at the beginning of a syllable and indicate the tone with which that syllable should be pronounced. However, in the case of "double vowel" (diphthong) sounds, i.e. "oo-uh", "ee-uh", etc., a tone symbol before the first vowel indicates that the entire double vowel should follow that tone. Ex: (f)choo-ay, ช่วย, to help.

4. **Exclamation mark (!)** A syllable followed by an exclamation mark is to be pronounced rapidly or quickly. In most cases, syllables not followed with an exclamation mark are pronounced either slowly or normally. Note that where a Thai word or syllable ends with the sound of "-ah!" (or "-eh!", "-ih!", "-oh!"), the phonetics in many cases show simply "-a", (or "-e", "-i", "-o"). For instance, the Thai word for "a dramatic play" could be written "lah!-kawn", but this dictionary shows it as "la-kawn" in order to simplify reading the phonetics.

5. **The double vowels,** or diphthongs ("aa-oh" "ee-oh", etc.), can be considered as being made up of two single vowels pronounced one after the other forming one continuous vowel sound.

6. **Consonants "bp-" and "dt-".** The letter combinations "bp-" and "dt-" represent simple sounds common in Thai but are unknown in English. The "bp-" sounds like a combined explosive "b" and "p", and the "dt-" sounds like a combined explosive "d" and "t". Consequently, the actual sound is somewhere "between" the two letters.

7. **The sound of "ng"** is the same in Thai as in English, where it normally occurs (in English) only at the end of a syllable. In Thai, however, "ng" is also used at the beginning of words or syllables, thus creating a sound probably never used in English. The following steps are offered as practice to help the reader pronounce a Thai word beginning with the sound of "ng-".

    a. Consider the word "ngahn" (งาน) meaning "work".

    b. Precede the word with the sound "ree-", which combines with the "ng" to form the familiar English word "ring". The entire sound is then "ring-ahn".

    c. Practice saying "ring-ahn", gradually separating and eliminating the beginning "ree-" sound. Finally, the remaining sound of "ngahn" will be the properly pronounced word.

8. **When two or more Thai words** are listed under one English entry without any explanation of differences, any one of the Thai words may be used. In some cases the difference between two Thai words is too subtle or difficult to explain simply, and one must

learn the difference through usage. Also, the Thai language often has both an elegant and a common or colloquial word for the same thing. This dictionary may list either form or both, depending on their frequency of use in colloquial speech.

9. It is recommended that Classifiers, described in Appendix 5, be studied as a requisite for speaking proper Thai.

10. The use of the words meaning "Sir" in Thai: "(h)krahp!"-ครับ-(spoken by males only) and "ka!" -คะ- (spoken by females only), is encouraged when speaking with Thai people of any social status (or even Thai people in general) in order to show friendly respect. These words should always follow the usual Thai salutation—"sa-waht! dee (h)**krahp**!", สวัสดีครับ; or "sa-waht! dee **ka**!" สวัสดีคะ—and be used after questions asked of a Thai, or after a reply to a question asked by a Thai. Appendix VI, "Yes and No", describes further meanings of "(h)krahp!" and "ka!".

11. Empty pages are provided at the end for writing your own notes and additional words not found in the dictionary.

ROBERTSON'S PRACTICAL

THAI DICTIONARY

a, an (No direct translation. Omit in most cases.
If necessary, use an equivalent word such as
"one".)

able (to be able, capable, can, can do)

	(r)sah-(f)maht	สามารถ
	"	(f)dy!	ได้
	"	bpen!	เป็น
(to be able to, physically)	(r)wy	ไหว

about (almost, nearly) (l)geu-up เกือบ
  (approximately) bpra-mahn ประมาณ
  (around, approximately) rao ราว
  (concerning) (l)gee-oh gahp! เกี่ยวกับ
  (relating to, concerning) (f)reu-ung เรื่อง

above (upper part, on top, upstairs)

  (f)kahng bohn! ข้างบน

  (over, to be higher in rank or status,
  be superior to) (r)neu-uh เหนือ
  (higher, to be higher than)

  (r)soong (l)gwah สูงกว่า

absent (to be absent, not to be in the usual
  location) (f)my! (l)yoo ไม่อยู่

accident oo-(l)baht!-dtih!-(l)het อุบัติเหตุ

1

(automobile accident, collision)

(h)roht! chohn! รถชน

(I want to report an accident.)

(r)chahn! (f)dtawng!-gahn (f)jaang
kwahm (f)reu-ung oo-(l)baht!-dtih-(l)het ฉันต้องการแจ้ง
ความเรื่องอุบัติเหตุ

accidentally (by accident, by chance,
unexpectedly) bahng!-un บังเอิญ

account (an account) bahn-chee บัญชี
(bank account)
bahn-chee ngun! (l)fahk ta-nah-kahn บัญชีเงินฝากธนาคาร

ache (to ache, be in pain) (l)bpoo-ut ปวด
(to hurt, be painful) (l)jep! เจ็บ

across (opposite) dtrohng! (f)kahm ตรงข้าม
(to lie across, to obstruct) (r)kwahng ขวาง

actor, actress (h)nahk! sa-daang la-kawn นักแสดงละคร
dah-rah la-kawn ดาราละคร
(character in a play) dtoo-uh la-kawn ตัวละคร
(movie star) dah-rah (r)nahng! ดาราหนัง
,, dah-rah (f)pahp-pa-yohn! ดาราภาพยนตร์

add (to combine, add up, sum up, include)
roo-um รวม
(to add mathematically, plus) (l)boo-uk บวก

2

---

address   (f)tee (l)yoo   ที่อยู่

adjust (to adjust, improve) (l)bprahp! bproong!   ปรับปรุง

   (an adjustment)   gahn (l)bprahp! bproong!   การปรับปรุง

administer (to administer)   baw-ri-(r)hahn   บริหาร

   (administration)   gahn baw-ri-(r)hahn   การบริหาร

   (administrator)   (f)poo baw-ri-(r)hahn   ผู้บริหาร

admiral   pohn! reu-uh   พลเรือ

   (rear adm.)   pohn! reu-uh dtree   พลเรือตรี

   (vice adm.)   pohn! reu-uh toh   พลเรือโท

   (4-star)   pohn! reu-uh (l)ehk   พลเรือเอก

   (5-star)   jawm pohn! reu-uh   จอมพลเรือ

admire (to admire, to look at with pleasure)

                 chohm!   ชม

   (to admire, praise, compliment)

                 chohm! chuh-ee   ชมเชย

admission (or entrance price, gate fee)

           (f)kah (l)pahn bpra-dtoo   ค่าผ่านประตู

adult   (f)poo (l)yai!   ผู้ใหญ่

advantage (or usefulness, benefit, profit)

               bpra-(l)yoht   ประโยชน์

3

advertise (to advertise, publicize)

(f)ko-sa-nah โฆษณา

(advertisement) gahn (f)ko-sa-nah การโฆษณา

(propaganda) gahn (f)ko-sa-nah choo-un

(f)cheu-uh การโฆษณาชวนเชื่อ

advice kahm! naa!-nahm! คำแนะนำ

advise (to advise, suggest, recommend)

naa!-nahm! แนะนำ

(to consult) (l)bpreuk!-(r)sah ปรึกษา

advisor (consultant) (f)tee (l)bpreuk!-(r)sah ที่ปรึกษา

afraid (to be afraid of, fear) gloo-uh กลัว

after (r)lahng! (l)jahk หลังจาก

afternoon (l)by บ่าย

(in the afternoon) dtawn (l)by ตอนบ่าย

(the afternoon, in the afternoon)

weh-lah (l)by เวลาบ่าย

(late this afternoon) yen! (h)nee เย็นนี้

afterwards py (r)lahng! ภายหลัง

(later, any time after this) tee (r)lahng! ที่หลัง

again (l)eek อีก

(once more, again) (l)eek tee อีกที

(one more time, once again)

(l)eek (h)krahng! (l)neung! อีกครั้งหนึ่ง

(Please say that again.) (l)bproht (f)poot

(l)eek (h)krahng! (l)neung! โปรดพูดอีกครั้งหนึ่ง

age   ah-(h)yoo! อายุ

(How old are you?) ah-(h)yoo!

(f)tao!-(l)ry! อายุเท่าไร

(I am.........years old.) (r)chahn!

ah-(h)yoo!.........bpee ฉันอายุ.........ปี

Note : A child under 12-13 years would
answer: (r)chahn!

ah-(h)yoo!.........(l)koo-up ฉันอายุ......ขวบ

ago   (f)tee (h)laa-oh ที่แล้ว

(*Example :* two months ago)

(r)sawng deu-un (f)tee (h)laa-oh สองเดือนที่แล้ว

agree (to agree, I agree, Agreed!)

(l)dtohk! lohng! ตกลง

(to agree with)   (r)hen! (f)doo-ay เห็นด้วย

,,   (r)hen! (f)chawp

(f)doo-ay เห็นชอบด้วย

5

agriculture	gahn ga-(l)set	การเกษตร
air	ah-(l)gaht	อากาศ
air-conditioner	(f)kreu-ung tahm! kwahm yen!	เครื่องทำความเย็น
	aar (air)	แอร์
(to be air-conditioned)	mee air	มีแอร์
air force	gawng (h)tahp! ah-(l)gaht	กองทัพอากาศ
airmail	bpry!-sa-nee ah-(l)gaht	ไปรษณีย์อากาศ
airplane	(f)kreu-ung bin!	เครื่องบิน
	reu-uh bin!	เรือบิน
airport	sa-(r)nahm bin!	สนามบิน
	(f)tah ah-(l)gat-sa-yahn	ท่าอากาศยาน
alarm clock	nah-li-gah (l)bplook!	นาฬิกาปลุก
alcohol	al-gaw-haw	แอลกอฮอล์
(liquor, alcoholic beverage)	(f)lao!	เหล้า
algebra	(h)pit!-cha-ka-(h)nit!	พีชคณิต
alive (to have life, to be alive)	mee chee-(h)wit!	มีชีวิต
,,	mee chee-(h)wit! (l)yoo	มีชีวิตอยู่
(to be alive, of plants)	bpen!	เป็น

6

all (everything)	(h)tahng! (1)moht!	ทั้งหมด
(throughout, all during)	dta-(l)lawt	ตลอด
(all **day**)	dta-(l)lawt **wahn!**	ตลอดวัน
alligator	jaw-ra-(f)keh	จระเข้
allow (to allow, permit)	yawm (f)hy!	ยอมให้
all right (alright)	O.K.	โอ เค
(Agreed!)	(l)dtohk! lohng!	ตกลง
(Correct!)	(l)took (f)dtawng	ถูกต้อง
(That's alright, it's nothing.)		
	(f)my! bpen! ry!	ไม่เป็นไร
(to be well, happy)	sa-by dee	สบายดี
(Are you alright?)	koon! sa-by dee (r)reu	คุณสบายดีหรือ
almost (or nearly)	(l)geu-up	เกือบ
alone (to be alone, one person)	kohn! dee-oh	คนเดียว
„	dtahm lahm!-pahng!	ตามลำพัง
along (or around, in)	dtahm	ตาม
alphabet letter (letter of the alphabet)		
	dtoo-uh (l)ahk!-(r)sawn	ตัวอักษร
already	(h)laa-oh	แล้ว

alright (see "all right")

also   (f)doo-ay   ด้วย
  (likewise, the same)   (r)meu-un gahn!   เหมือนกัน

always   sa-(r)muh   เสมอ

am (see "be")

amazed (to be amazed, surprised)

                    (l)bplaak jy!   แปลกใจ

ambassador (l)ehk-(l)ahk!-ka-ra

              (f)raht-cha-(f)toot   เอกอัครราชทูต

ambulance   (h)roht! pa-yah-bahn   รถพยาบาล
  (I want to call an ambulance.)
  (r)chahn! (f)dtawng! gahn (f)ree-uk (h)roht!
                      pa-yah-bahn   ฉันต้องการเรียก
                                 รถพยาบาล

America   ah-meh-rih!-gah   อเมริกา
  (American person) chow ah-meh-rih!-gahn   ชาวอเมริกัน
      ,,   kohn! ah-meh-rih!-gahn   คนอเมริกัน
  (United States of America)
       sa-(l)ha-(h)raht! ah-meh-rih!-gah   สหรัฐอเมริกา
  (South America)   ah-meh-rih!-gah (f)dty   อเมริกาใต้

8

among	ny! (h)ra-(l)wahng	ในระหว่าง
amount (quantity)	jahm!-noo-un	จำนวน
amplifier (electronic)	(f)kreu-ung ka-(r)yai (r)see-ung	เครื่องขยายเสียง

ampur, ampoe (subdiv. of changwat, a district)
ahm!-puh อำเภอ

(district officer, chief of ampur)
ny ahm!-puh นายอำเภอ

an, a (No direct translation. Omit in most cases. If necessary, use an equivalent word such as "one".)

and laa! (with a short, emphatic vowel sound) และ
(and then) (h)laa-oh (f)gaw! แล้วก็
(And you?) (spoken by males) (h)laa-oh koon! (f)lah (h)krahp! แล้วคุณล่ะครับ
(And you?) (spoken by females) (h)laa-oh koon! (f)lah (h)ka! แล้วคุณล่ะคะ

angle (or corner) moom! มุม
(right angle, 90°) moom! (l)chahk มุมฉาก
" (f)dtahng (l)chahk ตั้งฉาก

9

angry (to be angry)	(l)groht	โกรธ
,, (suddenly)	moh-(r)hoh	โมโห
animal (l)saht!		สัตว์
(classifier for animals)	dtoo-uh	ตัว
Ex. two animals (l)saht! (r)sawng dtoo-uh		สัตว์สองตัว
ankle	(f)kaw (h)tao	ข้อเท้า
announce (to announce, an announcement)		
	bpra-(l)gaht	ประกาศ
annoy (to annoy, bother)	rohp! goo-un	รบกวน
(to annoy by teasing) (f)glaang (h)law (f)lehn		แกล้งล้อเล่น
another (or other)	(l)eun	อื่น
(another person)	kohn (l)eun	คนอื่น
answer (to answer, reply)	(l)dtawp	ตอบ
(an answer, a reply)	kahm! (l)dtawp	คำตอบ
ant	(h)moht!	มด
(red ants)	(h)moht! daang	มดแดง
(black ants)	(h)moht! dahm!	มดดำ
antenna	(r)sow! ah-(l)gaht	เสาอากาศ
(TV antenna)	(r)sow! tee-wee	เสาทีวี
any (or some)	(pronoun) (f)bahng	บ้าง
,,	(adjective) bahng	บาง

10

anybody (or somebody)	kry!	ใคร
,,	bahng kohn!	บางคน
(anybody will do)	kry! (f)gaw! (f)dy!	ใครก็ได้
,,	kry! kry!	ใคร ๆ
anyone (or someone)	kry!	ใคร
,,	bahng kohn!	บางคน
,,	kry! kry!	ใคร ๆ
anything	ah!-ry!	อะไร
(anything will do)	ah!-ry! (f)gaw! (f)dy!	อะไรก็ได้
anywhere	(f)tee (r)ny! (f)gaw! (f)dy!	ที่ไหนก็ได้
apartment	(f)hawng! (f)chow!	ห้องเช่า
(a flat)	flaat!	แฟล็ต
apologize (to apologize, Excuse me!)		
	(r)kaw (f)toht	ขอโทษ
appendicitis	(f)rohk (f)sy! (l)dting!	โรคไส้ติ่ง
appetite	kwahm (r)hue!	ความหิว
apple	aa!-puhn!	แอ๊ปเปิ้ล
apply (to apply, make application)	sa-(l)mahk!	สมัคร
(an application form)	by sa-(l)mahk!	ใบสมัคร
April	meh-(r)sah yohn!	เมษายน

apron	(f)pah gahn! (f)bpeu-un	ผ้ากันเปื้อน
architect	sa-(r)tah-bpa-(h)nik!	สถาปนิก
are (see "be")		
area (region, environs, vicinity)	baw-ri-wen	บริเวณ
(area of a surface, geometrical area)		
	(h)neu-uh (f)tee	เนื้อที่
argue (to argue, quarrel)	ta-law! gahn!	ทะเลาะกัน
(to argue, contradict, talk back to)	(r)tee-ung	เถียง
arithmetic	(f)lek ka-(b)nit!	เลขคณิต
arm (of the body)	(r)kaan	แขน
army	gawng (h)tahp! (l)bohk!	กองทัพบก
around	(f)rawp	รอบ
(completely around)	(f)rawp (f)rawp	รอบ ๆ
(about, approximately)	bpra-mahn	ประมาณ
"	rao	ราว
arrest (to arrest)	(l)jahp! goom!	จับกุม
(to be arrested, get arrested)		
	(l)took (l)jahp! goom!	ถูกจับกุม
arrive (to arrive)	(r)teung!	ถึง
(to arrive here)	mah (r)teung!	มาถึง

(to arrive there)	bpy! (r)teung!	ไปถึง
(We have arrived !)	(r)teung! (h)laa-oh	ถึงแล้ว
art (arts and crafts)	(r)sin!-la-(l)bpa!	ศิลป
artist	(r)sin!-la-bpin!	ศิลปิน
as soon as (just as, when)	paw	พอ
ash, ashes	(f)kee (f)tao!	ขี้เถ้า
ashamed (to be ashamed)	(h)la!-I	ละอาย
ashtray	(f)tee (l)kee-uh boo!-(1)ree	ที่เขี่ยบุหรี่
ask (to ask for, request, beg)	(r)kaw	ขอ
(to ask a question)	(r)tahm	ถาม
asleep (to be asleep, to sleep) nawn (l)lahp!		นอนหลับ
(an arm or leg to be asleep, be numb)		
	(h)roo-(l)seuk chah	รู้สึกชา
,,	(l)nep! chah	เหน็บชา
assist (to assist, help)	(f)choo-ay	ช่วย
(to help others, give help)	(f)choo-ay(r)leu-uh	ช่วยเหลือ
assistance (aid) kwahm (f)choo-ay (r)leu-uh		ความช่วยเหลือ
assistant	(f)poo (f)choo-ay	ผู้ช่วย
association (or club, society, organization)		
	sa-mah-kohm!	สมาคม

astrology	(r)ho-rah-(l)saht	โหราศาสตร์
(astrologer)	(r)hohn	โหร
(fortune teller)	(r)maw doo	หมอดู
astronomy	dah-rah-(l)saht	ดาราศาสตร์
at (at a location)	(f)tee	ที่
(at a certain time)	weh-lah	เวลา
(at least, as a minimum)	(l)yahng (h)nawy	อย่างน้อย
(at once, immediately)	tahn!-tee	ทันที
attach (to attach, connect)	(l)dtit! (h)wy	ติดไว้
auction (to auction)	(r)ky leh-(r)lahng!	ขายเลหลัง
(an auction)	gahn (r)ky leh-(r)lahng!	การขายเลหลัง
audience (listeners)	(f)poo fahng!	ผู้ฟัง
August	(r)sing!-(r)hah-kohm!	สิงหาคม
aunt (younger sister of one's mother)	(h)nah	น้า
(younger sister of one's father)	ah	อา
(elder sister of mother or father)	(f)bpah	ป้า
author (or writer)	(h)nahk! bpra-pahn!	นักประพันธ์
,,	(n)nahk! (r)kee-un	นักเขียน
authority (or power, influence)	ahm!-(f)naht	อำนาจ

14

automobile	(h)roht!-yohn!	รถยนตร์
(general term for autos, trucks, etc.)	(h)roht!	รถ
(classifier for vehicles)	kahn!	คัน
autumn	(h)reu!-doo by!-my (f)roo-ung	ฤดูใบไม้ร่วง
awake (to wake up, to be awake)	(l)dteun(f)keun	ตื่นขึ้น
(to awaken someone)		
	(l)bplook! (f)hy (l)dteun	ปลุกให้ตื่
award (prize)	rahng-wahn!	วางวัล
away (to be far away)	(l)yoo gly!	อยู่ไกล
(Go away!)	(h)bpy!	ไป
(to take something away)	ow!——bpy!	เอา——ไป
ax, axe	(r)kwahn	ขวาน
baby	(l)dek! (l)awn	เด็กอ่อน
	tah-(h)rohk!	ทารก
(offspring of animals)	(f)look	ลูก
bachelor	chy (l)soht	ชายโสด
(to be single, unmarried)	bpen! (l)soht	เป็นโสด
back (of the body)	(r)lahng!	หลัง
(in back, behind)	(f)kahng (r)lahng!	ข้างหลัง
(to go back)	(l)glahp!	กลับ
	(l)glahp! bpy!	กลับไป

,,

15

(to back up, go backwards)	(r)tawy	ถอย
,,	(r)tawy bpy!	ถอยไป
(to back up, to step back)	(r)tawy (r)lahng!	ถอยหลัง
(to give back, return)	keun	คืน
,,	(l)sohng! keun	ส่งคืน
,,	keun (f)hy!	คืนให้
(a sore back, backache)	(l)bpoo-ut (r)lahng!	ปวดหลัง

backwards (to put something on backwards)

	(l)sy!——(l)glahp!	ใส่——กลับ
bacon	(r)moo beh-kawn	หมู-เบคอน
bacteria (germs)	(h)cheu-uh (f)rohk	เชื้อโรค
bad (to be bad, not good)	(f)my! dee	ไม่ดี
(to be bad, vile, wicked)	(f)choo-uh	ชั่ว
(to be bad, poor in quality or character)	leh-oh	เลว
(to be rotton, of fruit, food)	(f)now!	เน่า
(That's too bad.)	(f)nah (r)see-uh-dy	น่าเสียดาย
(What a pity!)	(f)nah (r)sohng!-(r)sahn	น่าสงสาร
badge (or trademark, brand, seal)	dtrah	ครา
bag (or sack, any kind)	(r)toong!	ถุง
(paper bag)	(r)toong! gra-(l)daht	ถุงกระดาษ

16

(suitcase, handbag)	gra-(r)bpow!	กระเป๋า
baht (or tical, 100 satang)	(l)baht	บาท
($\frac{1}{4}$ baht, 25 satang)	sa-(r)leung	สลึง
bake (to bake in an oven)	(l)ohp	อบ
(to bake, roast, barbecue, toast)	(f)bping!	ปิ้ง
bald (to be bald)	(r)hoo-uh! (h)lahn	หัวล้าน
ball	bawl	บอลล์
	(f)look bawl	ลูกบอลล์
(rattan ball, used for playing takraw)	dta-(f)graw	ตะกร้อ
balloon (toy balloon)	(f)look (l)bpohng	ลูกโป่ง
bamboo	(h)my-(l)py!	ไม้ไผ่
banana	(f)gloo-ay	กล้วย
(most common kind, a fragrant variety, further classified below)	(f)gloo-ay (r)hawm	กล้วยหอม
1. (yellow)	(f)gloo-ay (r)hawm tawng	กล้วยหอมทอง
2. (green)	(f)gloo-ay (r)hawm (r)kee-oh	กล้วยหอมเขียว
(very small kind)	(f)gloo-ay (l)ky!	กล้วยไข่
(short and fat)	(f)gloo-ay (h)nahm! (h)wah	กล้วยน้ำว้า
(short and fat, has seeds, eaten by animals)	(f)gloo-ay dtah-nee	กล้วยตานี

band–barbed wire

band (a brass or musical band)	dtraa wohng!	แตรวง
(rubber band)	yahng wohng!	ยางวง
,,	yahng (h)raht	ยางรัด
,,	(r)nahng yahng	หนังยาง
bandage (n.)	(f)pah pahn!-(r)plaa	ผ้าพันแผล
	plahs-dtuhr (plaster)	ปลาสเต้อร์
bandit (armed bandit, robber)	john (rhymes with "bone")	โจร
(guerilla band, robber gang) (terrorist, revolutionist)	gawng john	กองโจร
	(f)poo (l)gaw gahn (h)rai	ผู้ก่อการร้าย
Bangkok groong!-(f)tep (normal short form, an abbreviation of the full longer name)		กรุงเทพ ฯ
bank (for money)	ta-nah-kahn	ธนาคาร
(savings bank)	ta-nah-kahn awm-(r)sin!	ธนาคารออมสิน
(bankbook, passbook)	sa-(l)moot! (l)fahk ngun!	สมุดฝากเงิน
(river bank)	(l)fahng! (h)nahm	ฝั่งน้ำ
barbecue (to roast over an open fire)	(f)yahng	ย่าง
barbed wire	(f)loo-ut (r)nahm	ลวดหนาม

18

barbershop	(h)rahn (l)dtaht! (r)pohm!	ร้านตัดผม
bargain (to bargain)	(l)dtaw! rah-kah	ต่อราคา
,,	(l)dtohk!-lohng! rah-kah	ตกลงราคา
bark (to bark)	(l)how!	เห่า
(tree bark)	(l)bpleu-uk (h)my	เปลือกไม้
asket	dta-(f)grah	ตะกร้า
at (animal)	(h)kahng kow	ค้างคาว
ath, bathe (to bathe, take a bath)		
	(l)ahb-(h)nahm	อาบน้ำ
athmat	(f)pah (h)chet! (h)tao	ผ้าเช็ดเท้า
bathroom (or restroom)	(f)hawng! (h)nahm	ห้องน้ำ
(toilet—common)	(f)hawng! (f)soo-um	ห้องส้วม
(toilet—more elegant)	(h)hawng! soo!-(r)kah	ห้องสขา
bathtub	(l)ahng (l)ahb-(h)nahm	อ่างอาบน้ำ
battery	baat-dtuh-(f)ree	แบตเตอรี่
	tahn	ถ่าน
(large battery)	(f)maw fy!	หม้อไฟ
,,	(f)maw baat-btuh-(f)ree	หม้อแบตเตอรี่
(flashlight battery)	(l)tahn fy! (r)chy	ถ่านไฟฉาย
bay (or gulf)	(l)ow	อ่าว

19

be (to be, am, are, been, is, was, were) bpen! เป็น

Note : The verb "to be" and all of its forms are used much less in the Thai language then they are used in English. Usually the words "be, is, am, are" etc. are understood to be already included in the Thai adjectives and modifiers.

(there is, there are)	mee	มี
(to be in a location)	(l)yoo	อยู่
beach (sandy beach)	(l)haht sy	หาดทราย
(seashore)	chy ta-leh	ชายทะเล
bean (or pea, nut)	(l)too-uh!	ถั่ว
bear (animal)	(r)mee	หมี
beard (or whiskers, mustache)	krao!	เครา
(beard including mustache)	(l)noo-ut krao!	หนวดเครา
beat (to beat, hit, strike)	dtee	ตี
(rhythm, timing, as in music)	jahng!-(l)wa!	จังหวะ
(to beat, win, as in sports)	cha-(h)na!	ชนะ
beautiful (to be beautiful, in appearance)		
	(r)soo-ay	สวย
,,	ngahm	งาม

(to be beautiful, of sounds)	(h)praw!	เพราะ
,,	pai-(h)raw!	ไพเราะ
because	(h)praw!	เพราะ
	(h)praw! (f)wah	เพราะว่า
bed	dtee-ung nawn	เตียงนอน
(mattress)	(f)tee nawn	ที่นอน
(to go to bed)	bpy! nawn	ไปนอน
,,	(f)kow nawn	เข้านอน
bedroom	(f)hawng! nawn	ห้องนอน
bee	(f)peung!	ผึ้ง
(bee's nest, beehive)	rahng! (f)peung!	รังผึ้ง
beef	(h)neu-uh woo-uh	เนื้อวัว
(tenderloin)	(h)neu-uh (r)sahn!	เนื้อสัน
been (see "be")		
(Where have you been ?)	bpy! (r)ny mah	ไปไหนมา
beer	bee-uh	เบียร์
(Singha, a Thai brand)	bee-uh dtrah (r)sing!	เบียร์ตราสิงห์
(Krating Thong, a Thai brand)		
	bee-uh gra-ting! tawng	เบียร์กระทิงทอง
before	(l)gawn	ก่อน

beg (to beg, ask for alms)	(r)kaw tahn	ขอทาน
beggar	kohn! (r)kaw tahn	คนขอทาน
begin (to begin, start)	(f)ruhm	เริ่ม
,,	(f)ruhm (f)dtohn!	เริ่มต้น
beginning (the beginning, first part)		
	dtawn (f)dtohn!	ตอนต้น
behind	(f)kahng (r)lahng	ข้างหลัง
believe (to believe)	(f)cheu-uh	เชื่อ
bell (large)	ra-kahng!	ระฆัง
(small)	gra-(l)ding!	กระดิ่ง
(bell, buzzer, to ring, to buzz)	(l)gring!	กริ่ง
belong (to belong to, belonging to, showing ownership)		
	(r)kawng	ของ
below	(f)kahng (f)lahng	ข้างล่าง
belt (for pants)	(r)kem!-(l)kaht!	เข็มขัด
(for machinery)	(r)sy pahn	สายพาน
bench (or stool)	(h)mah (f)nahng!	ม้านั่ง
bend, bent (to be bent, curved)	(h)kohng	โค้ง
(to bend)	tahm! (f)hy! (h)kohng	ทำให้โค้ง
(to bend, fold, curl)	ngaw	งอ

22

(to bend over, stoop)	(f)gohm!	ก้ม
beside	(f)kahng (f)kahng	ข้าง ๆ
best	dee (f)tee (l)soot!	ดีที่สุด
bet (to bet, wager, gamble, a bet)	pa-nahn!	พนัน
better to be better than––	dee (l)gwah––	ดีกว่า––
(to improve, be better than before)		
	dee (f)keun!	ดีขึ้น
(had better, probably should)		
	(r)hen! ja! (f)dtawng!	เห็นจะต้อง
between	ra-(l)wahng	ระหว่าง
(between A and B)	ra-(l)wahng A laa! B	ระหว่างAและB
„	ra-(l)wahng A (l)gahp! B	ระหว่างA กับB
beverage	(f)kreu-ung (f)deum	เครื่องดื่ม
(see "drink")		
bicycle (l)jahk!-ra-yahn (Sounds like		
"jahk-a-yahn")		จักรยาน
big (to be big, large) (l)yai! (rhymes with "my")		ใหญ่
(to be big, large, mature)	dtoh	โต
(to have a large body)	dtoo-uh dtoh	ตัวโต
bill (or check)	bin	บิล
„	chek!	เช็ค

(receipt)	by (h)rahp! ngun!	ใบรับเงิน
(water bill)	bin (h)nahm! bpra-bpah	บิลค่าน้ำประปา
(electric bill)	bin (f)kah fy!-(h)fah	บิลค่าไฟฟ้า
(telephone bill)	bin (f)kah toh-ra-(l)sahp	บิลค่าโทรศัพท์
(garbage bill)	bin (f)kah (r)kohn! ka-(l)ya!	บิลค่าขนขยะ
binoculars	(f)glawng (l)sawng tahng gly!	กล้องส่องทางไกล
bird	(h)nohk!	นก
birthday	wahn! (l)gut	วันเกิด
bite (to bite)	(l)gaht!	กัด
bitter (to be bitter in taste)	(r)kohm!	ขม
black (to be black)	dahm!	ดำ
(the color of black)	(r)see dahm!	สีดำ
blackboard	gra-dahn dahm!	กระดานดำ
blame (to blame, criticize)	(l)dtih! dtee-un	ติเตียน
(to blame, blame)	(f)toht	โทษ
blanket	(f)pah (l)hohm nawn	ผ้าห่มนอน
bleach (powder)	(f)bpaang	แป้ง
(to bleach, to make white)	tahm! (f)hy!(r)kow	ทำให้ขาว
bleed (to bleed)	(f)leu-ut (l)awk	เลือดออก
„	mee (f)leu-ut (l)awk	มีเลือดออก

---

blind (to be blind)   dtah (l)bawt   ตาบอด

  (venetian blinds, bamboo blinds) moo-(f)lee   มู่ลี่

block (to block, obstruct, get in the way)

                  (l)kaht! (r)kwahng   ขัดขวาง

  (a block of wood)   (f)tawn (h)my   ท่อนไม้

  (a city block)   (l)dteuk!-(r)taaow   ตึกแถว

Note: Distances along streets are not counted or measured in blocks, but rather by streets or cross streets.

Examples:

(How many blocks to— —?)

(l)eek (l)gee ta-(r)nohn! (r)teung— —   อีกกี่ถนนถึง— —

(in the next block) (l)yoo ta-(r)nohn! (f)nah   อยู่ถนนหน้า

blood   (f)leu-ut, lo-hit   เลือด, โลหิต

  (blood vessel, vein)   (f)sen! lo-hit   เส้นโลหิต

blotter (blotting paper) gra-(l)daht (h)sahp!   กระดาษซับ

blow (the wind to blow, to fan)   (h)paht!   พัด

  (the wind is blowing)   lohm! (h)paht!   ลมพัด

  (to blow, by mouth)   (l)bpow!   เป่า

blowout (of a tire)   yahng ra-but   ยางระเบิด

                yahng (l)dtaak   ยางแตก

25

blue	(r)see (h)nahm! ngun!	สีน้ำเงิน
(light blue, sky blue)	(r)see (h)fah	สีฟ้า
board (of wood)	(h)my gra-dahn	ไม้กระดาน
(to board a vehicle)	(f)keun! (h)roht!	ขึ้นรถ
boast (to boast, brag, talk big)	kooy! dtoh	คุยโต
,,	(l)oh-(l)oo-ut	โอ่อวด
boat (or ship)	reu-uh	เรือ
body	dtoo-uh	ตัว
(human body)	(f)rahng-gy	ร่างกาย
boil (to boil)	(f)dtohm!	ต้ม
(to be boiling)	(l)deu-ut	เดือด
(boiled water)	(h)nahm! (f)dtohm!	น้ำต้ม
bolt (latch, sliding bolt)	glawn	กลอน
(to bolt or latch a door, etc.)	(l)sy! glawn	ใส่กลอน
(threaded bolt, machine screw)	nawt!	น็อต
1. (the threaded shaft)	nawt!dtoo-uh(f)poo	น็อตตัวผู้
2. (the nut)	nawt! dtoo-uh mee-uh	น็อตตัวเมีย
bomb (to bomb)	(h)ting! ra!-but	ทิ้งระเบิด
(a bomb)	(f)look ra!-but	ลูกระเบิด
bone	gra-(l)dook	กระดูก

book	nahng!-(r)seu	หนังสือ
(notebook, ledger)	sa-(l)moot!	สมุด
(classifier for books)	(f)lem!	เล่ม
(to book, reserve)	(h)book!	บุ๊ค
bookcase	(f)dtoo nahng!-(r)seu	ตู้หนังสือ
border (boundary, limit)	(l)ket	เขต
(border, frontier)	chy-daan	ชายแดน
(border police)		
dtahm!-(l)roo-ut dtra-wen chy daan		ตำรวจตระเวน
		ชายแดน
(border police) dtahm!-(l)roo-ut chy daan		ตำรวจชายแดน
bored (to be bored with, tired of)	(l)beu-uh	เบื่อ
born (to be born)	(l)gut	เกิด
(to give birth)	(f)klawt	คลอด
"	(f)klawt (l)boot!	คลอดบุตร
borrow (to borrow)	yeum	ยืม
(to borrow, to ask to borrow)	(r)kaw yeum	ขอยืม
(to borrow with interest)	(f)goo	กู้
boss (supervisor)	ny ngahn	นายงาน
both	(h)tahng! (r)sawng	ทั้งสอง

27

	(h)tahng! (f)koo	ทั้งคู่
bother (to bother, annoy)	rohp goo-un	รบกวน
bottle	(l)koo-ut	ขวด
bottom	(f)gohn!	ก้น
boundary (or border, limit)	(l)ket	เขต
bowl (dish)	chahm	ชาม
(small bowl, cup)	(f)too-ay	ถ้วย
box (container)	(l)heep	หีบ
(boxing)	moo-ay	มวย
(to box)	(b)chohk! moo-ay	ชกมวย
(a boxer)	(h)nahk! moo-ay	นักมวย
boy	(f)poo-chy	ผู้ชาย
(a child)	(l)dek! (f)poo-chy	เด็กผู้ชาย
(children)	(l)dek! (l)dek	เด็ก ๆ
bracelet	(f)sawy (f)kaw-meu	สร้อยข้อมือ
brag (to brag, boast, talk big)	kooy! dtoh	คุยโต
„	(l)oh-(l)oo-ut	โอ่อวด
brain	sa-(r)mawng	สมอง
brake, brakes	(l)brek	เบรค
branch (of a plant or tree)	(l)ging! (h)my	กิ่งไม้

28

(branch office, subsidiary, offshoot)

(r)sah-(r)kah   สาขา

brand (trademark) dtrah (f)khreu-ung-

(r)mai gahn-ka   ตราเครื่องหมาย
การค้า

brass   tawng (r)leu-ung   ทองเหลือง

brassiere   brah-see-uh   บราเซียร์

(f)seu-uh (h)yohk! sohng!   เสื้อยกทรง

bread   ka-(r)nohm!-bpahng   ขนมปัง

(a roll)   ka-(r)nohm!-bpahng! glohm!   ขนมปังกลม

break (to break,to be broken,smashed) (l)dtaak   แตก

(to break apart, get broken off)   (l)hahk!   หัก

breakfast   ah-(r)hahn (h)chow   อาหารเช้า

breath   lohm! (r)hy jy!   ลมหายใจ

breathe   (r)hy jy!   หายใจ

bribe (n.)   (r)sin!-bohn!   สินบน

(to bribe)   (l)dtit! (r)sin!-bohn!   ติดสินบน

brick   (l)it!   อิฐ

bridge   sa-pahn   สะพาน

bright (of light)   sa-(l)wahng   สว่าง

29

bring (to bring something)	ow!––mah	เอา––มา
(to go get and bring something)		
	bpy! ow––mah	ไปเอา––มา
(to bring someone)	pah––mah	พา––มา
(to bring someone by leading or guiding him along)		
	nahm!––mah	นำ––มา
broil (to broil, barbecue)	(f)yahng	ย่าง
broken-hearted (over a love affair)		
	(l)ohk!-(l)bahk!	อกหัก
(to be sad, sorrowful)	(l)sohk-(f)sow!	โศกเศร้า
bronze	tawng brawn	ทองบรอนซ์
broom	(h)my (l)gwaht	ไม้กวาด
brother (younger)	(h)nawng-chy	น้องชาย
(elder)	(f)pee-chy	พี่ชาย
(brothers; sisters; brother and sister; brothers and sisters; cousins)	(f)pee-(b)nawng	พี่น้อง
brother-in-law (younger)	(h)nawng (r)kuh-ee	น้องเขย
(elder)	(f)pee (r)kuh-ee	พี่เขย
brown	(r)see (b)nahm! dtahn	สีน้ำตาล
brush (a brush, to brush)	bpraang	แปรง

30

bubbles (or foam)	fawng	ฟอง
bucket	(r)tahng!	ถัง
Buddha (the Lord Buddha)		
	(h)pra! (h)poot!-ta-(f)jow	พระพุทธเจ้า
Buddhism	(l)saht-sa-(r)nah (h)poot!	ศาสนาพุทธ
buffalo	kwy	ควาย
build (to make)	tahm!	ทำ
(to construct)	(f)sahng	สร้าง
,,	(l)gaw (f)sahng	ก่อสร้าง
building (structure)	ah-kahn	อาคาร
(a building of stone or brick)	(l)dteuk!	ตึก
(building, construction)	gahn(l)gaw(f)sahng	การก่อสร้าง
bull	woo-uh dtoo-uh poo	วัวตัวผู้
bullet	(f)look bpeun	ลูกปืน
bullfight	chohn! woo-uh	ชนวัว
bump (to bump into, run into, collide)	chohn!	ชน
(a bumpy road, rough road)		
	ta-(r)nohn! (l)kroo!-(l)kra!	ถนนขรุขระ
bumper (as of an automobile)		
	(f)tee gahn! chohn!	ที่กันชน

burglar (or thief)	ka-moy	ขโมย
Burma	pa-(f)mah	พม่า
burn (to burn, burn up)	(r)pow!	เผา
(to be burned, burnt, a fire ι burn)	(f)my!	ไหม้
bury (to bury, to be buried)	(r)fahng!	ฝัง
bus (local bus)	(h)roht! meh	รถเมล์
(up-country or inter-city bus)		
	(h)roht! doy-(r)sahn	รถโดยสาร
(busline)	(f)sehn-tahng (h)roht! meh	เส้นทางรถเมล์
(bus stop)	(f)tee (l)yoot! (h)roht! meh	ที่หยุดรถเมล์
(bus-stop sign)	(f)bpy (l)yoot!(h)roht! meh	ป้ายหยุดรถเมล์
bush (or shrub, bushes)	(f)poom! (h)my	พุ่มไม้
business (affairs)	(h)too!-(h)ra!	ธุระ
,,	(h)too!-(h) ra! (l)git!	ธุรกิจ
(work)	ngahn	งาน
(It is none of your business.)		
(f)my!(f)chy!(h)too!-(h)ra!(r)kawngkoon!	ไม่ใช่ธุระของคุณ
busy (to be busy)	mee (h)too!-(h)ra!	มีธุระ
(not to be free)	(f)my! (f)wahng	ไม่ว่าง
(telephone line is busy)	(r)sy(f)my!(f)wahng	สายไม่ว่าง

but	(l)dtaa	แต่
butter	nuh-ee	เนย
	nuh-ee (l)awn	เนยอ่อน
	nuh-ee (r)leh-oh	เนยเหลว
(fresh butter)	nuh-ee (l)soht!	เนยสด
butterfly	(r)pee (f)seu-uh	ผีเสื้อ
button (a button)	gra-doom!	กระดุม
(to button)	(l)glaht! gra-doom!	กลัดกระดุม
„	(l)dtit! gra-doom!	ติดกระดุม
(to unbutton)	(l)bploht! gra-doom!	ปลดกระดุม
buy (to buy)	(h)seu	ซื้อ
buzzer (or bell, to buzz, to ring)	(l)gring!	กริ่ง
by (by means of)	doy	โดย
(written by)	doy	โดย
(by way of)	tahng	ทาง
(by automobile)	tahng (h)roht! yohn!	ทางรถยนต์
(by rail, by train)	tahng (h)roht! fy!	ทางรถไฟ
„	doy tahng (h)roht! fy!	โดยทางรถไฟ
(by airplane)	tahng reu-uh bin!	ทางเรือบิน
(to be nearby)	(l)yoo (f)gly!	อยู่ใกล้
(A by B, A times B)	A koon B	A คูณ B

33

cabbage	ga-(l)lahm!-bplee	กะหล่ำปลี
cabinet (cupboard, bookcase, etc.)	(f)dtoo	ตู้
cable (wire rope, any size)	(f)loo-ut sa-ling!	ลวดสลิง
cage	grohng!	กรง
cake	ka-(r)nohm! kehk	ขนมเค็ก
calendar	(l)bpa!-dtih!-tin!	ปฏิทิน
calf (animal)	(f)look woo-uh	ลูกวัว
call (to call, to be called)	(f)ree-uk	เรียก
(to cry out)	(h)rawng	ร้อง
(to shout, yell)	dta-gohn	ตะโกน
(What do you call this?)		
(r)kawng (h)nee (f)ree-uk (f)wah ah!-ry!		ของนี้เรียกว่าอะไร
Cambodia, Cambodian, Khmer	ka-(r)men	เขมร
"	gahm!-poo-chah	กัมพูชา
(the country of)	bpra-(f)tet ka-(r)men	ประเทศเขมร
(the Khmer language)	pah-(r)sah ka-(r)men	ภาษาเขมร
camera	(f)glawng (l)ty (f)roop	กล้องถ่ายรูป
camp n.	(f)ky	ค่าย
(army camp)	(f)ky ta-(r)hahn (l)bohk!	ค่ายทหารบก

34

(quarters, resting place, lodging)

	(f)tee (h)pahk!	ที่พัก
can (or could, might, may, to be able to)	(f)dy!	ได้
„	bpen!	เป็น
(to be able to, physically)	(r)wy	ไหว
(can you?)	(f)dy! (r)my	ได้ไหม
„	bpen! (r)my	เป็นไหม
(tin can)	gra-(r)bpawng!	กระป๋อง
(garbage can)	(r)tahng! ka-(l)ya!	ถังขยะ
(trash can, wastebasket)	(r)tahng!(r)pohng!	ถังผง
canal	klawng	คลอง
cancel (to cancel, nullify)	(h)yohk! (f)luk	ยกเลิก
cancer	(f)rohk ma-reng!	โรคมะเร็ง
candidate	(f)poo sa-(l)mahk!	ผู้สมัคร
candle	tee-un	เทียน
candy	ka-(r)nohm! (r)wahn	ขนมหวาน
(candies, hard candies)	(f)look (l)gwaht	ลูกกวาด
cannot (to be unable to)	(f)my! (f)dy!	ไม่ได้
„	(f)my! bpen!	ไม่เป็น

35

(to be unable to, due to physical weakness)

(f)my! (r)wy! ไม่ไหว

(to be impossible) bpen! bpy! (f)my! (f)dy! เป็นไปไม่ได้

canvas (f)pah by! ผ้าใบ

capital city meu-ung (r)loo-ung เมืองหลวง

  ,, (of Thailand, Bangkok) pra! na-kawn พระนคร

captain (army) (h)rawy (l)ehk ร้อยเอก

  (navy) nah-wah (l)ehk นาวาเอก

  (air force) reu-uh ah-(l)gaht (l)ehk เรืออากาศเอก

capture (to catch) (l)jahp! จับ

  (to capture a person) (l)jahp! dtoo-uh จับตัว

car (automobile) (h)roht! yohn รถยนต์

  (general term for vehicle) (h) roht! รถ

  (rented car, taxi) (h)roht! (f)chow! รถเช่า

  (classifier for vehicles) kahn! คัน

card (l)baht! บัตร

  (business card) nahm (l)baht! นามบัตร

  (playing cards) (f)py! ไพ่

cardboard gra-(l)daht (r)kaang กระดาษแข็ง

care (to take care of) doo-laa ดูแล

(to care for, take care of, watch over, keep)

(h)rahk!-(r)sah   รักษา

(to take care of, as a baby or puppy)

(h)lee-ung doo   เลี้ยงดู

(to care, to be interested)   kaa   แคร์

(to care about, to be concerned) gahng!wohn!   กังวล

(Handle with Care.)

ra-wahng! (r)kawng! (l)dtaak   ระวังของแตก

careful (to be careful, Be Careful!) ra-wahng!   ระวัง

careless (to be careless)   sa-(f)prow   สะเพร่า

carnival (or fair, festival)   ngahn   งาน

   ,,   ngahn cha-(r)lawng   งานฉลอง

carpenter   (f)chahng (h)my   ช่างไม้

carrot   (r)hoo-uh! (l)pahk!-(l)gaht daang   หัวผักกาดแดง

carry (to carry something light in the hands)

(r)teu   ถือ

(to carry something heavy in the hands)

(f)hue!   หิ้ว

(to carry a heavy load on the back or shoulder)

(l)baak   แบก

37

(to carry a baby or animal in one's arms)

	(f)oom!	อุ้ม
cart (wagon, general term)	(h)roht!	รถ
(a pull cart)	(h)roht! lahk	รถลาก
(a pushcart)	(h)roht! (r)ken!	รถเข็น
(ox-cart)	gwee-un	เกวียน
carton (cardboard carton)	(l)heep gra-(l)daht	หีบกระดาษ
cash (currency)	ngun! (l)soht!	เงินสด
(coins, small change)	ngun! (l)bpleek	เงินปลีก
(to cash a check)	(f)keun (h)chek!	ขึ้นเช็ค
,,	(f)laak (h)chek	แลกเช็ค
cashier	pa-(h)nahk! ngahn (l)gep! ngun!	พนักงานเก็บเงิน
	(f)poo (h)rahk!-(r)sah ngun!	ผู้รักษาเงิน
casket (or coffin)	(l)heep! (l)sohp!	หีบศพ
cat	maa-oh	แมว
catch (to catch, seize, hold on to)	(l)jahp!	จับ
(to catch cold)	bpen! (l)waht!	เป็นหวัด
caterpillar (non-hairy type)	dtoo-uh(f)gaa-oh	ตัวแก้ว
(hairy type)	(f)boong!	บุ้ง
(caterpillar tractor)		
	(h)roht! dteen dta-(l)kahp	รถตีนตะขาบ

38

cauliflower	(l)dawk ga-(l)lahm!	ดอกกะหล่ำ
cause (the cause, reason)	(l)het	เหตุ
(to cause)	tahm! (f)hy!	ทำให้
cave (or tunnel)	(f)tahm!	ถ้ำ
ceiling	peh-dahn	เพดาน
celebrate (to celebrate)	cha-(r)lawng	ฉลอง
(celebration, festival)	ngahn cha-(r)lawng	งานฉลอง
celery	(l)pahk seh-luh-(f)ree	ผักเซเลอรี่
cement	bpoon sih!-men	ปูนซิเมนต์
cemetery	(l)bpah-(h)chah	ป่าช้า
center (middle)	glahng	กลาง
(at the center)	dtrohng! glahng	ตรงกลาง
centimeter	sen!-dti!-(h)met	เซนติเมตร
centipede	dta-(l)kahp	ตะขาบ
ceremony	(h)pih!-tee	พิธี
certain (to be certain, sure)	(f)naa	แน่
"	(f)naa jy	แน่ใจ
certainly (definitely, of course)	(f)naa nawn	แน่นอน
"	(f)naa la!	แน่ละ
certificate	by! (h)rahp! rawng	ใบรับรอง

chain	(f)soh	โซ่
chair	(f)gow!-ee	เก้าอี้
(rocking chair)	(f)gow!-ee (f)yohk	เก้าอี้โยก
chance (or opportunity)	oh-(l)gaht	โอกาส
change (to change, alter, vary)	(l)bplee-un	เปลี่ยน
(to change one's mind)	(l)bplee-un jy!	เปลี่ยนใจ
"	(l)glahp! jy!	กลับใจ
(to change money into smaller pieces)	tawn	ทอน
(change, money returned)	ngun! tawn	เงินทอน
(coins, small change)	ngun! (l)bpleek	เงินปลีก
(to exchange, trade)	(f)laak (l)bplee-un	แลกเปลี่ยน
(I want to exchange A for B.)		
	(r)kaw (l)bplee-un A bpen! B	ขอเปลี่ยนAเป็นB
changwat (province)	jahng!-(l)waht	จังหวัด
charcoal	(l)tahn	ถ่าน
charge (to charge a fee)	(h)keet! rah-kah	คิดราคา
chase	(f)ly!	ไล่
(to chase, run after)	(f)ly! goo-ut	ไล่กวด
(to chase away)	(l)kahp! (f)ly!	ขับไล่

chat (to chat, talk, converse)	kooy!	คุย
(to chat together)	kooy! gahn	คุยกัน
cheap (to be cheap, inexpensive)	(l)took	ถูก
cheat (to cheat, swindle)	gohng	โกง
check (to check, examine)	(l)droo-ut	ตรวจ
(a check, paycheck)	(h)chek!	เช็ค
cheese	nuh-ee (r)kaang!	เนยแข็ง
chemistry	keh-mee	เคมี
chew (to chew)	(h)kee-oh	เคี้ยว
chicken	(l)gy!	ไก่
(chick)	(f)look (l)gy!	ลูกไก่
chief (head, leader)	(r)hoo-uh (f)nah	หัวหน้า
child	(l)dek!	เด็ก
	(f)look	ลูก
(children)	(l)dek! (l)dek!	เด็ก ๆ
chili (pepper)	(h)prik!	พริก
,,	(h) prik! ty	พริกไทย
chin (or jaw)	kahng	คาง
China, Chinese	jeen	จีน
(the country of China)	bpra-(f)tet jeen	ประเทศจีน

41

(a Chinese person)	kohn! jeen	คนจีน
(the Chinese)	chow jeen	ชาวจีน
(the Chinese language)	pah-(r)sah jeen	ภาษาจีน
(Red China)	jeen daang	จีนแดง
chisel (handtool)	(l)siw! (rhymes with "few")	สิ่ว
(to chisel out)	sa-(l)gaht!	สกัด
choice (or selection)	gahn (f)leu-uk	การเลือก
choke (to choke on)	(r)sahm!-(h)lahk!	สำลัก
cholera	(l)ah-hih!-wah	อหิวาต์
(to have the disease of cholera)		
	bpen! (f)rohk (l)ah-hih!-wah	เป็นโรคอหิวาต์
choose (to choose, pick out, select)	(f)leu-uk	เลือก
chopsticks	dta-(l)gee-up	ตะเกียบ
Christ	(h)pra! yeh-soo	พระเยซู
Christianity	(l)saht-sa-(r)nah (h)krit!	ศาสนาคริสต์
Christmas	(l)dtroot! fa-(l)rahng!	ครุมฝรั่ง
church	(l)boht	โบสถ์
(temple, wat)	(h)waht	วัด
cigar	sih!-gah	ซิการ์
cigarette	boo!-(l)ree	บุหรี่

(cigarette lighter)	fy! (h)chaak!	ไฟแช็ก
„	(f)tee (l)joot! boo!-(l)ree	ที่จุดบุหรี่

cinema (see "movie")

cinnamon (l)ohp! chuhy อบเชย

circle (geometric figure) wohng! glohm! วงกลม

(traffic circle) wohng! wee-un วงเวียน

circuit (electrical circuit) wohng! jawn วงจร

(electrical circuit diagram)

(r)paan (r)pahng fy! (h)fah แผนผังไฟฟ้า

(radio circuit diagram)

(r)paan (r)pahng (h)wih!-ta-(h)yoo! แผนผังวิทยุ

circus (with animals) la-kawn (l)saht! ละครสัตว์

city meu-ung เมือง

na-kawn! (often spelled "nakorn") นคร

civil service (govt. service, govt. job)

(f)raht-cha-gahn ราชการ

(civil servant, govt. official)

(f)kah (f)raht-cha-gahn ข้าราชการ

civilian pohn!-la-reu-un พลเรือน

clam (shellfish, oyster) (r)hawy หอย

43

clap (to clap hands)	(l)dtohp! meu	ตบมือ
class (or level, rank, grade)	(h)chahn!	ชั้น
(1st class)	(h)chahn! (l)neung!	ชั้นหนึ่ง
(2nd class)	(h)chahn! (r)sawng	ชั้นสอง
(3rd class)	(h)chahn! (r)sahm	ชั้นสาม
(group, type, species)	jahm-(f)poo-uk	จำพวก
classroom	(f)hawng! ree-un	ห้องเรียน
claw, claws	grohng! (h)lep!	กรงเล็บ
clean (to be clean)	sa-(l)aht	สะอาด
(to clean, to make clean)		
	tahm! (f)hy! sa-(l)aht	ทำให้สะอาด
(not dirty)	(f)my! sohk!-ga-bprohk!	ไม่สกปรก
clear (to be transparent)	(l)bprohng-(r)sy!	โปร่งใส
(to be clear weather)	(l)jaam!-(r)sy!	แจ่มใส
(to be clear)	(h)chaht!	ชัด
,,	(h)chaht!-jen	ชัดเจน
(clear soup)	(h)soop! (h)nahm! (r)sy!	ซุปน้ำใส
clerk (store clerk, shop assistant)		
	kohn! (r)ky (r)kawng	คนขายของ
(office worker)	sa!-(r)mee-un	เสมียน

clever (to be clever, smart, intelligent)

	cha-(l)laht	ฉลาด
climate (the weather)	ah-(l)gaht	อากาศ
climb (to climb)	bpeen	ปีน
clock	nah-li-gah	นาฬิกา
close (to close, to shut)	(l)bpit!	ปิด
(close, near)	(f)gly!	ใกล้
cloth	(f)pah	ผ้า
(dust cloth) (f)pah (h)chet! (l)foon!		ผ้าเช็ดฝุ่น
(a rag, old cloth) (f)pah (f)kee (h)riw!		ผ้าขี้ริ้ว
(washcloth) (f)pah (r)kohn (r)noo (h)lek		ผ้าขนหนูเล็ก
clothes	(f)seu-uh (f)pah	เสื้อผ้า
(clothespin,-pins) (h)my (l)neep! (f)pah		ไม้หนีบผ้า
clothing store (h)rahn (r)ky (f)seu-uh (f)pah		ร้านขายเสื้อผ้า
cloud, clouds	(f)mehk	เมฆ
(to be cloudy)	mee (f)mehk	มีเมฆ
(to be cloudy, overcast)	(h)kreum!	ครึ้ม
(the weather is cloudy) ah-(l)gaht(h)kreum!		อากาศครึ้ม
coast (or seacoast, seashore, shore) chy ta-leh		ชายทะเล
,,	(l)fahng! ta-leh	ฝั่งทะเล

coat	(f)seu-uh (f)nawk	เสื้อนอก
coat hanger	(r)kaw (r)kwaan (f)seu-uh	ขอแขวนเสื้อ
	(f)mai (r)kwaan (f)seu-uh	ไม้แขวนเสื้อ
cobra	ngoo (l)how!	งูเห่า
(king cobra)	ngoo johng!-ahng	งูจงอาง
Coca-cola, Coke	ko-(f)lah	โคล่า
cockfight	chohn! (l)gy!	ชนไก่
cockroach	ma-laang (l)sahp	แมลงสาบ
	maang (l)sahp	แมงสาบ
cocktail	kawk-tel	ค๊อกเทล
cocoa	go-(f)go	โกโก้
coconut	ma-(h)prow	มะพร้าว
(coconut meat)	(h)neu-uh ma-(h)prow	เนื้อมะพร้าว
(coconut juice, natural)		
	(h)nahm! ma-(h)prow	น้ำมะพร้าว
(coconut milk or cream, the liquid squeezed from the grated meat added to water)		
	(h)nahm! ga-(h)tih!	น้ำกะทิ
coffee	gah-faa	กาแฟ
(coffee pot)	gah gah-faa	กากาแฟ

(coffee to drink, black)	gah-faa dahm!	กาแฟดำ
(coffee with cream)	gah-faa (l)sy! nohm	กาแฟใส่นม
(coffee with sugar)		
	gah-faa (l)sy! (h)nahm!-dtahn	กาแฟใส่น้ำตาล
coffin (or casket)	(l)heep (l)sohp!	หีบศพ
coins (small change)	ngun! (l)bpleek	เงินปลีก
	sa-dtahng (f)yawy	สตางค์ย่อย
cold	yen!	เย็น
(to feel cold)	(r)now	หนาว
(to catch cold)	bpèn! (l)waht!	เป็นหวัด
collar	(l)bplawk kaw	ปลอกคอ
	kaw (f)seu-uh	คอเสื้อ
collect (to collect, keep, store)	(l)gep!	เก็บ
college	(h)wit!-ta-yah-ly!	วิทยาลัย
collide (to collide, bump into, run into)	chohn!	ชน
(to collide together)	chohn! gahn!	ชนกัน
collision	gahn chohn! gahn!	การชนกัน
(auto collision)	(h)roht! chohn!	รถชน
colonel (army)	pahn! (l)ehk	พันเอก
(air force)	nah-wah ah-(l)gaht (l)ehk	นาวาอากาศเอก

(lt. col., army)	pahn! toh	พันโท
(lt. col., air force)	nah-wah ah-(l)gaht toh	นาวาอากาศโท
color	(r)see	สี
comb n.	(r)wee	หวี
(to comb the hair)	(r)wee (r)pohm	หวีผม
come	mah	มา
(come in, enter)	(f)kow! mah	เข้ามา
(Come here!)	mah (f)nee	มานี่
(Where do you come from ?)		
	koon! mah (l)jahk (r)ny	คุณมาจากไหน
(What country do you come from ?)		
	koon! mah (l)jahk meu-ung (r)ny	คุณมาจากเมืองไหน
comedy	(f)reu-ung dta-(l)lohk!	เรื่องตลก
comfortable (to be comfortable)	sa-by	สบาย
,,	sa-(l)doo-uk sa-by	สะดวกสบาย
commander (navy)	nah-wah toh	นาวาโท
(lt. cmdr., navy)	nah-wah dtree	นาวาตรี
(commanding officer)		
	(f)poo bahn!-chah gahn	ผู้บัญชาการ
commodore	pohn! reu-uh (l)jaht!-dta-wah	พลเรือจัตวา

communist, communism	kawm-miw!-(h)nis!	คอมมิวนิสต์
(Communist China)	jeen daang	จีนแดง
company (firm)	baw-ri-(l)saht!	บริษัท
(guests)	(l)kaak	แขก
compass (for drawing circles)	wohng! wee-un	วงเวียน
(magnetic)	(r)kem! (h)tit!	เข็มทิศ
complain (to complain)	(h)rawng (h)took!	ร้องทุกข์
(a complaint)	gahn (h)rawng (h)took!	การร้องทุกข์
(to have a grievance, complain to)		
	(l)dtaw (f)wah	ต่อว่า
concerning	(l)gee-oh gahp	เกี่ยวกับ
concrete (cemented material)	kawn-(l)greet	คอนกรีต
condition (of health)	ah-gahn	อาการ
confidence	kwahm (f)cheu-uh (f)mahn!	ความเชื่อมั่น
confuse (to be confused)	(f)yoong!	ยุ่ง
connect (to connect, attach, stick to)	(l)dtit	ติด
(to be connected together)	(l)dtit! gahn!	ติดกัน
(to connect, continue, extend)	(l)dtaw	ต่อ
consonant	(h)pa-yahn!-(h)cha!-(h)na!	พยัญชนะ
constitution	(h)raht!-ta-tahm-ma-noon	รัฐธรรมนูญ

contruct (to construct, to build)	(f)sahng	สร้าง
,,	(l)gaw (f)sahng	ก่อสร้าง
consul	gohng!-(r)soon!	กงสุล
consulate	sa-(r)tahn gohng!-(r)soon!	สถานกงสุล
consult (to consult)	(l)bpreuk!-(r)sah	ปรึกษา
consultant (advisor)	(f)tee (l)bpreuk!-(r)sah	ที่ปรึกษา
contact (to contact, get in touch with)		
	(l)dtit! (l)dtaw	ติดต่อ
content (to be content, contented)	sa-by jy!	สบายใจ
(to be content, happy, at ease)	bpen!(l)sook!	เป็นสุข
continue (to continue)	(l)dtaw bpy!	ต่อไป
contract (agreement)	(r)sahn!-yah	สัญญา
(to sign a contract)	sen! (r)sahn!-yah	เซ็นสัญญา
(to break a contract)	(l)pit! (r)sahn!-yah	ผิดสัญญา
convenient (to be convenient)	sa-(l)doo-uk	สะดวก
cook (to cook **food**)	tahm! ah-(r)hahn	ทำอาหาร
(a cook)	kohn! kroo-uh	คนครัว
(a cook, female)	(f)maa kroo-uh	แม่ครัว
(a cook, male)	(f)paw kroo-uh	พ่อครัว
(to heat **something** up)		
	tahm! **something** (f)hy! (h)rawn	ทำ—ให้ร้อน

(to roast, bake, toast)	(f)bping!	ปิ้ง
(to roast, bake, broil in an oven)	(l)ohp!	อบ
(to barbecue over an open fire)	(f)yahng	ย่าง
(to fry)	(f)tawt	ทอด
(to boil)	(f)dtohm!	ต้ม
(to steam)	(f)neung!	นึ่ง
cookie, cookies ka-(r)nohm! bpahng! (r)wahn		ขนมปังหวาน
cool (to be cool or cold)	yen!	เย็น
(to be comfortably cool)	yen! se-by	เย็นสบาย
(to cool **something**)		
tahm! **something** (f)hy! yen!		ทำ—ให้เย็น
cooperate (to cooperate) (f)roo-um meu gahn!		ร่วมมือกัน
copper	tawng daang	ทองแดง
copy (to copy, redraw the same)	(f)lawk	ลอก
(a duplicate copy)	(r)sahm!-now!	สำเนา
(to make a duplicate copy)		
tahm! (r)sahm!-now!		ทำสำเนา
(a copy machine, any kind)		
(f)kreu-ung (l)aht! (r)sahm! now!		เครื่องอัดสำเนา
(no. of copies)	**no.** cha-(l)bahp!	—ฉบับ

51

cork (stopper)	(l)jook! (h)my! (h)gawk	จุกไม้ก๊อก
(a stopper for a bottle, any kind)		
	(l)jook! (l)koo-ut	จุกขวด
corn	(f)kow-(f)poht	ข้าวโพด
corner (or angle)	moom!	มุม
(street corner)	moom! ta-(r)nohn	มุมถนน
(corner of a room)	moom! (f)hawng!	มุมห้อง
(intersection of four streets)	(l)see (f)yaak	สี่แยก
corporal	(l)sip!-toh	สิบโท
corral (or pen)	(f)kawk	คอก
correct (to be right)	(l) took	ถูก
(to be right, correct!)	(l)took (f)dtawng	ถูกต้อง
,,	(l)took (h)laa-oh	ถูกแล้ว
corrugated roofing (cement-board material)		
	gra-(f)beu-ung (f)look (f)fook	กระเบื้องลูกฟูก
(galvanized iron)		
	(r)sahng!-ga-(r)see (f)look (f)fook	สังกะสีลูกฟูก
cost	(f)kah	ค่า
(price)	rah-kah	ราคา
(fare)	(f)kah doy-(r)sahn	ค่าโดยสาร

cotton	(f)fy	ผ้าย
(cloth)	(f)pah (f)fy	ผ้าผ้าย
(cotton wool, surgical cotton)	(r)sahm!-lee	สำลี
(cotton flannel cloth)	(f)pah (r)sahm!-lee	ผ้าสำลี
cough (to cough)	I!	ไอ
count (to count)	(h)nahp!	นับ
country	bpra-(f)tet	ประเทศ
	meu-ung	เมือง
(countryside, upcountry, rural)		
	(f)bahn (f)nawk	บ้านนอก

(What country do you come from ?)

koon! mah (l)jahk meu-ung (r)ny	คุณมาจากเมืองไหน

course (course of study, curriculum)		
	(l)lahk! (l)soot	หลักสูตร
(golf course)	sa-(r)nahm gawlf	สนามก๊อลฟ์
(Of course!)	(f)naa nawn	แน่นอน
,,	(f)naa la!	แน่ละ
court (of law)	(r)sahn	ศาล
cousin, consins (f)look(f)pee(f)look(h)nawng		ลูกพี่ลูกน้อง
	(f)pee-(h)nawng	พี่น้อง

53

cover (a cover, top, lid)	(r)fah-(l)bpit!	ฝาปิด
(to cover, to put on the cover)	(l)bpit! (r)fah	ปิดฝา
(to cover up, cover over)	kloom!	คลุม
(to uncover, to take off the cover)		
	ow! (r)fah (l)bpit! (l)awk	เอาฝาเปิดออก
„	(l)bpuht (l)awk	เปิดออก
cow	woo-uh dtoo-uh mee-uh	วัวตัวเมีย
crab	bpoo	ปู
crackers (salty crackers)		
	ka-(r)nohm! bpahng! kem!	ขนมปังเค็ม
(crisp crackers)		
	ka-(r)nohm! bpahng! (l)grawp	ขนมปังกรอบ
crawl (to crawl)	klahn	คลาน
(to crawl, slither, as of snakes)	(h)leu-ay	เลื้อย
crazy (to be crazy)	(f)bah	บ้า
(to be halfwit)	(f)bah (f)bah baw baw	บ้า ๆ บอ ๆ
cream	kreem	ครีม
creek (or brook, stream)	(f)hoo-ay	ห้วย
cremate (to cremate)	(r)pow! (l)sohp	เผาศพ
(cremation)	gahn (r)pow! (l)sohp	การเผาศพ

cricket (insect)	(f)jing!-(l)reet	จิ้งหรีด
crocodile	jaw-ra-(f)keh	จระเข้
crops (plants, vegetation)	(f)peut	พืช
(farm crops)	(f)peut (f)ry!	พืชไร่
cross (to cross, cross over)	(f)kahm	ข้าม
(to cross the street)	(f)kahm ta-(r)nohn!	ข้ามถนน
(a cross, form of a cross)	gahng-(r)ken	กางเขน
corssroads (four corners)	(l)see (f)yaak	สี่แยก
crosswalk (pedestrian crosswalk)		
	tahng (f)kahm	ทางข้าม
crowded (to be crowded,tight,packed)	(f)naan!	แน่น
cry (to cry with tears, weep)	(h)rawng (f)hy!	ร้องไห้
(to cry out)	(h)rawng	ร้อง
cucumber	dtaang-gwah	แตงกวา
cup	(f)too-ay	ถ้วย
cupboard (or cabinet)	(f)dtoo	ตู้
curry	gaang	แกง
(Indian curry)	gaang ga-(l)ree	แกงกะหรี่
(hot curry)	gaang (l)pet!	แกงเผ็ด
(pepper sauce)	(h)nahm! (h)prik!	น้ำพริก

curtain	(f)mahn	ม่าน
(window curtains)	(f)mahn(f)nah-(l)dtahng	ม่านหน้าต่าง
curve (to be bent, curved)	(h)kohng	โค้ง
(curve in a road)	(r)hoo-uh (h)kohng	หัวโค้ง
cuspidor (spittoon)	gra-(r)tohn	กระโถน
custom (or tradition)	bpra!-peh-nee	ประเพณี
customs department		
	grohm! (r)soon!-la-gah-gawn	กรมศุลกากร
customer	(f)look (h)kah	ลูกค้า
cut (to cut)	(l)dtaht!	ตัด
(a cut, wound)	(l)baht (r)plaa	บาดแผล
(to cut into pieces, to slice)	(l)hahn!	หั่น
cute (to be cute, lovely)	(f)nah (h)rahk!	น่ารัก
cylinder	(l)soop	สูบ
(cylinder of an engine)	gra-(l)bawk(l)soop	กระบอกสูบ
daily (every day)	(h)took! wahn!	ทุกวัน
(——per day)	wahn! la!——	วันละ——
(a daily issue or publication)	ry wahn!	รายวัน
(daily, everyday)	bpra-jahm! wahn!	ประจำวัน
dam (or dike, embankment, breakwater, general term)	(l)keu-un	เขื่อน

(small dam)	tahm!-(b)nohp!	ทำนบ
damage (to be damaged)	(r)see-uh (r)hy	เสียหาย
(to damage **something**)		
tahm! **something**	(r)see-uh (r)hy	ทำ——เสียหาย
(a damage, loss) kwahm	(r)see-uh (r)hy	ความเสียหาย
(to become damaged, be defective)		
	chahm!-(b)root!	ชำรุด
damp (to be damp, moist, humid)	(h)cheun	ชื้น
dance (to dance)	(f)dten-rahm!	เต้นรำ
,,	lee-(f)laht	ลีลาศ
(Thai folk dance)	rahm!-wohng!	รำวง
(Thai classical dance)	rahm! ty	รำไทย
danger	ahn!-dta-ry	อันตราย
(to be dangerous)	mee ahn!-dta-ry	มีอันตราย
dark	dahm!	ดำ
(no light)	(f)meud	มืด
(to be dark in **color**)	**color** (l)gaa	——แก่
date (the **no.** day of the month) wahn!(f)tee **no.**		วันที่——
(What is the date today ?)		
wahn! (h)nee bpen! wahn! (f)tee (f)tow!-ry		วันนี้เป็นวันที่เท่าไร
(to go out on a date)	bpy! (f)tee-oh	ไปเที่ยว

57

daughter	(f)look (r)sow	ลูกสาว
dawn (or daybreak)	(f)roong!	รุ่ง
(at daybreak)	(f)roong! (h)chow	รุ่งเช้า
(dawn, at dawn)	(f)roong! ah-roon!	รุ่งอรุณ
day	wahn	วัน
(in the daytime)	glahng wahn!	กลางวัน
dead (to be dead, to die)	dty	ตาย
,,	dty (h)laa-oh	ตายแล้ว
deaf (to be deaf)	(r)hoo (l)noo-uk	หูหนวก
dear (beloved)	(f)tee (h)rahk!	ที่รัก
dear (expensive)	paang	แพง
debt	(f)nee	หนี้
(debts, liabilities)	(f)nee (r)sin	หนี้สิน
(to owe, be indebted)	bpen! (f)nee	เป็นหนี้
December	tahn!-wah-kohm!	ธันวาคม
decide (to decide)	(l)dtaht!-(r)sin!	ตัดสิน
(to make up one's mind)	(l)dtaht!-(r)sin!jy!	ตัดสินใจ
,,	(l)dtohk!-lohng! jy!	ตกลงใจ
decision	gahn (l)dtaht!-(r)sin!	การตัดสิน
	gahn (l)dtohk!-lohng! jy!	การตกลงใจ

decrease (to decrease)	(b)loht!	ลด
(to decrease **something**)		
	(b)loht! **something** lohng!	ลด――ลง
deep	(b)leuk!	ลึก
deer	gwahng	กวาง
defecate (see "excrement")		
defective (to be, defective, become damaged)		
	chahm!-(h)root!	ชำรุด
degree, degrees (of temperature or angular		
measure)	ohng!-(r)sah	องศา
(educational degree) (See "diploma".)		
delicious	ah!-(l)rawy	อร่อย
deliver (to deliver)	(l)sohng!	ส่ง
,,	(l)sohng! (f)hy	ส่งให้
democracy	bpra!-chah-(h)tip!-bpa!-dty	ประชาธิปไตย
dentist	(r)maw fahn!	หมอฟัน
	(f)paat fahn!	แพทย์ฟัน
	tahn!-dta-(f)paat	ทันตแพทย์
department (subdiv. of a ministry)	grohm!	กรม
(dept., section, division)	pa-(l)naak	แผนก

depend (to depend on, be dependent upon)

ah-(r)sy! อาศัย

(to be dependent on for subsistence)

ah-(r)sy! (l)yoo อาศัยอยู่

deposit (to deposit money)   (l)fahk ngun! ฝากเงิน

depth   kwahm (h)leuk! ความลึก

describe (to describe)   pahn-na-nah พรรณนา

desk   (h)dto! (r)kee-un (r)nahng-(r)seu โต๊ะเขียนหนังสือ

dessert (sweets)   (r)kawng (r)wahn ของหวาน

detour   tahng (f)awm ทางอ้อม

develop (to develop, progress, advance)

ja-run เจริญ

(to develop film)   (h)lahng feem ล้างฟิล์ม

development (progress, advancement)

kwahm ja-run ความเจริญ

diamond   (h)pet เพชร

diarrhea   (f)rohk (h)tawng (f)roo-ung โรคท้องร่วง

dice (game dice)   (r)dtow! เต๋า

(f)look (r)dtow! ลูกเต๋า

dictionary   (b)poht!-ja!-nah (h)noo!-grohm! พจนานุกรม

dik (colloquial)	ดิค
(l)bpa-tah-(h)noo!-grohm!	ปทานุกรม

die (to die, to be dead)   dty   ตาย

diesel oil, diesel fuel
         (h)nahm!-mahn! (h)roht! dee-sen   น้ำมันรถดีเซล

different   (l)dtahng   ต่าง
   (to be different)   (l)dtaak (l)dtahng   แตกต่าง
   (to be different from)
         (l)dtaak (l)dtahng (l)gwah   แตกต่างกว่า
   (to differ from)   (l)dtahng (l)gahp!   ต่างกับ
   (various)   (l)dtahng (l)dtahng   ต่าง ๆ

difficult (to be difficult, hard)   (f)yahk   ยาก
   (troublesome)   lahm!-(l)bahk   ลำบาก

dig (to dig)   (l)koot!   ขุด
   (to dig the ground)   (l)koot! din!   ขุดดิน

diligent (to be diligent, industrious) ka-(r)yahn   ขยัน

dining (dining room) (f)hawng! ah-(r)hahn   ห้องอาหาร
     ,,   (f)hawng!(h)rahp!-(l)bpra-tahn
                        ah-(r)hahn   ห้องรับประทาน
                                อาหาร

61

(dining table)	(h)dto! ah-(r)hahn	โต๊ะอาหาร
dinner (or supper)	ah-(r)hahn yen!	อาหารเย็น
(the evening meal)	ah-(r)hahn (f)kahm!	อาหารค่ำ
diploma (academic degree)	bpa-rin!-yah	ปริญญา
(bachelor's degree)	bpa-rin!-yah dtree	ปริญญาตรี
(master's degree)	bpa-rin!-yah toh	ปริญญาโท
(doctor's degree)	bpa-rin!-yah (l)ehk	ปริญญาเอก
direction (of the compass)	(h)tit	ทิศ
(way, route, path, road)	tahng	ทาง
director (administrator)		
	(f)poo ahm!-noo-ay gahn	ผู้อำนวยการ
dirt (dirt, ashes, residue)	(f)kee	ขี้
(mud)	(f)kee klohn	ขี้โคลน
(dirt, from the ground)	(f)kee din!	ขี้ดิน
dirty	sohk!-ga-bprohk!	สกปรก
(to get stained, soiled)	(f)bpeu-un	เปื้อน
disappear (to vanish, be missing)	(r)hy	หาย
„	(r)hy bpy!	หายไป
„	(r)soon (r)hy	สูญหาย
discouraged (to be discouraged)	(h)taw jy!	ท้อใจ

disease   (f)rohk!   โรค
  (to have **name** disease) bpen! (f)rohk! **name**   เป็นโรค—
disgusted (to be disgusted with or disapprove
  of someone)   (l)mahn!-(f)sy!   หมั่นไส้
dish (or plate, dishes)   jahn   จาน
  (bowl)   chahm   ชาม
  (dishes, dishware)   (f)too-ay! chahm   ถ้วยชาม
  (dishcloth, dishrag) (f)pah (h)lahng chahm   ผ้าล้างชาม
  (dishtowel)   (f)pah (h)chet! chahm   ผ้าเช็ดชาม
dismiss (to dismiss, discharge, fire **someone**
  from work)   (f)ly! **someone** (l)awk   ไล่—ออก
dissolve (to dissolve or melt)   la!-ly   ละลาย
distance   ra!-(h)ya! tahng   ระยะทาง
distilled water   (h)nahm! (l)glahn!   น้ำกลั่น
district (ampur,subdiv.of changwat)ahm!-puh   อำเภอ
  (tambon, subdiv. of ampur) dtahm!-bohn!   ตำบล
  (district officer,chief of ampur)ny ahm!-puh   นายอำเภอ
dive (to dive into water)   dahm! (h)nahm   ดำน้ำ
divide (to divide mathematically)   (r)hahn   หาร
  (A divided by B is C) B (r)hahn A bpen! C   B หาร A เป็น C

(to divide, to share)	(l)baang	แบ่ง
divorce (to divorce)	(l)yah gahn!	หย่ากัน
dizzy (to feel dizzy)	wee-un (r)hoo-uh	เวียนหัว
do (to do, did, does, done)	tahm!	ทำ
(do not, Don't!, imperative)	(l)yah	อย่า
(do not, it is forbidden to)	(f)hahm	ห้าม
dock (or pier, wharf, port, harbor)	(f)tah	ท่า
doctor	(r)maw	หมอ
	ny (f)paat	นายแพทย์
dog	(r)mah	หมา
	soo!-(h)nahk	สุนัข
doll	(h)dtook!-ga-dtah	ตุ๊กตา
dollar	dawn-(f)lah	ดอลล่า
	(r)ree-un	เหรียญ
done (to have finished, completed)		
	(l)set! (h)laa-oh	เสร็จแล้ว
(to have come to the end, as a book)		
	(l)johp! (h)laa-oh	จบแล้ว
(to be done, be cooked thoroughly)	(l)sook!	สุก
(to be well done)	(l)sook! dee	สุกดี
"	(l)sook! (l)sook!	สุก ๆ

door	bpra!-dtoo	ประตู
doormat	(f)tee (h)chet! (h)tao!	ที่เช็ดเท้า
double (pair)	(f)koo	คู่
(double room)	(f)hawng! (f)koo	ห้องคู่
doubt (to doubt, to be doubtful, to suspect)		
	(r)sohng!-(r)sy!	สงสัย
dove (bird)	(h)nohk! (r)kow!	นกเขา
down	lohng!	ลง
downstairs	(h)chahn! (f)lahng	ชั้นล่าง
	(f)kahng (f)lahng	ข้างล่าง
downtown	ny! meu-ung	ในเมือง
dozen	(r)loh	โหล
dragonfly	ma-laang bpaw	แมลงปอ
drain (to drain)	ra!-by	ระบาย
(drainage ditch, gutter)		
	rahng ra!-by (h)nahm!	รางระบายน้ำ
(drain pipe)	(f)taw ra!-by (h)nahm!	ท่อระบายน้ำ
(drainspout, drainpipe for rainwater)		
	(f)taw (h)nahm! (r)fohn!	ท่อน้ำฝน
(roof gutter)	rahng (h)nahm! (r)fohn!	รางน้ำฝน

draw (to draw)	(f)waht (r)kee-un	วาดเขียน
(to draw a picture)	(r)kee-un (f)roop	เขียนรูป
(to withdraw money)	(l)buk ngun!	เบิกเงิน
drawer (of a cabinet)	(h)lin!-(h)chahk!	ลิ้นชัก
dream (to dream)	(r)fahn!	ฝัน
(a dream)	kwahm (r)fahn!	ความฝัน
(to daydream)	(h)keet! (r)fahn!	คิดฝัน
,,	(b)kluhm (r)fahn	เคลิ้มฝัน
dress (a dress, skirt)	gra-bprohng	กระโปรง
	(sounds like "ga-prohng")	
(to dress)	(l)dtaang dtoo-uh	แต่งตัว
dresser	(f)dtoo (f)seu-uh (f)pah	ตู้เสื้อผ้า
(dressing table)	(h)dto! (l)dtaang dtoo-uh	โต๊ะแต่งตัว
drill (to drill, bore, puncture)	(l)jaw!	เจาะ
(hand drill)	sa-(l)wahn	สว่าน
(drill bit)	(l)dtawk sa-(l)wahn	ดอกสว่าน
drink (to drink)	(l)deum	ดื่ม
(to drink, eat)	geen!	กิน
(bottled drinks, soda pop)		
	(f)kreu-ung (l)deum	เครื่องดื่ม

(Coca-Cola)	ko-(f)lah	โคล่า
(Pepsi Cola)	pep!-(f)see	เป๊ปซี่
(Bring me two bottles of Coke.)		
(r)kaw! ko-(f)lah (r)sawng (l)koo-ut		ขอโคล่าสองขวด
drip (to drip)	(l)yoht!	หยด
drive (to drive a vehicle)	(l)kahp!	ขับ
,,	(l)kahp! (h)roht!	ขับรถ
driver (of a vehicle) kohn! (l)kahp! (h)roht!		คนขับรถ
drop (to drop, fall)	(l)dtohk!	ตก
(to drop **something**)		
tahm! **something** (l)dtohk!		ทำ——ตก
(a drop or drops of liquid)	(l)yoht!	หยด
(a drop or drops of water)	(l)yoht!(h)nahm	หยดน้ำ
drown (to drown) johm! (h)nahm! dty		จมน้ำตาย
drugstore (or pharmacy)	(h)rahn(r)ky yah	ร้านขายยา
drum	glawng	กลอง
drunk (to be drunk, intoxicated)	mao!	เมา
(to be habitually drunk)	(f)kee mao!	ขี้เมา
dry (to be dry, dried)	(f)haang	แห้ง
(to dry the hands, wipe hands)	(h)chet!meu	เช็ดมือ

67

dry-clean (to be dry-cleaned) (b)sahk!(f)haang ซักแห้ง

  (dry-cleaners) (b)rahn (h)sahk! (f)haang ร้านซักแห้ง

duck (l)bpet! เป็ด

dull (to be dull, not sharp) (f)teu ทื่อ

         ,, (f)my! kohm! ไม่คม

dump (to dump, discard) (h)ting! (f)kwahng ทิ้งขว้าง

  (a dump heap, rubbish pile) gawng ka-(l)ya! กองขยะ

  (a dump, dumping place)

           (f)tee (h)ting! moon-(r)fawy ที่ทิ้งมูลฝอย

durian (a large, rich, meaty fruit) (h)too!-ree-un ทุเรียน

during (or between, among) ra-(l)wahng ระหว่าง

         ,, ny! ra-(l)wahng ในระหว่าง

dust (l)foon! ฝุ่น

  (to dust, wipe up dust) (h)chet! (l)foon! เช็ดฝุ่น

  (dustcloth) (f)pah (h(chet! (l)foon! ผ้าเช็ดฝุ่น

dustpan (f)tee (l)dtahk! (r)pohng! ที่ตักผง

dye (to dye) (h)yawm ย้อม

dysentery (f)rohk (l)bit! โรคบิด

each (or every)	(h)took!	ทุก
(each and every)	(h)took! (h)took!	ทุก ๆ
ear	(r)hoo	หู
(earring, earrings)	(f)dtoom! (r)hoo	ตุ้มหู
,,	(l)dtahng (r)hoo	ต่างหู
early (to be early)	reh-oh	เร็ว
(to come early)	mah reh-oh	มาเร็ว
(early in the morning)	(h)chow	เช้า
,,	(h)chow (l)dtroo	เช้าตรู่
earn (to earn money)	(r)hah ngun!	หาเงิน
,,	(f)dy ngun!	ได้เงิน
earth (the ground, soil)	din!	ดิน
(the world, globe)	(f)lohk	โลก
east	dta-wahn! (l)awk	ตะวันออก
(the direction of)	(h)tit! dta-wahn! (l)awk	ทิศตะวันออก
easy (to be easy, simple)	(f)ngy	ง่าย
eat	geen!	กิน
	(h)rahp!-bpra!-tahn	รับประทาน
(to eat rice, to eat food)	geen! (f)kow	กินข้าว
,,	tahn (f)kow	ทานข้าว

69

ebony (the wood)	(h)my! ma-gleu-uh	ไม้มะเกลือ
edge	(l)kawp	ขอบ
	rim!	ริม
educate (to study, be educated)	(l)seuk!-(r)sah	ศึกษา
education	gahn (l)seuk!-(r)sah	การศึกษา
egg	(l)ky!	ไข่
(fried eggs)	(l)ky! dow	ไข่ดาว
(hard-boiled eggs)	(l)ky! (f)dtohm!	ไข่ต้ม
(soft-boiled eggs)	(l)ky! (f)loo-uk	ไข่ลวก
(scrambled eggs)	(l)ky! kohn!	ไข่คน
,,	(l)ky! goo-un	ไข่กวน
(poached eggs)	(l)ky! lawy (h)nahm!	ไข่ลอยน้ำ
(omelet)	(l)ky! jee-oh	ไข่เจียว
(egg yolk)	(l)ky! daang	ไข่แดง
(egg white)	(l)ky! (r)kow	ไข่ขาว
eight (8)	(l)bpaat	แปด
either (either A or B, either one, either one will do)	A (r)reu B (f)gaw! (f)dy	A หรือ B ก็ได้
elect (to elect, choose)	(f)leu-uk	เลือก
(election)	gahn (f)leu-uk (h)dtahng!	การเลือกตั้ง

electrician	(f)chahng fy! (h)fah	ช่างไฟฟ้า
electricity, electric, electrical	fy! (h)fah	ไฟฟ้า
elephant	(h)chahng	ช้าง
elevator (lift)	lift	ลิฟต์
eleven (11)	(l)sip-(l)et!	สิบเอ็ด
embarrassed (to feel embarrassed)	la!-I	ละอาย
(to feel self-conscious)	(r)koo-ay (r)kuhn	ขวยเขิน
embassy	sa-(r)tahn (f)toot	สถานทูต
employ (to employ, hire)	(f)jahng	จ้าง
employee	(f)look (f)jahng	ลูกจ้าง
employer	ny (f)jahng	นายจ้าง
employment	gahn ngahn	การงาน
empty (to be empty, vacant)	(f)wahng (l)bplao	ว่างเปล่า
(contents to have been used up)		
	(l)moht (h)laa-oh	หมดแล้ว
(to empty **something**)		
tahm! (f)hy! **something**	(f)wahng (l)bplao	ทำให้—ว่างเปล่า
end (or tip)	bply	ปลาย
(to end, finish, as a book or movie)	(l)johp	จบ
(the end of the road)	(l)soot! ta-(r)nohn!	สุดถนน

71

(the end of the bus or train line)

(l)soot! tahng (h)roht!   สุดทางรถ

(the end of the month)   (f)sin! deu-un   สิ้นเดือน

enemy   (f)kah-(l)seuk   ข้าศึก

energy   gahm!-lahng!   กำลัง

engaged (to be engaged to be married)

(f)mahn!   หมั้น

engine (or machinery, device, general term)

(f)kreu-ung   เครื่อง

(reciprocating engine, gasoline engine)

(f)kreu-ung yohn!   เครื่องยนต์

(automobile engine)

(f)kreu-ung (h)roht yohn!   เครื่องรถยนต์

(electric motor)   dy-na-mo   ไดนาโม

engineer (professional) (h)wiht!-sa-wa-gawn   วิศวกร

engineering   (h)wiht!-sa-wa-gahm!   วิศวกรรม

England, English   ahng!-(l)grit!   อังกฤษ

(the country of) bpra-(f)tet ahng!-(l)grit!   ประเทศอังกฤษ

(an English person) kohn! ahng!-(l)grit!   คนอังกฤษ

(the English language)

	pah-(r)sah ahng!-(l)grit!	ภาษาอังกฤษ
enjoy (to enjoy oneself)	sa-(l)nook	สนุก
(to have a good time	sa-(l)nook!dee	สนุกดี
enough (to be enough)	paw	พอ
(That's enough!)	paw (h)laa-oh	พอแล้ว
(good enough)	paw dee	พอดี
ensign (naval officer)	reu-uh dtree	เรือตรี
enter (to enter, go in)	(f)kow! bpy!	เข้าไป
(to enter, come in)	(f)kow! mah	เข้ามา
(do not enter, keep out)	(f)hahm (f)kow	ห้ามเข้า
entertain (to entertain)	(h)rahp! rawng	รับรอง
(to entertain guests)	(h)rahp! rawng (l)kaak	รับรองแขก
(to give a banquet, to feast)		
	(h)lee-ung (l)kaak	เลี้ยงแขก
(to provide enjoyment)		
	tahm! (f)hy! sa-(l)nook!	ทำให้สนุก
entrance	tahng (f)kow!	ทางเข้า
(entrance to a **canal, street, lane, river,** etc.)		
	(l)bpahk––	ปาก––

envelope (general term)	sawng	ซอง
(mail envelope)	sawng (l)joht!-(r)my	ซองจดหมาย
equal	(f)tao!	เท่า
(to be equal with each other)	(f)tao!gahn!	เท่ากัน
(to be equal to)	(f)tao! gahp!	เท่ากับ
equipment (implements, accessories, etc., general term)	(l)oop-bpa-gawn	อุปกรณ์
erase (to erase)	(h)lohp!	ลบ
,,	(h)lohp! (l)awk	ลบออก
(a rubber eraser)	yahng (h)lohp!	ยางลบ
escape (to escape)	(r)nee	หนี
(to run away)	(f)wing! (r)nee	วิ่งหนี
especially	cha-(h)paw!	เฉพาะ
(particularly)	doy cha-(h)paw	โดยเฉพาะ
evening (in the evening, eveningtime)	weh-lah yen!	เวลาเย็น
(this evening)	yen! (h)nee	เย็นนี้
(early in the evening)	(r)hoo-uh (f)kahm!	หัวค่ำ
ever (at some time, used to)	kuh-ee	เคย
every (or each)	(h)took!	ทุก

(each and every)	(h)took! (h)took!	ทุก ๆ
everybody, everyone	(h)took! kohn!	ทุกคน
	(h)took! (h)took! kohn!	ทุก ๆ คน
every day	(h)took! wahn!	ทุกวัน
everything	(h)took! sing!	ทุกสิ่ง
	(h)took! (l)yahng	ทุกอย่าง
	(h)took! (l)sing! (h)took! (l)yahng	ทุกสิ่งทุกอย่าง
everywhere, every place	(h)took! (l)haang!	ทุกแห่ง
	(h)took! (r)hohn! (h)took! (l)haang	ทุกหนทุกแห่ง
exact (to be exactly, exactly)	dtrohng!	ตรง
(at 12 o'clock noon sharp)		
	(f)tee-ung dtrohng!	เที่ยงตรง
(exactly, precisely, just right, in size or quantity)	paw dee	พอดี
examine (to check, inspect)	(l)dtroo-ut	ตรวจ
(to test, take an exam)	(l)sawp	สอบ
(an examination, test)	gahn (l)sawp	การสอบ
example (an example, a sample)		
	dtoo-uh (l)yahng	ตัวอย่าง

75

except (f) nawk (l)jahk นอกจาก

exchange (to exchange, trade)

(f)laak (l)bplee-un แลกเปลี่ยน

(to change money into smaller pieces) tawn ทอน

(the rate of exchange)

(l)aht!-dtrah (f)laak (l)bplee-un อัตราแลกเปลี่ยน

(I want to exchange A for B)

(r)kaw (l)bplee-un A bpen! B ขอเปลี่ยนAเป็นB

excrement (fecal matter, feces, to defecate)

(f)kee (vulgar) ขี้

,, (l)oot!-jah-(h)ra! อุจจาระ

(to have the urge to defecate)

(l)bpoo-ut (h)tawng (f)kee ปวดท้องขี้

excuse (to excuse, Excuse me!) (r)kaw (f)toht ขอโทษ

,, (r)kaw ah-py! ขออภัย

(an excuse, reason) (f)kaw (f)gaa dtoo-uh ข้อแก้ตัว

exercise (to exercise one's body)

(l)awk gahm!-lahng! gy ออกกำลังกาย

exhaust pipe (f)taw I (r)see-uh ท่อไอเสีย

exit tahng (l)awk ทางออก

expect (to expect that)	(f)kaht (f)wah	คาดว่า
expense, expenses	(f)kah (h)chy (l)jy	ค่าใช้จ่าย
expensive (to be expensive)	paang	แพง
expert (authority)	(f)poo chahm!-nahn gahn	ผู้ชำนาญการ
(artisan, specialist, one skilled at)	(f)chahng	ช่าง
(one who is skilled or experienced at——)		
	(h)nahk!——	นัก——
expire (to expire, terminate, end)		
	(f)sin (l)soot!	สิ้นสุด
„	(l)moht! ah-(h)yoo	หมดอายุ
explain (to explain)	ah-tih!-by	อธิบาย
(explantion)	kahm! ah-tih!-by	คำอธิบาย
explode (to explode, burst, blast)	ra-(l)but	ระเบิด
explosion	gahn ra-(l)but	การระเบิด
extinguish (to extinguish, put out)	(l)dahp!	ดับ
(to put out a fire)	(l) dahp! fy!	ดับไฟ
„	(l)dahp! plung	ดับเพลิง
(fire extinguisher)		
	(f)kreu-ung (l)dahp! plung	เครื่องดับเพลิง
eye, eyes	dtah	ตา

eyebrow	(h)kue (pronounced like "cue")	คิ้ว
eyelashes	(r)kohn! dtah	ขนตา
face	(f)nah	หน้า
fact	kwahm jing!	ความจริง
factory	rohng ngahn	โรงงาน
fair (or ceremony, festival)	ngahn	งาน
"	ngahn cha-(r)lawng	งานฉลอง
(to be fair, just)	(h)yoot!-dtih!-tahm	ยุติธรรม
faith (or trust)	kwahm (f)cheu-uh	ความเชื่อ
(to be faithful, true, loyal)	(f)seu-(l)saht!	ซื่อสัตย์
fall (to fall, drop)	(l)dtohk!	ตก
(to fall over)	(h)lohm!	ล้ม
(to trip and fall)	(l)hohk! (h)lohm!	หกล้ม
(to fall off, come off, become detached)		
	(l)loot!	หลุด
(autumn) (h)reu!-doo by! (h)my (f)roo-ung		ฤดูใบไม้ร่วง
false (to be false, fake, be an imitation)		
	bplawm	ปลอม
(to be not real)	(f)my! jing!	ไม่จริง
(to be not the truth) (f)my!bpen!kwahm jing		ไม่เป็นความจริง

family	(f)krawp kroo-uh	ครอบครัว
fan (a fan, to fan)	(h)paht!	พัด
(an electric fan)	(h)paht! lohm!	พัดลม
far (to be far, distant)	gly!	ไกล
(to be located far away)	(l)yoo gly!	อยู่ไกล
fare (cost of passage)	(f)kah doy-(r)sahn	ค่าโดยสาร
farm (or field, rice paddy)	nah	นา
(farm, plantation)	(f)ry!	ไร่
farmer	chow nah	ชาวนา
fast (to be fast, swift, quick)	reh-oh!	เร็ว
„	reh-oh! reh-oh!	เร็ว ๆ
fasten (to fasten, attach)	(l)dtit!	ติด
(to tie, bind, fasten)	(l)pook	ผูก
(to unfasten, untie, undo, unwrap)	(f)gaa	แก้
fat (to be fat, obese)	(f)oo-un	อ้วน
(oil, grease, any kind)	(h)nahm! mahn!	น้ำมัน
(grease, of foods)	(r)ky! mahn	ไขมัน
(lard)	(h)nahm! mahn! (r)moo	น้ำมันหมู
father	(f)paw	พ่อ
	(l)bee!-dah	บิดา

79

father-in-law (of a man)   (f)paw dtah   พ่อตา

  (of a woman)   (f)paw (r)poo-uh   พ่อผัว

faucet (tap, spigot)   (h)gawk!   ก๊อก

fault (guilt, mistake)   kwahm (l)pit!   ความผิด

fear (to fear, be afraid of)   gloo-uh   กลัว

feather, feathers   (r)kohn! (h)nohk!   ขนนก

February   goom!-pah pahn!   กุมภาพันธ์

feed (to feed)   (h)lee-ung   เลี้ยง

feel (to feel)   (h)roo-(l)seuk!   รู้สึก

  (to feel by touch, feel around)   klahm!   คลำ

feet (of the body)   (h)tao   เท้า

  (see "foot")

female (of people)   (r)ying!   หญิง

  (of animals)   dtoo-uh mee-uh   ตัวเมีย

fence   (h)roo-uh   รั้ว

fender (or mudguard of any vehicle)

                   bahng! klohn   บังโคลน

fertilizer (or manure)   (r)bpoo-ee   ปุ๋ย

fever   (f)ky!   ไข้

  (to have a fever)   bpen! (f)ky   เป็นไข้

few	(h)nawy!	น้อย
(two or three)	(r)sawng (r)sahm	สองสาม
field (paddy)	nah	นา
,,	(f)toong! nah	ทุ่งนา
(field, as for sports)	sa-(r)nahm	สนาม
(airfield)	sa-(r)nahm bin	สนามบิน
fight (to fight)	(l)dtaw-(f)soo	ต่อสู้
(fist fight)	(h)chohk! gahn!	ชกกัน
,,	dtee gahn!	ตีกัน
(bullfight)	chohn! woo-uh	ชนวัว
(cockfight)	chohn! (l)gy!	ชนไก่
file (hand tool)	dta!-by!	ตะไบ
(to file)	(r)too dta!-by!	ถูตะไบ

fill (to fill full with **something**)		
	(l)sy! **something** (h)hy! dtem!	ใส่——ให้เต็ม
(to make full, to fill up)	tahm! (f)hy! dtem!	ทำให้เต็ม
(to be full, filled)	dtem!	เต็ม
film (photographic)	feem!	ฟิล์ม
	feem! (l)ty (f)roop	ฟิล์มถ่ายรูป
finally (at last, in the end)	ny! (f)tee (l)soot!	ในที่สุด

find (to find, meet)	(h)pohp!	พบ
(to look for **something** or **someone** and find it, him)	(r)hah——(h)pohp	หา——พบ
"	(r)hah——juh	หา——เจอ
("juh" often sounds like "(h)juh!")		
(to look for, but cannot find)		
	(r)hah (f)my! juh	หาไม่เจอ
fine (to be fine, well, happy)	sa-by	สบาย
"	sa-by dee	สบายดี
(a fine, penalty)	(f)kah (l)bprahp! (r)my	ค่าปรับไหม
finger (of the hand)	(h)nue!	นิ้ว
(rhymes with "hue")		
"	(h)nue! meu	นิ้วมือ
fingernail	(h)lep! meu	เล็บมือ
fingerprint (or handwriting)	ly meu	ลายมือ
finish (to be finished, be done)	(l)set!	เสร็จ
(to have finished already)	(l)set!(h)laa-oh	เสร็จแล้ว
(to finish, make finished)	tahm! (l)set	ทำเสร็จ
"	tahm! (f)hy! (l)set	ทำให้เสร็จ
"	(f)hy! (l)set!	ให้เสร็จ

(to finish, as with a book, play, or movie)

(l)johp! จบ

(to finish, end, quit, to be over, be through)

(f)luk เลิก

(to be finished up, all used up, all gone)

(l)moht! (h)laa-oh หมดแล้ว

(to be finished eating, be full of food) (l)im! อิ่ม

     ,,   (l)im! (h)laa-oh อิ่มแล้ว

fire (to be on fire, a fire)   fy! (f)my ไฟไหม้

(fire station) sa-(r)tah-nee (l)dahp! plung! สถานีดับเพลิง

(fire engine)   (h)roht! (l)dahp! plung! รถดับเพลิง

(I want to report a fire.) (r)chahn! (f)dtawng!

gahn (f)jaang kwahm (f)reu-ung fy! (f)my ฉันต้องการแจ้ง
ความเรื่องไฟไหม้

(to fire, to dismiss **someone** from work)

(f)ly! **someone** (l)awk ไล่——ออก

firefly   (l)hing! (h)hawy! หิ่งห้อย

first (to be first)   (f)raak แรก

(the first one, first time, first place)

(f)tee (f)raak ที่แรก

(1st, ordinal number)	(f)tee (l)neung!	ที่หนึ่ง
(before, ahead of)	(l)gawn	ก่อน
(beforehand, in advance)	(r)see-uh(l)gawn	เสียก่อน
(the first part, the beginning)	(f)dtohn!	ต้น
fish	bplah	ปลา
(to fish, catch fish with a line)	(l)dtohk! bplah	ตกปลา
,,	(l)jahp! bplah	จับปลา
(to catch fish with a net)	(r)hah bplah	หาปลา
fisherman	kohn! (l)jahp! bplah	คนจับปลา
	chow bpra-mohng!	ชาวประมง
fishhook	(l)bet!	เบ็ด
fishing pole, rod	kahn! (l)bet!	คันเบ็ด
fit (to be a good fit, as with clothing)		
	(l)maw! (r)sohm	เหมาะสม
five (5)	(f)hah	ห้า
fiix (to fix, repair, mend)	(f)gaa	แก้
,,	(f)sawm	ซ่อม
(to be fixed in place, rigid)	dty dtoo-uh	ตายตัว
flag (banner)	tohng!	ธง
(the national flag)	tohng! (f)chaht	ธงชาติ

flashlight	fy! (r)chy	ไฟฉาย
flat (to be flat)	baan	แบน
(to have a flat tire)	yahng baan	ยางแบน
,,	yahng (l)dtaak	ยางแตก
(apartment)	flaat!	แฟลต
,,	(f)hawng! (f)chow!	ห้องเช่า
flea, fleas	(l)maht!	หมัด
float (to float on water)	lawy	ลอย
(Floating Market)	dta-(l)laht (h)nahm	ตลาดน้ำ
flood n.	(h)nahm! (f)too-um	น้ำท่วม
floor	(h)peun	พื้น
(story, level)	(h)chahn!	ชั้น
flour (wheat flour)	(f)bpaang (r)sah-lee	แป้งสาลี
flow (to flow, run, as a liquid)	(r)ly!	ไหล
flower	(l)dawk-(h)my	ดอกไม้
flowerpot	gra-(r)tahng	กระถาง
flu (influenza)	(f)ky! (l)waht (l)yai	ไข้หวัดใหญ่
fly (insect)	ma-laang wahn!	แมลงวัน
(to fly)	bin!	บิน
(to fly, to travel by airplane)		

85

	bpy! tahng reu-uh bin!	ไปทางเรือบิน
(to fly a kite)	(h)chahk! (f)wow!	ชักว่าว
,,	(f)len! (f)wow!	เล่นว่าว
foam (or bubbles)	fawng	ฟอง
(foam rubber)	fawng (h)nahm	ฟองน้ำ
fog (or mist)	(l)mawk	หมอก
(to be foggy)	mee (l)mawk	มีหมอก
foil (tin foil)	gra-(l)daht dee-(l)book!	กระดาษดีบุก
fold (to fold)	(h)pahp!	พับ
follow	dtahm	ตาม
food	ah-(r)bahn	อาหาร
(food, rice)	(f)kow	ข้าว
(food that is eaten with rice)	(l)gahp!(f)kow	กับข้าว
foolish (to be foolish, stupid)	(f)ngoh	โง่
foot, feet (of the body)	(h)tao	เท้า
(foot, paw)	dteen	ตีน
(of length)	(h)foot!	ฟุต
footprint	rawy (h)tao	รอยเท้า
for	(r)sahm!-(l)rahp!	สำหรับ

(for the purpose of)   (f)peu-uh   เพื่อ

forbid (to forbid, prohibit, it is forbidden to)

            (f)hahm   ห้าม

  (to not allow, not permit)(f)my!yawm(f)hy!   ไม่ยอมให้

force (to force, compel, require)

            bahng!-(h)kahp!   บังคับ

  (strength, energy)   gahm!-lahng!   กำลัง

foreign(foreign country) (l)dtahng bpra-(f)tet   ต่างประเทศ

  (outside the country) (f)nawk bpra-(f)tet   นอกประเทศ

foreigner (westerner, European, occidental)

            (l)fa-(l)rahng!   ฝรั่ง

forest (or woods, jungle)   (l)bpah   ป่า

forever (indefinitely, everlasting)

            dta-(l)lawt gahn   ตลอดกาล

  (on and on, all the time) dta-(l)lawt bpy!   ตลอดไป

forget (to forget)   leum   ลืม

forgive (to forgive) (h)yohk! (f)toht (f)hy!   ยกโทษให้

  (to forgive, pardon, excuse **someone**)

          (f)hy! ah-py! **someone**   ให้อภัย——

(Forgive me!, Excuse me!) (r)kaw (f)toht	ขอโทษ
„ (r)kaw ah-py!	ขออภัย
„ (h)yoht! (f)toht (f)hy!	
(r)chahn (f)doo-ay	ยกโทษให้ฉันด้วย
„ ah-py!(f)hy!(r)chahn(f)doo-ay	อภัยให้ฉันด้วย
fork (for eating) (f)sawm	ซ่อม
fortune teller (r)maw doo	หมอดู
fountain (water fountain) (h)nahm! (h)poo!	น้ำพุ
four (4) (l)see	สี่
fourth (4th) (f)tee (l)see	ที่สี่
(one-fourth, $\frac{1}{4}$) (l)set(l)neung!(l)soo-un(l)see	เศษหนึ่งส่วนสี่
„ (l)neung! ny (l)see	หนึ่งในสี่
(three-fourths, 3/4)	
(l)set (r)sahm (l)soo-un (l)see	เศษสามส่วนสี่
fraction (remainder, remnant) (l)set	เศษ
(arithmetic fraction) (l)set (l)soo-un	เศษส่วน
(To say any fraction : A/B)	
(l)set A (l)soo-un B	เศษ A ส่วน B
fragile (to be fragile, be easily broken)	
(l)dtaak (f)ngy	แตกง่าย

(Fragile. Handle with care.)

	ra-wahng! (r)kawng (l)dtaak	ระวังของแตก
France, French	fa-(l)rahng!-(l)set	ฝรั่งเศส
(the country of)		
	bpra-(f)tet fa-(l)rahng!-(l)set	ประเทศฝรั่งเศส
(the French people)	chow fa-(l)rahng!-(l)set	ชาวฝรั่งเศส
(the French language)		
	pah-(r)sah fa-(l)rahng!-(l)set	ภาษาฝรั่งเศส
free (to be free, of no cost)	free	ฟรี
(to be at leisure; be vacant)	(f)wahng	ว่าง
freedom	(l)iht!-(l)sa-(h)ra!	อิสสระ
freeze (to freeze **something**) tahm! **something**		
(f)hy! yen! bpen! (h)nahm! (r)kaang!		ทำ—ให้เย็นเป็น น้ำแข็ง
fresh (to be fresh)	(l)soht!	สด
(fresh water)	(h)nahm! (l)jeut	น้ำจืด
Friday	wahn! (l)sook!	วันศุกร์
fried (to fry, to be fried)	(f)tawt	ทอด
friend	(f)peu-un	เพื่อน
(to be friends)	bpen! (f)peu-un gahn	เป็นเพื่อนกัน

friendly—full

friendly (to be friendly)　　bpen! (f)peu-un　เป็นเพื่อน

frighten (to be frightened)　　(l) dtohk! jy!　ตกใจ
　(to frighten **someone**)
　　　　tahm! **someone** (f)hy! (l)dtohk! jy　ทำ——ให้ตกใจ

frog　　　　　　　　　(l)gohp!　กบ

from　　　　　　　　　(l)jahk　จาก
　(since, starting from)　(f)dtahng! (l)dtaa　ตั้งแต่

front　　　　　　　　　(f)nah　หน้า
　(the front, in front, the front side)
　　　　　　　　(f)kahng (f)nah　ข้างหน้า

frozen (to be frozen) bpen! (h)nahm! (r)kaang!　เป็นน้ำแข็ง

fruit　　　　　　　(r)pohn!-la-(h)my　ผลไม้

fry (to fry, to be fried)　　　　(f)tawt　ทอด
　(to fry chopped meat with other things)
　　　　　　　　　　(l)paht!　ผัด

full (to be full, filled)　　　　dtem!　เต็ม
　(to be already filled)　　dtem! (h)laa-oh　เต็มแล้ว
　(to make full, to fill up) tahm! (f)hy! dtem!　ทำให้เต็ม
　(to be full of people, crowded)　(f)naan!　แน่น

90

(to be full from eating)	(l)im!	อิ่ม
,,	(l)im! (h)laa-oh	อิ่มแล้ว
fun (enjoyment)	kwahm sa-(l)nook!	ความสนุก
(to have fun, to be having a good time)		
	sa-(l)nook	สนุก
funeral	ngahn (l)sohp!	งานศพ
fungus (mold)	rah	รา
funnel	groo-ay	กรวย
funny (to be funny, amusing)	(r)kahn!	ขัน
,,	(l)kohp! (r)kahn!	ขบขัน
,,	kahm!	ขำ
(to act funny, to clown)	dta-lohk!	ตลก
fur	(r)kohn! (l)saht!	ขนสัตว์
furniture	(f)kreu-ung reu-un	เครื่องเรือน
fuse	few! (Thai pronun. of "fuse")	ฟิวส์
future	ah-nah-(h)koht!	อนาคต
galvanized iron	(r)sahng!-ga-(r)see	สังกะสี
(corrugated for roofing)		
	(r)sahng!-ga-(r)see (f)look (f)fook	สังกะสีลูกฟูก
gamble (to gamble, bet, wager)	pa-nahn!	พนัน

91

(to gamble, play at gambling)

	(f)len! gahn pa-nahn!	เล่นการพนัน
(gambling)	gahn pa-nahn!	การพนัน
game	gehm	เกม
(athletic sport)	gee-lah	กีฬา

garage (for parking or storing a vehicle)

	rohng (h)roht!	โรงรถ
,,	rohng (l)gep! (h)roht!	โรงเก็บรถ
(repair garage)	(l)oo (h)roht!	อู่รถ
,,	rohng (f)sawm (h)roht!	โรงซ่อมรถ
garbage (food wastes)	(l)set ah-(r)hahn	เศษอาหาร
(waste, garbage, trash, refuse)	ka-(l)ya!	ขยะ
,,	moon (r)fawy	มูลฝอย
(garbage can, pail)	(r)tahng! ka-(l)ya!	ถังขยะ
garden	(r)soo-un	สวน
gardener	kohn! (r)soo-un	คนสวน
	kohn! tahm! (r)soo-un	คนทำสวน
garlic	gra!-tee-um	กระเทียม
gas	(h)gaas	แก๊ส

92

(gas station)

sa-(r)tah-nee dtum (h)nahm! mahn!   สถานีเติมน้ำมัน

gasoline   (h)nahm! mahn! ben!-seen!   น้ำมันเบนซิน

gate (any kind)   bpra-dtoo   ประตู

   (fence gate)   bpra-dtoo (h)roo-uh   ประตูรั้ว

   (gate of a wall) bpra-dtoo gahm!-paang   ประตูกำแพง

gear   gee-uh   เกียร์

general (military rank) (army) ny pohn!   นายพล

     ,, (air force) pohn! ah-(l)gaht   พลอากาศ

(1-star, air force)   pohn! ah-(l)gaht (l)jaht!-dta-wah   พลอากาศจัตวา

(2-star, ,,) pohn! ah-(l)gaht dtree   พลอากาศตรี

(3-star, ,,) pohn! ah-(l)gaht toh   พลอากาศโท

(4-star, ,,) pohn! ah-(l)gaht (l)ehk   พลอากาศเอก

(brig. gen., army) pohn! (l)jaht!-dta-wah   พลจัตวา

(maj. gen., ,,) pohn! dtree   พลตรี

(lt. gen., ,,) pohn! toh   พลโท

(4-star gen., ,,) pohn! (l)ehk   พลเอก

(in general) (f)too-uh bpy!   ทั่วไป

(Ex : people in general, the public)

                         kohn! (f)tʊʊ-uh bpy!   คนทั่วไป

gentle (gently, lightly, softly)   bao! bao!   เบา ๆ

gentleman,-men   soo!-(f)pahp-boo!-(l)root!   สุภาพบุรุษ

geometry   reh-(r)kah ka-nit!   เรขาคณิต

germ germs, (bacteria)   (h)cheu-uh (f)rohk   เชื้อโรค

Germany, German   yuh-ra-mahn!   เยอรมัน

   (the country of) bpra-(f)tet yuh-ra-mahn!   ประเทศเยอรมัน

   (a German person) kohn! yuh-ra-mahn!   คนเยอรมัน

   (the German people) chow yuh-ra-mahn!   ชาวเยอรมัน

   (the German language)

                       pah-(r)sah yuh-ra-mahn!   ภาษาเยอรมัน

get (to get something)   ow! **something**   เอา——

        ,,   (f)dy! **something**   ได้——

   (to go get something) bpy! ow! **something**   ไปเอา——

   (to go get something and come back)

                 bpy! ow! **something** mah   ไปเอา——มา

   (Get something and give to me.)

        ow! **something** mah (f)hy! (r)chahn!   เอา——มาให้ฉัน

(to get, receive)	(h)rahp!	รับ
,,	(f)dy! (h)rahp!	ได้รับ
(to get off or out of a vehicle)	lohng!	ลง
(to get on or aboard a vehicle)	(f)keun!	ขึ้น
(to get sick)	(f)my! sa-by	ไม่สบาย
(to get well)	(r)hy	หาย
(to get up)	(h)look! (f)keun!	ลุกขึ้น
ghost	(r)pee	ผี
gibbon	cha!-nee	ชะนี
ginger	(r)king	ขิง
(ginger ale)	(h)nahm! (r)king!	น้ำขิง
girl	(f)poo-(r)ying!	ผู้หญิง
(a child)	(l)dek! (f)poo-(r)ying!	เด็กผู้หญิง
	(l)dek! (r)ying!	เด็กหญิง
give (to give, let)	(f)hy!	ให้
(to give to **someone**)	(f)hy! **someone**	ให้——
(to give **something** to **someone**		
	ow! **something** (f)hy! **someone**	เอา——ให้——
(to go give **something** to **someone**)		
	ow! **something** bpy! (f)hy! **someone**	เอา—ไปให้—

(Give me **something**.)

      ow! **something** (f)hy! (r)chahn!   เอา - —ให้ฉัน

(Give me **something**)

      ow! **something** mah (f)hy! (r)chahn!   เอา——มาให้ฉัน

glad (to be glad, pleased)	yin!-dee	ยินดี
(to be glad)	dee jy!	ดีใจ
glass (the material)	(f)gaa-oh	แก้ว
(a pane of glass, a mirror)	gra-(l)johk!	กระจก
(drinking glass)	(f)too-ay (f)gaa-oh	ถ้วยแก้ว
,,	(f)gaa-oh	แก้ว
(water glass) (f)too-ay (f)gaa-oh (h)nahm		ถ้วยแก้วน้ำ
(liquor glass) (f)too-ay (f)gaa-oh (f)lao!		ถ้วยแก้วเหล้า
glasses (spectacles)	(f)waan! dtah	แว่นตา

(sun glasses, dark glasses)

      (f) waan! dtah gahn! (l)daat   แว่นกันแดด

gloves	(r)toong! meu	ถุงมือ
glue	gow	กาว
(to glue)	(l)dtit! gow	ติดกาว
gnat, gnats	(h)rin!	ริ้น

go (to go, goes, going, gone, went)	bpy!	ไป
(to go in)	(f)kow! bpy!	เข้าไป
(to go out, leave)	(l)awk bpy!	ออกไป
(to go away, disappear, as a sickness)	(r)hy	หาย
(Go away!)	(h)bpy!	ไป
(Get out of here!)	(l)awk (h)bpy!	ออกไป
(Let's go!)	bpy!	ไป
,,	bpy! gahn! tuh!	ไปกันเถอะ
(to go up)	(f)keun!	ขึ้น
,,	(f)keun! bpy!	ขึ้นไป
(to go down)	lohng!	ลง
,,	lohng! bpy!	ลงไป
goat	(h)paa!	แพะ
God	(h)pra!-(f)jow!	พระเจ้า
going (going to **do something**, will **do** something)	(l)ja!——	จะ——
(to be going **somewhere**)	bpy!——	ไป——
(Where are you going?)	bpy! (r)ny	ไปไหน
gold	tawng	ทอง
(the color of)	(r)see tawng	สีทอง

97

golf	gawlf	ก็อล์ฟ
(golf course)	sa-(r)nahm gawlf	สนามก็อล์ฟ
gone (to have gone, go already)	bpy! (h)laa-oh	ไปแล้ว
(to be all gone, to have been used up)		
	(l)moht! (h)laa-oh	หมดแล้ว
gong	(h)kawng	ฆ้อง
gonorrhea (the clap)	(f)rohk (r)nawng-ny	โรคหนองใน
good	dee	ดี
(no good)	(f)my! dee	ไม่ดี
(no good at all)	(f)my! dee luh-ee	ไม่ดีเลย
(to do good)	tahm! (f)hy! dee	ทำให้ดี
(to be good-natured, warm at heart)		
	(l)ohp! (l)oon!	อบอุ่น
(to have a good time)	sa-(l)nook!	สนุก

Good morning!, Good afternoon!,
Good evening!, Good night!

(as spoken by males)	sa-waht! dee (h)krahp	สวัสดีครับ
(as spoken by females)	sa-waht! dee ka!	สวัสดีค่ะ
goodbye (same as above) (as spoken by males)		
	sa-waht! dee (h)krahp!	สวัสดีครับ

(as spoken by females)   sa-waht! dee ka!   สวัสดีค่ะ
(goodbye, said by the person leaving)

                      lah (l)gawn   ลาก่อน

goose   (l)hahn   ห่าน

gossip (to gossip)   nin!-tah   นินทา

  (to chat)   kooy!   คุย

government   (h)raht!-ta-bahn   รัฐบาล
(govt. service, civil service, govt. job)

           (f)raht-cha!-gahn   ราชการ
(govt. official, civil servant)

        (f)kah (f)raht-cha!-gahn   ข้าราชการ

governor (of a changwat or province)

    (f)poo (f)wah (f)raht-cha!-gahn
          jahng!-(l)waht!   ผู้ว่าราชการจังหวัด

  (of a changwat or province)

           (f)kah (r)loo-ung   ข้าหลวง

grade (or level, class, rank)   (h)chahn!   ชั้น

graduate (to graduate)

    (r)sahm!-(l)ret! gahn (l)seuk!-(r)sah   สำเร็จการศึกษา

  (to graduate)   ree-un (r)sahm!-(l)ret!   เรียนสำเร็จ

99

(to graduate from)

	(r)sahm!-(l)ret! (l)jahk——	สำเร็จจาก——
grandchild	(r)lahn	หลาน
grandfather (paternal)	(l)bpoo	ปู่
(maternal)	dtah	ตา
grandmother (paternal)	(f)yah	ย่า
(maternal)	yai	ยาย
grape	ah-(l)ngoon!	องุ่น
grass	(f)yah	หญ้า
grasshopper	(h)dtahk!-ga-dtaan	ตั๊กแตน

grave (a grave, burial spot)

	(r)loom!-(r)fahng! (l)sohp!	หลุมฝังศพ
gravel (or pebbles)	(l)groo-ut	กรวด
gray (to be gray)	tao!	เทา
(the color of)	(r)see tao!	สีเทา

grease (oil, grease, general term)

	(h)nahm! mahn!	น้ำมัน
(fat, grease, of foods)	(r)ky! mahn!	ไขมัน
(to grease or lubricate a car)	(l)aht! (l)cheet	อัดฉีด
(a heavy lubricating grease)	jah-ra-bee	จาระบี

100

great-grandchild	(r)len	เหลน
great-grandfather,-grandmother	(f)too-ut	ทวด
green (to be green)	(r)kee-oh	เขียว
(the color of)	(r)see (r)kee-oh	สีเขียว
greet (to welcome, to receive)		
	(f)dtawn (h)rahp!	ต้อนรับ
grinder (meat grinder)		
	(f)kreu-ung (l)boht! (h)neu-uh	เครื่องบดเนื้อ
ground (earth, soil, land)	din!	ดิน
(the earth surface, ground surface)		
	(h)peun! din!	พื้นดิน
(to place **something** on the ground)		
	ow! **something** wahng (l)gahp! din!	เอา—วางกับดิน
group	(f)poo-uk	พวก
grow (to grow, get bigger)	dtoh (f)keun!	โตขึ้น
(to grow up, develop, mature)	(l)dtuhp dtoh	เติบโต
(to increase in size)	(l)yai! (f)keun!	ใหญ่ขึ้น
(to plant, cultivate)	(l)bplook	ปลูก
(to grow, sprout, multiply)	(f)ngawk	งอก
guarantee (to guarantee, insure)	bpra!-gahn!	ประกัน
(a guarantee, warranty)	gah-rahn-tee	การันตี

(a bank guaranty)

gahn (h)kahm! bpra!-gahn! การค้ำประกัน

guard (watchman)   kohn! yahm คนยาม

guerrilla band (or robber gang) gawng john กองโจร

(rhymes with "bone")

(revolutionist)   (f)poo gra-tahm! gahn!

bpa-tih!-waht! ผู้กระทำการปฏิวัติ

(Communist terrorist) (f)poo (l)gaw gahn

(h)ry kawm-miw!-(h)nis! ผู้ก่อการ
คอมมิวนิสต์

guess (to guess)   dow! เดา

guest, guests   (l)kaak แขก

(visitor)   (f)poo mah (r)hah ผู้มาหา

guide (to guide, lead, conduct)   nahm! นำ

(a guide, one who leads the way)

(f)poo nahm! tahng ผู้นำทาง

(tourist guide)   kohn! nahm! (f)tee-oh คนนำเที่ยว

guilty (to be guilty)   mee kwahm (l)pit! มีความผิด

gulf (or bay)   (l)ow อ่าว

(Gulf of Thailand)   (l)ow ty! อ่าวไทย

gum (chewing gum)   (l)mahk fa-(l)rahng! หมากฝรั่ง

(gums of the teeth)	(l)ngeu-uk	เหงือก
gun (any kind)	bpeun	ปืน
(pistol, revolver)	bpeun (h)pohk!	ปืนพก
(rifle)	bpeun yow	ปืนยาว
(machine gun)	bpeun (l)gohn!	ปืนกล
gutter (drainage ditch)	rahng ra!-by (h)nahm	รางระบายน้ำ
(roof gutter)	rahng (h)nahm! (r)fohn!	รางน้ำฝน
had (see "have")		
hair (general term)	(r)kohn!	ขน
(hair on the head)	(r)pohm!	ผม
haircut (a haircut, to cut the hair)		
	(l)dtaht! (r)pohm!	ตัดผม
hairpin	gip!	กิ๊บ
	gip! (l)nep! (r)pohm!	กิ๊บเหนีบผม
half	(f)kreung!	ครึ่ง
(one-half)	(f)kreung! (l)neung!	ครึ่งหนึ่ง

Note: "(f)kreung! **something**" means half of **something**.
   "**something** (f)kreung!" means 1½ or 3/2 of **something**

ham	haam	แฮม
	(r)moo haam	หมูแฮม

103

hammer (hand tool)	(h)kawn	ค้อน
(to hammer, nail, pound)	(l)dtawk	ตอก
(to hit something with a hammer)	(h)toop!	ทุบ
hammock	bpleh yoo-un	เปลญวน
hand (of the body)	meu	มือ
(of a clock)	(r)kem! nah-li-gah	เข็มนาฬิกา
handbag	gra-(r)pow!	กระเป๋า
	gra-(r)pow! (f)hue!	กระเป๋าหิ้ว
handkerchief	(f)pah (h)chet! (f)nah	ผ้าเช็ดหน้า
handle n.	meu (l)jahp!	มือจับ
(Handle with care.)		
	ra-wahng! (r)kawng (l)dtaak	ระวังของแตก
handsome (to be handsome)	(l)law	หล่อ
	(f)roop (l)law	รูปหล่อ
handwriting	ly meu	ลายมือ
hang (to hang, suspend)	(r)kwaan	แขวน
(to hang out clothes)	(l)dtahk (f)pah	ตากผ้า
hanger (coat hanger)		
	(r)kaw (r)kwaan (f)seu-uh	ขอแขวนเสื้อ

happen (to happen, occur, take place, be born)

		(l)gut	เกิด
(to occur, develop)	(l)gut (f)keun!		เกิดขึ้น
(What happened?)	(l)gut ah!-ry (f)keun!		เกิดอะไรขึ้น

happy (to be happy, content)   (l)sook!   สุข

	,,	(l)sook! sa-by	สุขสบาย
	,,	mee kwahm (l)sook!	มีความสุข
(to be glad)		dee jy!	ดีใจ
(happiness)		kwahm (l)sook!	ความสุข

harbor (port, pier, wharf, landing)   (f)tah   ท่า

| (harbor, port, seaport) | (f)tah reu-uh | ท่าเรือ |

hard (to be hard, strong, stiff)   (r)kaang   แข็ง

(to be hard or heavy, of work)	(l)nahk!	หนัก
(to be difficult)	(f)yahk	ยาก
(to be troublesome)	lahm!-(l)bahk	ลำบาก
(forcefully, powerfully, strongly)	raang	แรง

harvest (to harvest, reap)   (l)gee-oh   เกี่ยว

| (to harvest) | (l)gep! (l)gee-oh | เก็บเกี่ยว |

has (see "have")

hat   (l)moo-uk   หมวก

105

hate (to hate)   (l)glee-ut   เกลียด

have (to have, has, had, there is, there are)

                                              mee   มี

  (have to, need to, must)   (f)dtawng   ต้อง

hawk (bird)   (h)nohk! (l)yee-oh   นกเหยี่ยว

hay (dry grass)   (f)yah (f)haang   หญ้าแห้ง

he, him   (r)kow!   เขา

                            (r)kow! (f)poo-chy   เขาผู้ชาย

head   (r)hoo-uh!   หัว

  (chief, leader)   (r)hoo-uh! (f)nah   หัวหน้า

headache   (l)bpoo-ut (r)hoo-uh!   ปวดหัว

headlight   (of a vehicle) fy! (f)nah (h)roht!   ไฟหน้ารถ

headman (of a tambon, kamnan) gahm!-nahn!   กำนัน

  (of a village, puyaiban) (f)poo(l)yai(f)bahn   ผู้ใหญ่บ้าน

health   (l)sook!-ka-(f)pahp   สุขภาพ

  (to be healthy) mee (l)sook!-ka-(f)pahp dee   มีสุขภาพดี

      ,,   sa-by dee   สบายดี

  (health, in general)   gahn ah-nah-my!   การอนามัย

hear (to hear)   (f)dy! yin!   ได้ยิน

  (to listen)   fahng!   ฟัง

heart	(r)hoo-uh! jy!	หัวใจ
(to be broken-hearted over a love affair)		
	(l)ohk!-(l)hahk!	อกหัก
heat n.	kwahm (h)rawn	ความร้อน
(to heat **something** up)		
	tahm! **something** (f)hy! (h)rawn	ทำ——ให้ร้อน
heaven (or paradise)	sa-(r)wahn!	สวรรค์
heavy (to be heavy)	(l)nahk!	หนัก
hedge	(h)roo-uh (f)dtohn!-(h)my	รั้วต้นไม้
heel (of the foot)	(f)sohn! (h)tao	ส้นเท้า
(of a shoe)	(f)sohn! rawng-(h)tao	ส้นรองเท้า
height	kwahm (r)soong	ความสูง
hell	na-(h)rohk!	นรก
hello (said when answering a telephone) hal-lo		ฮัลโล
(polite greeting) (said by males)		
	sa-waht! dee (h)krahp!	สวัสดีครับ
(polite greeting) (said by females)		
	sa-waht! dee ka!	สวัสดีค่ะ
help (to help, assist)	(f)choo-ay	ช่วย

107

(to help others, give help)

　　　　　　　　　　　(f)choo-ay (r)leu-uh　ช่วยเหลือ

(help, assistance, aid)

　　　　　　kwahm (f)choo-ay (r)leu-uh　ความช่วยเหลือ

(Help!)　　　　　　　(f)choo-ay (f)doo-ay　ช่วยด้วย

hen　　　　　　(l)gy! dtoo-uh mee-uh　ไก่ตัวเมีย

　　　　　　　　　　　(f)maa (l)gy!　แม่ไก่

hepatitis (inflammation of the liver)

　　　　　(f)rohk (l)dtahp! (l)ahk!-(l)sep　โรคตับอักเสบ

(jaundice)　　　　(f)rohk dee (f)sahn　โรคดีซ่าน

her, she　　　　　　　　(r)kow!　เขา

(belonging to her)　　　(r)kawng (r)kow!　ของเขา

　,, (r)kawng(r)kow!(f)poo-(r)yeeng!　ของเขาผู้หญิง

(her **something**) something (r)kawng (r)kow!　——ของเขา

here　　　　　　　(f)tee (f)nee　ที่นี่

　　　　　　　　　　　(f)nee　นี่

hers (to be hers, belonging to her)

　　　　　　　　　　(r)kawng (r)kow!　ของเขา

(hers, her **something**)

　　　　　something (r)kawng (r)kow　——ของเขา

hiccup (to hiccup)	sa-(l)euk!	สะอึก
hide (to hide)	(f)sawn	ซ่อน
(to be hidden)	(l)took (f)sawn	ถูกซ่อน
(animal skin, leather)	(r)nahng! (l)saht!	หนังสัตว์
high (to be high, tall)	(r)soong	สูง
highschool	rohng ree-un (h)ma-ta-yohm!	โรงเรียนมัธยม
highway	tahng (r)loo-ung	ทางหลวง
hill (or mountain)	(r)kow	เขา
(mountain)	poo-(r)kow!	ภูเขา
(knoll, mound)	nun	เนิน
him, he	(r)kow!	เขา
	(r)kow! (f)poo-chy	เขาผู้ชาย
hinge n.	bahn (h)pahp!	บานพับ
hire (to hire, employ)	(f)jahng	จ้าง
his (belonging to him)	(r)kawng (r)kow!	ของเขา
,,	(r)kawng (r)kow! (f)poo-chy	ของเขาผู้ชาย
(his **something**) **something**(r)kawng (r)kow!		——ของเขา
history	bpra!-(l)waht!-saht	ประวัติศาสตร์
hit (to hit, beat, strike)	dtee	ตี
(to collide)	chohn!	ชน

hobby	ngahn ah!-dih!-(l)rek	งานอดิเรก
hoe (garden tool)	(l)jawp	จอบ
hog (pig)	(r)moo	หมู
hold (to hold in the hand)	(r)teu	ถือ
(to hold onto)	(l)jahp!	จับ
(to keep)	(l)gep!	เก็บ
hole	roo	รู
(pit, hole, as in the ground)	(r)loom!	หลุม
holiday	wahn! (l)yoot!	วันหยุด
(official holiday)		
	wahn! (l)yoot! (f)raht-cha-gahn	วันหยุดราชการ
hollow (to be hollow)	gloo-ung	กลวง
home	(f)bahn	บ้าน
	(f)bahn (h)pahk!	บ้านพัก
homesick (to miss home)		
	(h)keet! (r)teung! (f)bahn	คิดถึงบ้าน
homosexual	ga!-tuh-ee	กะเทย
honest (to be honest)	(f)seu dtrohng!	ซื่อตรง
honey	(h)nahm! (f)peung!	น้ำผึ้ง

110

hood (of an automobile) gra-bprohng (r)fah
(f)krawp (h)kreu-ung-yohn! กระโปรงฝาครอบ
เครื่องยนต์

hook n. (r)kaw ขอ
  (fish hook) (l)bet! เบ็ด
  (to hook, hitch) (l)gee-oh เกี่ยว
  (coat hook) (r)kaw (r)kwaan (f)seu-uh ขอแขวนเสื้อ
hop (to jump, leap, hop) gra-(l)doht กระโดด
hope n. kwahm (r)wahng! ความหวัง
  (to hope, hope for) (r)wahng! หวัง
  (to hope that) (r)wahng! (f)wah หวังว่า
  (to be hopeful) mee (r)wahng! มีหวัง
  (I hope so!)
    (r)chahn! (r)wahng! (f)chehn (h)nahn! ฉันหวังเช่นนั้น
horizontal (to be horizontal, perfectly level,
  a level surface) ra-(l)dahp! ได้ระดับ
horn (a horn, any kind) dtraa แตร
  (automobile horn) dtraa (h)roht! แตรรถ
horse (h)mah ม้า
  (horse racing, the races, to race)
    (l)kaang! (h)mah แข่งม้า

horsepower	gahm! lahng! (h)mah	กำลังม้า
	raang (h)mah	แรงม้า
hose (pipe, tube)	(f)taw	ท่อ
(rubber hose)	(f)taw yahng	ท่อยาง
hospital	rohng pa-yah-bahn	โรงพยาบาล
hot (to be hot in temperature)	(h)rawn	ร้อน
(to be hot with spices, pepper)	(l)pet!	เผ็ด
hotel	rohng raam	โรงแรม
hour	(f)choo-uh mohng	ชั่วโมง
house, home	(f)bahn	บ้าน
	(f)bahn (h)pahk!	บ้านพัก
(classifier for houses)	(r)lahng!	หลัง
how (how?, in what way?)	(l)yahng-ry!	อย่างไร
(often pronounced "yahng-I")		
(this is how, like this)	(l)yahng (h)nee	อย่างนี้
(How much? What is the price?)		
	(f)tao!-(l)ry!	เท่าไร
(How many-- ?)	(l)gee--	กี่--
(How many? of things)	(l)gee ahn!	กี่อัน
(How many people?)	(l)gee kohn!	กี่คน

(How much?, of something)		
	(f)mahk (f)tao!-(l)ry!	มากเท่าไร
(How long?, in length)	yow (f)tao!-(l)ry!	ยาวเท่าไร
(How long?, in time)	nahn (f)tao!-(l)ry!	นานเท่าไร
(How far?)	gly! (f)tao!-(l)ry!	ไกลเท่าไร
(How are you?)	(f)tahn sa-by dee (r)reu	ท่านสบายดีหรือ
hug (to hug, embrace, caress)	(l)gawt	กอด
huge (to be huge, enormous)	(l)yai! dtoh	ใหญ่โต
humid (to be damp, moist, humid)	(h)cheun	ชื้น
(humidity)	kwahm (h)cheun	ความชื้น
hundred	(h)rawy	ร้อย
(one hundred, 100)	(l)neung! (h)rawy	หนึ่งร้อย
„	(h)rawy (l)neung!	ร้อยหนึ่ง
hungry (to be hungry)	(r)hue	หิว
(rhymes with "cue" or "few")		
(Are you hungry?)	(r)hue! (r)my!	หิวไหม
hunt (to hunt **animals**)	(f)lah (l)**saht!**	ล่าสัตว์
(to hunt for, look for)	(r)hah	หา
hurry (to be in a hurry)	(f)reep (h)rawn	รีบร้อน
(Hurry!, Hurry up!)		
	(h)reh-oh (h)reh-oh (f)kow!	เร็ว ๆ เข้า

113

hurt (to feel pain)	(l)jep!	เจ็บ
(to pain, ache)	(l)bpoo-ut	ปวด
(to injure)	tahm! (h)ry	ทำร้าย
(to smart, sting)	(l)saap	แสบ
husband	(r)sah-mee	สามี
(colloquial)	(r)poo-uh	ผัว
I, me (polite form, spoken by males)	(r)pohm!	ผม
(spoken by females, and is familiar form		
for males)	(r)chahn!	ฉัน
ice	(h)nahm! (r)kaang!	น้ำแข็ง
ice cream	I-sa greem	ไอสกรีม
I-dtim (Thai pronun. of "ice cream")		ไอติม
idea	kwahm (h)keet!	ความคิด
	kwahm (r)hen!	ความเห็น
idiom	(r)sahm!-noo-un	สำนวน
if	(f)tah	ถ้า
(in the event that)	(f)tah (l)hahk (f)wah	ถ้าหากว่า
ignite (to ignite a fire)	(l)dtit! fy!	ติดไฟ
„	(l)joot! fy!	จุดไฟ

114

ill (to be sick, not well) (f)my! sa-by ไม่สบาย

  ,,   (l)jep! (f)ky! เจ็บไข้

  ,,   (l)bpoo-ay ป่วย

illegal (to be illegal, unlawful)

      (l)pit! (l)goht!-(r)my ผิดกฎหมาย

immediately   tahn!-tee ทันที

immigration department

 grohm! (l)droo-ut kohn! (f)kow! meu-ung กรมตรวจคน

               เข้าเมือง

 (immigrant) kohn! (f)kow! meu-ung คนเข้าเมือง

important (to be important, significant)

      (r)sahm-kahn! สำคัญ

impossible (to be impossible)

   bpen! bpy! (f)my! (f)dy! เป็นไปไม่ได้

 (cannot do) tahm! (f)my! (f)dy! ทำไม่ได้

in   ny! ใน

 (inside)   (f)kahng ny! ข้างใน

 (in order to)   (f)peu-uh เพื่อ

incense (joss sticks) (f)toop ธูป

inch (h)nue! (rhymes with "cue" or "few") นิ้ว

    (h) nue! (h)foot! นิ้วฟุต

115

include (to include, combine, add, including)

roo-um รวม

increase (to increase, add on) (f)puhm เพิ่ม

(to increase, be increased) (f)puhm (f)keun! เพิ่มขึ้น

(to make bigger) tahm! (f)hy!(l)yai!(f)keun! ทำให้ใหญ่ขึ้น

India, Indian in!-dee-uh อินเดีย

(the country of) bpra-(f)tet in!-dee-uh ประเทศอินเดีย

(the Indian people) chow in!-dee-uh ชาวอินเดีย

(an Indian) (l)kaak in!-dee-uh แขกอินเดีย

,, (l)kaak แขก

industry (as opposed to agriculture)

oot!-(r)sah-(l)hah!-gahm! อุตสาหกรรม

infect (to be infected, inflamed) (l)ahk!-(l)sep อักเสบ

inflammable (combustible substance)

(h)cheu-uh pluhng เชื้อเพลิง

(to be inflammable) wy! fy! ไวไฟ

influenza (flu) (f)ky! (l)waht! (l)yai! ไข้หวัดใหญ่

inject (to inject, inoculate) (l)cheet yah ฉีดยา

(an injection) gahn (l)cheet yah การฉีดยา

injure (to injure, do harm) tahm! (h)ry ทำร้าย

116

(to injure, hurt)	tahm! ahn!-dta!-ry	ทำอันตราย
(injury, wound)	(l)baht (l)jep!	บาดเจ็บ
ink	(l)meuk!	หมึก
(fountain pen ink)	(h)nahm! (l)meuk!	น้ำหมึก
innocent (to be innocent, pure, not guilty)		
	baw-ri-(l)soot!	บริสุทธิ์
(to be innocent, naive, childish)		
	(h)ry! dee-ung-(r)sah	ไร้เดียงสา
insect	ma-laang	แมลง
	dtoo-uh ma-laang	ตัวแมลง
insecticide (or DDT)	D D T	ดีดีที
	yah (f)kah ma-laang	ยาฆ่าแมลง
inside	(f)kahng ny!	ข้างใน
insignia (of rank)	(f)kreu-ung (h)yoht!	เครื่องยศ
inspect (to inspect, examine, check)		
	(l)droo-ut	ตรวจ
inspection	gahn (l)droo-ut	การตรวจ
install (to install)	(l)dtit! (f)dtahng	ติดตั้ง
insure (to insure, to guarantee)	bpra!-gahn!	ประกัน

(to insure against loss or damage)

	bpra!-gahn! py!	ประกันภัย
(insurance)	gahn bpra!-gahn! py!	การประกันภัย
(life insurance)	bpra!-gahn! chee-(h)wit!	ประกันชีวิต

intelligent (to be intelligent)

	(r)wy!-(h)prip! dee	ไหวพริบดี
(to be clever, smart)	cha-(l)laht	ฉลาด

interest (liking) kwahm (r)sohn! jy! ความสนใจ

(financial, interest) (l)dawk (f)bee-uh ดอกเบี้ย

interested (to be interested) (r)sohn! jy! สนใจ

interesting (to be interesting)

(f)nah (r)sohn jy! น่าสนใจ

interpreter (one who translates)

pa-nahk-ngahn! bplaa พนักงานแปล

interview (to interview, an interview)

(r)sahm!-(f)paht สัมภาษณ์

into, in ny! ใน

(to go in, go into, enter) (f)kow! เข้า

    ,, (f)kow! bpy! เข้าไป

introduce (to introduce someone to someone else)

(h)naa! nahm! (f)hy! (h)roo-(l)jahk! แนะนำให้รู้จัก

invite (to invite)	chuhn	เชิญ
,,	(h)cheu-uh chuhn	เชื้อเชิญ
(invitation)	kahm! chuhn	คำเชิญ
iron (the metal)	(l)lek!	เหล็ก
(clothes iron)	dtow! (f)reet	เตารีด
(to iron clothes)	(f)reet (f)pah	รีดผ้า
irrigate (to irrigate)	(h)toht! (h)nahm	ทดน้ำ
(irrigation)	gahn (h)toht! (h)nahm	การทดน้ำ
,,	gahn chohn! bprah!-tahn	การชลประทาน

is (see "be") (Usually omitted or already included in the grammar.)

(is, are, be)	bpen!	เป็น
(to be in a location)	(l)yoo	อยู่
(there is, there are)	mee	มี
(is, is namely, to be as follows)	keu	คือ
island	(l)gaw!	เกาะ
it	mahn!	มัน

Note : The word "it" is used much less often in Thai than in English and is usually omitted because it is understood.   Usually, the word "it" is used when referring to a specific animal or thing.

119

itch (to itch, be itchy)	kahn!	คัน
ivory	ngah	งา
jack (for lifting)	(f)maa-raang	แม่แรง
jackfruit	ka-(r)noon!	ขนุน
jail (prison)	(h)kook!	คุก
	dta-rahng	ตะราง

(to go to jail, be imprisoned)

	(l)dtit! dta-rahng	ติดตะราง
jam	yaam	แยม
janitor (or custodian)	pahn rohng	ภารโรง
January	(h)mohk!-ga-rah kohm!	มกราคม
Japan, Japanese	(f)yee-(l)bpoon!	ญี่ปุ่น

(the country of) bpra-(f)tet(f)yee-(l)bpoon! ประเทศญี่ปุ่น
(the Japanese people) chow(f)yee-(l)bpoon! ชาวญี่ปุ่น
(the Japanese language)

	pah-(r)sah (f)yee-(l)bpoon!	ภาษาญี่ปุ่น

jar (large earthen jar for storing water)

	(l)dtoom!	ตุ่ม

(a small-mouthed, glazed, earthen jug)

	(r)hy	ไห

jaundice (f)rohk dee (f)sahn โรคดีซ่าน

jealous (to be jealous) (r)heung! หึง

jellyfish maang ga-proon! แมงกะพรุน

jerk (to jerk, pull suddenly) gra-(l)dtook! กระตุก

jewelery (ornaments worn on the body, general term)
(f)kreu-ung bpra-(l)dahp! gy เครื่องประดับกาย

(ornaments worn on the body, general term)
(f)peht-plawy เพชรพลอย

(jewelery shop) (h)rahn (r)ky (f)kreu-ung
bpra-(l)dahp! (l)sa-dtree ร้านขายเครื่อง
ประดับสตรี

job (work, task) ngahn งาน

joke (to joke, speak in fun) (f)poot (f)len พูดเล่น

(to tell a joke) (f)poot dta-(l)lohk! พูดตลก

(to be funny, comical) dta-(l)lohk! ตลก

joss sticks (incense) (f)toop ธูป

judge (to judge) (h)pih!-(f)pahk-(r)sah พิพากษา

(a judge) (f)poo (h)pih!-(f)pahk-(r)sah ผู้พิพากษา

juice (fruit juice) (h)nahm! (r)pohn!-la-(h)my น้ำผลไม้

July ga-(h)rah!-ga-dah-kohm! กรกฎาคม

121

jump (to jump)   gra-(l)doht!   กระโดด
June   (h)mih!-too!-nah-yohn!   มิถุนายน
jungle (or forest, woods)   (l)bpah   ป่า
just (very recently, just now)   (f)puhng!   เพิ่ง
  (just a moment ago, just now)

                (f)meu-uh (f)gee (h)nee   เมื่อกี้นี้
  (only)   (f)tow! (h)nahn!   เท่านั้น
  (merely, as little as)   (l)sahk!   สัก
  (just then, at that very moment, just the
  right moment)   paw dee   พอดี
kamnan (headman of a tambon) gahm!-nahn!   กำนัน
keep (to store, collect)   (l)gep!   เก็บ
  (to store or put away **something**)

            (l)gep! **something** (h)wy!   เก็บ——ไว้
  (to maintain, care for)   (h)rahk!-(r)sah   รักษา
  (Keep going!)   bpy! luh-ee   ไปเลย
  (keep out!, Do not enter.) (f)hahm (f)kow!   ห้ามเข้า
kerosene   (h)nahm!-mahn! (h)gaht   น้ำมันก๊าส
kettle (teakettle, pot with a spout)   gah   กา
            ,,   gah (h)nahm   กาน้ำ

key (for a lock)	(f)look goon!-jaa	ลูกกุญแจ
,,	goon!-jaa	กุญแจ
Khmer (see "Cambodia")		
kick (to kick)	(l)dteh!	เตะ
kill (to kill)	(f)kah	ฆ่า
kilogram	gih!-loh-grahm!	กิโลกรัม
kilometer	gih!-loh-(h)met!	กิโลเมตร
(kilo)	gih!-loh	กิโล
(**no.** km. per hr.)	**no.** gih!-loh-(h)met!	
	dtaw (f)choo-uh-mohng	—กิโลเมตรต่อ
		ชั่วโมง
kind (type, species)	cha-(h)nit!	ชนิด
(model, type, style)	(l)baap	แบบ
(to be kind, merciful)	ga-roo!-nah	กรุณา
(to be kind-hearted, good natured) jy! dee	ใจดี
(this kind, like this)	(l)yahng (h)nee	อย่างนี้
kindergarten (or nursery school)		
	rohng ree-un (l)ah!-noo!-bahn	โรงเรียนอนุบาล
king	(h)pra-(f)jow! (l)yoo (r)hoo-uh	พระเจ้าอยู่หัว
(king cobra)	ngoo johng!-ahng	งูจงอาง

123

kiss (to kiss)	(l)joop	จูบ
kitchen	kroo-uh	ครัว
kite	(f)wow	ว่าว
(to fly a kite)	(h)chahk (f)wow!	ชักว่าว
„	(f)len (f)wow!	เล่นว่าว
kitten	(f)look maa-oh	ลูกแมว
knee	(r)hoo-uh (l)kow!	หัวเข่า
knife	(f)meed	มีด
(sharp knife)	(f)meed kohm!	มีดคม
(butter knife)	(f)meed (l)dtaht! nuh-ee	มีดตัดเนย
knock (to knock, to knock on)	(h)kaw!	เคาะ
(to knock on a door)	(h)kaw! bpra-dtoo	เคาะประตู
know (to know)	(h)roo	รู้
„	(f)sahp	ทราบ
(to know a person)	(h)roo-(l)jahk!	รู้จัก
(to know how to do something)	bpen!	เป็น
„	tahm! bpen!	ทำเป็น
„	tahm! (f)dy	ทำได้
knowledge	kwahm (h)roo	ความรู้
Korea	gow!-(r)lee	เกาหลี

krait (banded krait snake)		
	ngoo (r)sahm (l)lee-um	งูสามเหลี่ยม
label (or tag)	(f)bpy	ป้าย
(brand, trademark)	dtrah	ตรา
laborer (or unskilled worker)	kohn! ngahn	คนงาน
,,	gahm!-ma-gawn	กรรมกร
ladder (or stairs)	bahn!-dy!	บันได
lady, ladies	soo! (f)pahp-(l)sa-dtree	สุภาพสตรี
lake	ta!-leh-(l)sahp	ทะเลสาบ
lamb (animal)	(f)look (l)gaa!	ลูกแกะ
(meat)	(h)neu-uh (f)look (l)gaa!	เนื้อลูกแกะ
lamp (electric)	kohm fy!-(h)fah	โคมไฟฟ้า
(lightbulb)	(l)lawt fy!	หลอดไฟ
land (ground, soil)	din!	ดิน
(land, earth, ground, kingdom)	(l)paan-din!	แผ่นดิน
(the countryside)	(f)bahn (f)nawk	บ้านนอก
(property)	(f)tee din!	ที่ดิน
(to land, as an airplane)	lohng!	ลง
landlord	(f)jow! (r)kawng (f)bahn	เจ้าของบ้าน

lane (soi)	sawy	ซอย
language	pah-(r)sah	ภาษา
lantern	kohm	โคม
Lao	lao (rhymes with "cow")	ลาว
(a Lao person)	kohn! lao	คนลาว
(the country of Laos)	bpra-(f)tet lao	ประเทศลาว
lard	(h)nahm!-mahn! (r)moo	น้ำมันหมู
large (to be big, large)	(l)yai!	ใหญ่
	(rhymes with "my")	
(to be large, mature)	dtoh	โต
(to have a large body)	dtoo-uh dtoh	ตัวโต
last (final)	(l)soot! (h)ty	สุดท้าย
(the last or final item)	ahn! (l)soot! (h)ty	อันสุดท้าย
(the last day of the month)		
wahn! (l)soot! (h)ty (r)kawng deu-un		วันสุดท้ายของเดือน
(the last day of the month)		
wahn! (f)sin! deu-un		วันสิ้นเดือน~
(to last, endure)	tohn!-tahn	ทนทาน
(last——, the preceding——)		
——(f)tee (h)laa-oh		——ที่แล้ว

126

(last night)	(f)meu-uh keun	เมื่อคืน
,,	(f)meu-uh keun (h)nee	เมื่อคืนนี้
late (to be late, slow)	(h)chah	ช้า
(late in the morning)	(r)sy	สาย
(late at night)	(l)deuk!	ดึก
later	tee (r)lahng!	ที่หลัง
laugh (to laugh)	(r)hoo-uh (h)raw!	หัวเราะ
laundry (shop)	(h)rahn (h)sahk! (f)pah	ร้านซักผ้า
(to wash clothes)	(h)sahk! (f)pah	ซักผ้า
(to wash and iron)	(h)sahk! (f)reet	ซักรีด
laundryman, laundress kohn! (h)sahk! (f)pah		คนซักผ้า
law (a rule, regulation)	(l)goht	กฎ
(the subject of law)	(l)goht!-(r)my	กฎหมาย
lawn	sa-(r)nahm (f)yah	สนามหญ้า
lawyer (attorney)	ta!-ny kwahm	ทนายความ
lay (to lay, lay down, to place, place on)		
	wahng	วาง
lazy (to be lazy)	(f)kee (l)gee-ut	ขี้เกียจ
lead (to lead, guide)	nahm!	นำ
(lead metal)	dta-(l)goo-uh	ตะกั่ว

leader—leech

leader (head, chief)	(r)hoo-uh (f)nah	หัวหน้า
leaf (of a tree)	by! (h)my	ใบไม้
leak (to leak)	(f)roo-uh	รั่ว
learn (to learn, study)	ree-un	เรียน
lease (to lease, let, rent out)	(f)hy! (f)chow!	ให้เช่า
(a lease, rental agreement)		
	(r)sahn!-yah (f)chow!	สัญญาเช่า
least (smallest)	(h)nawy (f)tee (l)soot!	น้อยที่สุด
(at least, as a minimum)	(l)yahng (h)nawy	อย่างน้อย
leather	(r)nahng! (l)saht!	หนังสัตว์
leave (to leave)	(l)awk	ออก
(to leave, go out)	(l)awk bpy!	ออกไป
(to leave, depart, go away)	(l)jahk	จาก
,,	(l)jahk bpy!	จากไป
(to intentionally leave **something** or **someone** somewhere)	(h)ting!——ow! (h)wy	ทิ้ง——เอาไว้
(to accidentally leave **something** somewhere)		
	leum——(h)ting! (h)wy	ลืม——ทิ้งไว้
leech (land leech)	(f)tahk	ทาก
(water leech)	bpling!	ปลิง

128

left (opposite of right)	(h)sy	ซ้าย
(on the left-hand side)	tahng (h)sy meu	ทางซ้ายมือ
(to turn left)	(h)lee-oh (h)sy	เลี้ยวซ้าย
(to be remaining, left over, to have left)		
	(r)leu-uh	เหลือ
(to have left something somewhere)		
(see "leave")		
legal (to be legal, according to the law)		
	dtahm (l)goht!-(r)my	ตามกฎหมาย
leg	(r)kah	ขา
lemon (or lime)	ma!-now	มะนาว
(lemonade, limeade)	(h)nahm! ma!-now	น้ำมะนาว
lend (to lend, loan)	(f)hy! yeum	ให้ยืม
length	kwahm yow	ความยาว
leprosy	(f)rohk (h)reu-un	โรคเรื้อน
less (less than **something**)		
	(h)nawy (l)gwah **something**	น้อยกว่า——
,,	(b)lek! (l)gwah **something**	เล็กกว่า——
(to be less, become less)	loht! lohng!	ลดลง
lesson (study lesson)	(l)boht! ree-un	บทเรียน

129

let	(f)hy!	ให้
(to request)	(r)kaw (f)hy!	ขอให้
(to permit, allow)	yawm (f)hy!	ยอมให้
(to let, to rent out)	(f)hy! (f)chow!	ให้เช่า
letter (postal)	(l)joht!-(r)my	จดหมาย
(classifier for letters, documents)		
	cha-(l)bahp!	ฉบับ
(of the alphabet)	dtoo-uh	ตัว
,,	dtoo-uh (l)ahk!-(r)sawn	ตัวอักษร
,,	dtoo-uh (r)nahng!-(r)seu	ตัวหนังสือ
lettuce	(l)pahk!-(l)gaht (r)hawm	ผักกาดหอม
level (to be level, a level surface)	ra-(l)dahp!	ระดับ
(carpenter's level)	ra-(l)dahp! (h)nahm	ระดับน้ำ
library	(f)hawng! sa-(l)moot!	ห้องสมุด
license (driver's license)	by! (l)kahp! (l)kee	ใบขับขี่
(a permit)	by! ah!-noo!-(f)yaht	ใบอนุญาต
(license plate)	by! ta-bee-un (h)roht!	ใบทะเบียนรถ
lick (to lick)	lee-uh	เลีย
lid (cover, top)	(r)fah	ฝา
,,	(r)fah (l)bpit!	ฝาปิด

lie (to lie down)	nawn	นอน
,,	nawn lohng!	นอนลง
(to tell a lie)	go-(l)hohk!	โกหก
,,	(f)poot go-(l)hohk!	พูดโกหก
lieutenant (1st Lt., army)	(h)rawy toh	ร้อยโท
(1st Lt., air force)	reu-uh ah-(l)gaht toh	เรืออากาศโท
(Lt., navy)	reu-uh ehk	เรือเอก
(Lt., jg, navy)	reu-uh toh	เรือโท
(2nd. Lt., sub-lt., army)	(h)rawy dtree	ร้อยตรี
(2nd Lt., air force)	reu-uh ah-(l)gaht dtree	เรืออากาศตรี
life	chee-(h)wit!	ชีวิต
lift (to lift up, raise)	(h)yohk!	ยก
,,	(h)yohk! (f)keun!	ยกขึ้น
(elevator)	lift!	ลิฟต์
light (ray, beam of light)	(r)saang	แสง
,,	(r)saang sa-(l)wahng	แสงสว่าง
(sunlight)	(r)saang (l)daat	แสงแดด
(to light a fire)	(l)joot! fy!	จุดไฟ
,,	(l)dtit! fy!	ติดไฟ
(light from a lamp or lightbulb)	fy!	ไฟ

(to be light in weight)	bao!	เบา
	(rhymes with "cow")	
(lightly, softly, gently)	bao! bao!	เบา ๆ
(to be light in **color**)	**color** (l)awn	——อ่อน
lightbulb (electric)	(l)lawt fy!	หลอดไฟ
lightning	(h)fah (f)laap	ฟ้าแลบ
like (to like, enjoy, want)	(f)chawp	ชอบ
(to be similar, be similar to)		
	(r)meu-un gahn!	เหมือนกัน
(like this, this way)	(l)yahng (h)nee	อย่างนี้
,,	(f)chen! (h)nee	เช่นนี้
(like that, that way)	(l)yahng (h)nahn!	อย่างนั้น
,,	(f)chen! (h)nahn!	เช่นนั้น
(would like to——)	(l)yahk——	อยาก——
,,	(l)yahk (l)ja!——	อยากจะ——
lime (or lemon)	ma!-now	มะนาว
(limeade, lemonade)	(h)nahm! ma!-now	น้ำมะนาว
line, lines	(f)sen!	เส้น
(a straight line)	(f)sen! dtrohng!	เส้นตรง
(to draw a line)	(l)keet (f)sen!	ขีดเส้น
,,	(f)lahk (f)sen!	ลากเส้น

(row, line)	(r)taa-oh	แถว
(to stand in a line)	(f)kow! (r)taa-oh	เข้าแถว
(boundary, limit)	(l)ket	เขต
(stripe, line, streak)	(h)riw!	ริ้ว
(bus line)	(r)sy (h)roht!-meh	สายรถเมล์
linoleum	prohm! (h)nahm!-mahn!	พรมน้ำมัน
lion	(r)sing!-dtoh	สิงโต
lip, lips	rim!-(r)fee-(l)bpahk	ริมฝีปาก
liquor (intoxicating beverage)	(f)lao!	เหล้า
	(rhymes with "cow")	
list (of items)	ry-gahn	รายการ
(of names)	ry (f)cheu	รายชื่อ
listen (to listen, listen to)	fahng!	ฟัง
liter (1,000 cc)	(h)lit!	ลิตร
little (to be little, small in size)	(h)lek!	เล็ก
"	(h)lek! (h)lek!	เล็ก ๆ
(little, a little bit)	(h)lek! (h)nawy	เล็กน้อย
(a little bit, very little)	(h)nit! (l)nawy	นิดหน่อย
(just a little bit)	(h)nit! dee-oh	นิดเดียว
live (to live, to be at a location)	(l)yoo	อยู่
"	(h)pahk! (l)yoo	พักอยู่

133

(to be alive, have life)	mee chee-(h)wit!	มีชีวิต
„	mee chee-(h)wit! (l)yoo	มีชีวิตอยู่
liver	(l)dtahp!	ตับ
living room	(f)hawng! (h)rahp! (l)kaak	ห้องรับแขก
lizard (house lizard, small)	(f)jing!-(l)johk!	จิ้งจก
(gecko, large house lizard)	(h)dtook!-gaa	ตุ๊กแก
(monitor, large lizard)	dta-(l)goo-ut	ตะกวด
load (to load, load on)	bahn!-(h)took!	บรรทุก
loaf, loaves (of bread)	bpawn	ปอนด์
„	(r)taa-oh	แถว
loan (a loan of money)	nguhn (f)goo	เงินกู้
(to loan, lend)	(f)hy! yeum	ให้ยืม
lobster	(f)goong! (l)yai!	กุ้งใหญ่
(mantis-shrimp)	(f)gahng!	กั้ง
located (to be located, to be at)	(l)yoo	อยู่
lock (a lock, padlock)	goon!-jaa	กุญแจ
„	(f)maa goon!-jaa	แม่กุญแจ
(to lock)	(l)sy! goon!-jaa	ใส่กุญแจ
log (a log, piece of wood)	(f)tawn (h)my	ท่อนไม้
lonely (to be lonely, lonesome)		
	(l)bplao (l)bplee-oh	เปล่าเปลี่ยว

(to be lonely, alone)	(l)yoo dee-oh dy	อยู่เดียวดาย
,,	(h)wah-(l)weh	ว้าเหว่
long (to be long, in size)	yow	ยาว
(to be long, in time)	nahn	นาน
look (to look, to look at)	doo	ดู
(to look at intently, to stare)	mawng	มอง
,,	mawng doo	มองดู
(to look for)	(r)hah	หา
,,	mawng (r)hah	มองหา

(to look for **something** or **someone** and find
it, him)　　　　　　　　(r)hah - -(h)pohp!　หา— —พบ

　　　　　　　　,,　　　(r)hah— —juh　หา— —เจอ

(to look for- -but cannot find)

　　　　　　　(r)hah— —(f)my! juh　หา— —ไม่เจอ

(to look carefully and see something)

　　　　　　　　　mawng (r)hen!　มองเห็น

(to look carefully but cannot find or see)

　　　　　　　mawng (f)my! (r)hen!　มองไม่เห็น

(to look like, seem, seems like)

　　　　　　　　doo (r)meu-un　ดูเหมือน

135

(Look out! Be careful!)	ra-wahng!	ระวัง
loose (to be loose, fit loosely, be too large)		
	(r)loo-um	หลวม
(to be slack, as with a rope)	(l)yawn	หย่อน
lose (to lose **something**) **something**	(r)hy	——หาย
(to waste, spend)	(r)see-uh	เสีย
(to not win)	(h)paa	แพ้
lost (to be lost, lose one's way)		
	(r)lohng! tahng	หลงทาง
lottery (or lottery ticket)	(h)lawt-dtuh-(f)ree	ล็อตเตอรี่
„ sa-(l)lahk	(h)lawt-dtuh-(f)ree	สลากล็อตเตอรี่
„ sa-(l)lahk-geen!-(l)baang!		สลากกินแบ่ง
loud (to be loud, noisy)	dahng!	ดัง
love (to love)	(h)rahk!	รัก
(love) n.	kwahm (h)rahk!	ความรัก
lovely (beautiful)	(f)nah-(h)rahk!	น่ารัก
„	(r)soo-ay	สวย
lover	kohn! (h)rahk!	คนรัก
(dear, sweetheart)	(f)tee (h)rahk!	ที่รัก
(boy or girl friend)	faan	แฟน

low (to be low in height, of things) (l)dtahm! ต่ำ

   (to be low in price, cheap)   (l)took ถูก

lower (to lower the position of **something**)

                ow! **something** lohng! เอา——ลง

   (to lower the price, to discount, put on sale)

                   (h)loht! rah-kah ลดราคา

loyal (to be loyal, true, faithful)

                 (f)seu-(l)saht! ซื่อสัตย์

lubricate (to oil)   (l)yawt (h)nahm!-mahn! หยอดน้ำมัน

   (to grease)   (l)aht!-(l)cheet อัดฉีด

luck   (f)chohk โชค

   (good luck)   (f)chohk dee โชคดี

   (to be lucky, to have luck) mee (f)chohk มีโชค

   (*Note :* see also "unlucky")

lumbermill   rohng (h)my โรงไม้

lump, lumps (as of sugar, etc.)   (f)gawn ก้อน

   (to be lumpy, have lumps) bpen! (f)gawn เป็นก้อน

lunch   ah-(r)hahn glahng wahn! อาหารกลางวัน

lung (the lungs)   (l)bpawt ปอด

machine (machinery, apparatus, devices, etc.)

   (general term)   (f)kreu-ung เครื่อง

(machine shop)	(h)rahn (f)sawm	ร้านซ่อม
mad (to be mad, crazy, insane)	(f)bah	บ้า
,,	bpen! (f)bah	เป็นบ้า
(to be angry)	(l)groht	โกรธ
,,	moh-(r)hoh	โมโห
Madam, Ma'am (as spoken by females)	ka!	คะ
(as spoken by males)	(h)krahp!	ครับ
made (see "make")		
(to be made of, made from)	tahm!(f)doo-ay	ทำด้วย
magazine	(r)nahng!-(r)seu (l)ahn	หนังสืออ่าน
	maak-ga-seen	แมกาซีน
magic	(h)wit-ta-yah gohn!	วิทยากล
(a trick)	gohn!-la-(h)met!	กลเม็ด
(to do tricks, stunts)	(f)len! gohn!	เล่นกล
maid	(f)poo-(r)ying! (h)rahp! (h)chy!	ผู้หญิงรับใช้
mail (letters)	(l)joht!-(r)my	จดหมาย
(to mail)	(l)sohng!	ส่ง
(to mail to, send to)	(l)sohng! bpy!	ส่งไป
(to mail or send by air, parcel post, etc.)		
	(l)sohng! tahng——	ส่งทาง——

138

(airmail)	bpry-sa-nee ah-(l)gaht	ไปรษณีย์อากาศ
(to register, for mail)	lohng! ta-bee-un	ลงทะเบียน
(registered mail)		
	bpry-sa-nee lohng! ta-bee-un	ไปรษณีย์ลงทะเบียน
(parcel post mail)	(h)paht!-sa-(l)doo!	พัสดุ
(classifier for letters, documents, newspapers)		
	cha-(l)bahp!	ฉบับ
major (army rank)	pahn! dtree	พันตรี
(air force rank)	nah-wah ah-(l)gaht dtree	นาวาอากาศตรี
make (to do, make, manufacture)	tahm!	ทำ
(to cause)	tahm! (f)hy!	ทำให้
(to make of, make from, be made of)		
	tahm! (f)doo-ay	ทำด้วย
malaria	(f)ky jahp!-(l)sahn!	ไข้จับสั่น
	mah-leh ree-uh	มาเลเรีย
Malaya	ma-lah-yoo	มลายู
male (of animals)	dtoo-uh (f)poo	ตัวผู้
(of people)	chy	ชาย
man	(f)poo-chy	ผู้ชาย
(person, in general)	kohn!	คน

139

manager	(f)poo (l)jaht! gahn	ผู้จัดการ
mango	ma-(f)moo-ung	มะม่วง
mangosteen	mahng!-(h)koot!	มังคุด
manufacture (to manufacture, produce)		
	pa-(l)lit!	ผลิต
,,	tahm!	ทำ
many (or much)	(f)mahk	มาก
(several)	(r)ly	หลาย
(a whole lot, plenty)	(h)yuh!	เยอะ
,,	(h)yuh! (h)yaa!	เยอะแยะ
,,	(f)mahk my	มากมาย
,,	(f)mahk tee dee-oh	มากที่เดียว
map	(r)paan (f)tee	แผนที่
March	mee-nah kohm!	มีนาคม
marine (the marines)	nah-(h)wik!-ga-yoh-tin!	นาวิกโยธิน
market	dta-(l)laht	ตลาด
(Floating Market)	dta-(l)laht (h)nahm	ตลาดน้ำ
(Sunday Market)	dta-(l)laht (h)naht!	ตลาดนัด
marry (to marry, to be married)		
	(l)dtaang ngahn	แต่งงาน

140

marsh	(r)nawng (h)nahm	หนองน้ำ
(a swamp)	beung!	บึง
marshal (field marshal, 5-star gen., army)		
	jawm pohn!	จอมพล
(air marshal, 5-star gen., air force)		
	jawn pohn! ah-(l)gaht	จอมพลอากาศ
massage (to massage, a massage)	(f)noo-ut	นวด
mat (woven grass mat)	(l)seu-uh	เสื่อ
(doormat)	(f)tee (h)chet! (h)tao	ที่เช็ดเท้า
(bathmat)	(f)pah (h)chet! (h)tao	ผ้าเช็ดเท้า
match, matches	(h)my (l)keet fy!	ไม้ขีดไฟ
(to match or fit in with a set)		
	(f)kow! (h)choot!	เข้าชุด
mathematics	ka-(h)nit!-dta-(l)saht	คณิตศาสตร์
mattress	(f)tee nawn	ที่นอน
	(f)fook	ฟูก
may	(f)dy!	ได้
(might)	(l)aht (l)ja!	อาจจะ
(may I ?)	(f)dy! (r)my	ได้ไหม
May	(h)preut!-sa-pah kohm!	พฤษภาคม

141

maybe (perhaps)	bahng tee	บางที
me, I (r)pohm! (polite, spoken by males)		ผม
(r)chahn! (spoken by females, and is familiar form for males)		ฉัน
meal (or food)	ah-(r)hahn	อาหาร
mean (to mean)	(r)my kwahm	หมายความ
(that means, by translation)	bplaa (f)wah	แปลว่า
(by means of)	doy	โดย
(to be mean, merciless)	jy! dahm!	ใจดำ
(What does——mean?)		
——(r)my kwahm (f)wah ah!-ry		——หมายความ ว่าอะไร
(What do you mean?)		
(f)tahn! (r)my kwahm (f)wah ah!-ry		ท่านหมายความ ว่าอะไร
meaning	kwahm (r)my	ความหมาย
measure (to measure)	(h)waht!	วัด
(measurement)	gahn (h)waht!	การวัด
meat	(b)neu-uh	เนื้อ
mechanic (machinist)	(f)chahng (f)kreu-ung	ช่างเครื่อง

medal (medals, decorations)	(r)ree-un dtrah	เหรียญตรา
medicine	yah	ยา
medium (or middle)	glahng	กลาง
meet (to meet, encounter)	(h)pohp!	พบ
"	juh	เจอ
(to make someone's acquaintance)		
	(h)roo-(l)jahk!	รู้จัก
(to go meet **someone**, pick up **someone**)		
	bpy! (h)rahp!——	ไปรับ——
meeting (a meeting, conference; to assemble, hold a meeting)	bpra-choom!	ประชุม
melon (watermelon)	dtaang-moh	แตงโม
(muskmelon, cantaloupe)	dtaang-ty	แตงไทย
melt (to melt or dissolve)	la!-ly	ละลาย
menu	ry-gahn ah-(r)hahn	รายการอาหาร
	ry (f)cheu ah-(r)hahn	รายชื่ออาหาร
message (a note, short letter)		
	(l)joht!-(r)my (f)sahn! (f)sahn!	จดหมายสั้น ๆ
(leave a message)	(l)sahng! (h)wy!	สั่งไว้
metal	loh-(l)ha!	โลหะ

meter (100 cm)	(h)met!	เมตร
(taxi meter)	mee-tuh	มิ่เตอร์
microscope	(f)glawng joon!-la-(h)taht!	กล้องจุลทรรศน์
middle	glahng	กลาง
(at the center)	dtrohng! glahng	ตรงกลาง
midnight	(f)tee-ung keun	เที่ยงคืน
	(r)sawng yahm	สองยาม
might, may	(l)aht (l)ja!	อาจจะ
mile	my!	ไมล์
milk	nohm!	นม
	(h)nahm! nohm!	น้ำนม
millimeter	min!-lih!-(h)met!	มิลลิเมตร
million (1,000,000)	(h)lahn	ล้าน
mimeograph machine (or duplicator, copy machine, any kind)		
	(f)kreu-ung (l)aht! (r)sahm!-now!	เครื่องอัดสำเนา
mind (or spirit, heart)	jy!	ใจ
(to mind, object, to dislike)	rahng! (l)gee-ut	รังเกียจ
mine (belonging to me)	(r)kawng (r)pohm!	ของผม
„	(r)kawng (r)chahn!	ของฉัน

144

(ore mine)	(r)meu-ung (f)raa	เหมืองแร่
(a bomb)	ra-(l)buht	ระเบิด
mineral, minerals	(f)raa	แร่
minister (of the government)		
	(h)raht!-ta-mohn!-dtree	รัฐมนตรี
ministry (of the government)	gra!-soo-ung	กระทรวง
minus (to subtract)	(h)lohp!	ลบ
minute (of time)	nah-tee	นาที
mirror	gra-(l)johk!	กระจก
mischievous (to be mischievous, naughty)		
	sohn!	ซน
miss, (to miss, as a bus, school, etc.)	(l)kaht	ขาด
(to miscalculate, fail)	(f)plaht	พลาด
(to be wrong, incorrect)	(l)peet!	ผิด
(to miss or long for **somebody** or **something**)		
	(h)keet! (r)teung!--	คิดถึง--
(Ex: to be homesick)		
	(h)keet! (r)teung! (f)bahn	คิดถึงบ้าน
Miss	koon!	คุณ
	nahng-(r)sow	นางสาว

145

missing (to be missing, to disappear)

	(r)hy bpy!	หายไป
(to be lacking)	(l)kaht	ขาด
mistake	kwahm (l)peet!	ความผิด
(to make a mistake)	tahm! (l)peet!	ทำผิด
Mister, Mr.	koon!	คุณ
	ny	นาย
misunderstand	(f)kow!-jy! (l)peet!	เข้าใจผิด
mix (to mix)	pa-(r)sohm!	ผสม
(to be mixed up, confused)	(f)yoong!	ยุ่ง
model (type, style)	(l)baap	แบบ
(kind, type, species)	cha-(h)nit!	ชนิด
(a girl in a fashion show)	nahng (l)baap	นางแบบ
modern	sa-(r)my! (l)my!	สมัยใหม่
mold (fungus)	rah	รา
moment	ka-(l)na!	ขณะ
	(r)dee-oh	เดี๋ยว
	(f)kroo	ครู่
(for a moment)	(f)choo-uh ka-(l)na!	ชั่วขณะ
(for just a moment)	(l)sahk! (f)kroo	สักครู่

(in a moment, just a moment)

bpra-(r)dee-oh ประเดี๋ยว

(a moment ago, just now)

(f)meu-uh (h)gee (h)nee เมื่อกี้นี้

(wait a moment)   (r)dee-oh dee-oh เดี๋ยวเดียว

    ,,   (r)dee-oh (l)gawn เดี๋ยวก่อน

Monday   wahn! jahn! วันจันทร์

money   ngun! เงิน

(baht, tical, monetary unit of Thailand,
equal to 100 satangs)   (l)baht บาท

(satang)   sa-dtahng สตางค์

money order (postal)   ta-nah-(h)naht! ธนาณัติ

monk (or Buddhist priest)   (h)pra! พระ

    ,,   (h)pra! (r)sohng! พระสงฆ์

(a monk or novice under the age of 20) nen เณร

(enter the monkhood)   (l)boo-ut บวช

monkey   ling! ลิง

month   deu-un เดือน

monthly   bpra-jahm! deu-un ประจำเดือน

ry deu-un รายเดือน

147

(each month, every month) (h)took! deu-un ทุกเดือน

(each and every month)

(h)took! (h)took! deu-un ทุก ๆ เดือน

monument (or memorial)

ah!-noo!-(r)sah-wa!-ree อนุสาวรีย์

mooban (village, group of houses)

(l)moo-(f)bahn หมู่บ้าน

(head of village, puyaiban)

(f)poo-(l)yai!-(f)bahn ผู้ใหญ่บ้าน

moon (h)pra-jahn! พระจันทร์

moonlight (r)saang jahn! แสงจันทร์

mop (h)my (r)too (f)bahn ไม้ถูบ้าน

more (more, again, another) (l)eek อีก

(more than **number**) **number** (l)gwah ——กว่า

(to be more than **something** else)

(f)mahk (l)gwah **something** มากกว่า—

morning (h)chow เช้า

(in the morning) dtawn (h)chow ตอนเช้า

(this morning) (h)chow (h)nee เช้านี้

mosquito yoong! ยุง

most (superlative)	(f)mahk (f)tee (l)soot!	มากที่สุด
(most of――, the majority of――)		
	――(l)soo-un (f)mahk	――ส่วนมาก
(Ex: most of the people)		
	kohn! (l)soo-un (f)mahk	คนส่วนมาก
moth	(f)mawt	มอด
	dtoo-uh (f)mawt	ตัวมอด
	dtoo-uh (f)mawt geen! (f)pah	ตัวมอดกินผ้า
(mothballs)	(f)look (r)men!	ลูกเหม็น
mother	(f)maa	แม่
	mahn-dah	มารดา
mother-in-law	(f)maa yai	แม่ยาย
motor (electric motor)	dy-na-mo	ไดนาโม
(reciprocating engine, gasoline engine)		
	(f)kreu-ung yohn!	เครื่องยนต์
(automobile engine)		
	(f)kreu-ung (h)roht! yohn!	เครื่องรถยนต์
motorcycle	(h)roht! moh-tuh sy	รถมอเตอร์ไซด์
	(l)jahk!-gra-yahn yohn!	จักรยานยนต์
mountain	(r)kow!	เขา

	poo (r)kow!	ภูเขา
mouse (or rat)	(r)noo	หนู
	(r)noo dtoo-uh (l)lek!	หนูตัวเล็ก
moustache	(l)noo-ut	หนวด
mouth	(l)bpahk	ปาก
move (to move **something**)		
	(f)kleu-un (h)yai **something**	เคลื่อนย้าย— —
(to have motion)	(f)kleu-un (r)wy!	เคลื่อนไหว
(to move house)	(h)yai (f)bahn	ย้ายบ้าน
movie	(f)pah-pa-yohn	ภาพยนตร์
	(r)nahng!	หนัง
(to go see a movie)	bpy! doo (r)nahng!	ไปดูหนัง
Mr., Mister	koon!	คุณ
	ny	นาย
Mrs.	koon!	คุณ
	nahng	นาง
much (or many)	(f)mahk	มาก
(too much of **something**)		
	something (f)mahk bpy!	— —มากไป
,,	**something** (f)mahk gun bpy!	— —มากเกินไป

mud	klohn	โคลน
(to be muddy)	bpen! klohn	เป็นโคลน
,,	bpen! dtohm!	เป็นตม
muffler (exhaust pipe)	(f)taw l! (r)see-uh	ท่อไอเสีย
multiply (to multiply mathematically)	koon	คูณ
(A times B is C)	A koon B bpen! C	—คูณ—เป็น—
municipal, municipality	(f)teh-sa-bahn	เทศบาล
murder (a murder) n.	(f)kaht-dta-gahm	ฆาตกรรม
(to kill)	(f)kah	ฆ่า
(a murderer)	kohn! (f)kah	คนฆ่า
museum	(h)pih!-pit!-ta-pahn!	พิพิธภัณฑ์
(sounds like "pipit-ta-pahn")		
mushroom	(l)het!	เห็ด
music	dohn!-dtree	ดนตรี
must	(f)dtawng!	ต้อง
mustache	(l)noo-ut	หนวด
mustard	(b)nahm! (f)jim! mahs!-(l)dtaht	น้ำจิ้มมัสตาด
mutton	(h)neu-uh (l)gaa!	เนื้อแกะ

151

my (my something)

	something	(r)kawng (r)pohm!	— — ของผม
,,	**something**	(r)kawng (r)chahn!	— —ของฉัน
,,	**something**	(r)pohm!	— —ผม
,,	**something**	(r)chahn!	— —ฉัน

myna bird (talking myna)

(h)nohk! (r)koon! tawng   นกขุนทอง

myself   eng   เอง

(r)chahn! eng   ฉันเอง

dtoo-uh eng   ตัวเอง

dtohn! eng   คนเอง

dtoo-uh (r)kawng (r)pohm! eng   ตัวของผมเอง

dtoo-uh (r)kawng (r)chahn! eng   ตัวของฉันเอง

mystery   kwahm (h)leuk! (h)lahp!   ความลึกลับ

(to be mysterious)   (h)leuk! (h)lahp!   ลึกลับ

(a mystery story)

(f)reu-ung (h)leuk! (h)lahp!   เรื่องลึกลับ

nail (carpenter's)   dtah-bpoo   คาปู

(to nail)   (l)dtawk dtah-bpoo   ดอกคาปู

(fingernail)   (h)lep! meu   เล็บมือ

152

(toenail)	(h)lep! (h)tao	เล็บเท้า
naked (to be naked)	bpleu-ay gy	เปลือยกาย
,,	(f)gaa (f)pah	แก้ผ้า
name	(f)cheu	ชื่อ
	nahm	นาม
(What is your name?)		
	(f)tahn (f)cheu ah!-ry	ท่านชื่ออะไร
(surname)	nahm sa-goon!	นามสกุล
(nickname)	(f)cheu (f)len!	ชื่อเล่น
(pen name)	nahm (l)bpahk-gah	นามปากกา
namely (is, to be as follows)	keu	คือ
napkin (table napkin, serviette)		
	(f)pah (h)chet! meu	ผ้าเช็ดมือ
narrow (to be narrow)	(f)kaap	แคบ
nation (or nationality, race)	(f)chaht	ชาติ
(the Thai nation, Thai nationality)		
	(f)chaht ty	ชาติไทย
naughty (to be naughty, mischievous)	sohn!	ซน
navy	gawng-(h)tahp! reu-uh	กองทัพเรือ
	nah-wee	นาวี

near	(f)gly!	ใกล้
(to be located nearby)	(l)yoo (f)gly!	อยู่ใกล้
nearly (or almost)	(l)geu-up	เกือบ
neat (to be neat, tidy, be in good order)		
	(f)ree-up (h)rawy	เรียบร้อย
necessary (to be necessary)	jahm!-bpen!	จำเป็น
(not necessary)	(f)my! jahm!-bpen!	ไม่จำเป็น
neck	kaw	คอ
necklace	(f)sawy kaw	สร้อยคอ
necktie	(h)nek!-ty!	เน็คไท
	(f)pah (l)pook kaw	ผ้าผูกคอ
need (to need, want, require)	(f)dtawng gahn	ต้องการ
(no need to, need not)	(f)my! (f)dtawng	ไม่ต้อง
needle	(r)kem!	เข็ม
negative (minus, opposite of positive)		
	(h)lohp!	ลบ
neighbor	(f)peu-un (f)bahn	เพื่อนบ้าน
nephew	(r)lahn-chy	หลานชาย
nest	rahng!	รัง
(bird's nest)	rahng! (h)nohk!	รังนก

net (mosquito net)	(h)moong!	มุ้ง
(fish net, small)	(r)haa	แห
(fish net, large)	oo-un	อวน
(ball net, e.g. tennis net)	dtah-(l)ky	ตาข่าย
(net profit)	gahm!-ry! (l)soot!-tee!	กำไรสุทธิ
never	(f)my! kuh-ee	ไม่เคย
(never mind, it doesn't matter, you're welcome)	(f)my! bpen! ry!	ไม่เป็นไร
new (to be new)	(l)my!	ใหม่
news	(l)kow	ข่าว
newspaper	(r)nahng!-(r)seu-pim!	หนังสือพิมพ์
(classifier for newspapers)	cha-(l)bahp!	ฉบับ
New Year	bpee (l)my!	ปีใหม่
next (to be next in a series)	(l)taht! bpy!	ถัดไป
(the house next door)	(f)bahn (l)taht! bpy!	บ้านถัดไป
(the next street)	ta-(r)nohn! (l)taht! bpy!	ถนนถัดไป
,,	ta-(r)nohn! (f)nah	ถนนหน้า
(next **month**)	**deu-un** (f)nah	เดือนหน้า
nice (to be nice, good)	dee	ดี
nickname	(f)cheu (f)len!	ชื่อเล่น

niece	(r)lahn-(r)sow	หลานสาว
night	keun	คืน
(at night, in the night)	glahng keun	กลางคืน
(all night)	dta-(l)lawt keun	ตลอดคืน
(last night)	(f)meu-uh keun (h)nee	เมื่อคืนนี้
nine (9)	(f)gow	เก้า
no, not	(f)my!	ไม่
(No!, is not)	(f)my! (f)chy	ไม่ใช่
(no, nothing)	(l)bplao	เปล่า
(no, not yet)	yahng!	ยัง
(I don't want it.)	(f)my! (f)dtawng gahn	ไม่ต้องการ
,,	(f)my! ow!	ไม่เอา
(Don't――!, Do not――!)	(l)yah――	อย่า――
nobody	(f)my! mee kry!	ไม่มีใคร
noise (or sound, tone)	(r)see-ung	เสียง
noisy (to be noisy)	(l)noo-uk (r)hoo	หนวกหู
,,	(l)euk!-ga-(h)teuk!	อึกทึก
none	(f)my! mee luh-ee	ไม่มีเลย
(no one, nobody)	(f)my! mee kry!	ไม่มีใคร

156

noodle (Chinese noodles, thin, white)

(h)goo-ay (r)dtee-oh	ก๋วยเตี๋ยว

(sounds like "gwit! dtee-oh")

(Chinese egg noodles, yellow) ba!-(l)mee บะหมี่

,, (f)sen!-(l)mee เส้นหมี่

noon (f)tee-ung เที่ยง

(at noon) weh-lah (f)tee-ung เวลาเที่ยง

(noontime) dtawn (f)tee-ung ตอนเที่ยง

(at noon sharp) (f)tee-ung dtrohng! เที่ยงตรง

normal (to be normal, usual, routine)

(l)bpo!-ga-(l)dtih! ปกติ

(as usual) bpen! (l)bpo!-ga-(l)dtih! เป็นปกติ

(to be ordinary, natural) tah-ma-dah ธรรมดา

north, northern (r)neu-uh เหนือ

(the direction of north) (h)tit! (r)neu-uh ทิศเหนือ

(the northern part of the country)

(f)pahk (r)neu-uh ภาคเหนือ

northeast (the northeastern part of Thailand)

(f)pahk ih!-(r)sahn ภาคอิสาณ

nose ja-(l)mook จมูก

157

not, no	(f)my!	ไม่
(No!, is not)	(f)my! (f)chy!	ไม่ใช่
(not yet)	yahng!	ยัง
note (message, short letter)		
	(l)joht!-(r)my (f)sahn! (f)sahn!	จดหมายสั้น ๆ
notebook	sa-(l)moot!	สมุด
nothing (there is nothing)	(f)my! mee ah!-ry	ไม่มีอะไร
(no, nothing)	(l)bplao	เปล่า
notice (to notice, observe)	(r)sahng!-(l)get	สังเกต
,,	(r)sahng!-(l)get (r)hen!	สังเกตเห็น
(a notice, an announcement)	bpra-(l)gaht	ประกาศ
November	(h)preut!-sa!-(l)jih!-gah yohn!	พฤศจิกายน
now	(r)dee-oh (h)nee	เดี๋ยวนี้
(at this time, nowadays)	weh-láh (h)nee	เวลานี้
numb (to be numb)	chah	ชา
,,	(l)nep! chah	เหน็บชา
(to feel numb)	(h)roo-(l)seuk! chah	รู้สึกชา
,,	bpen! (l)nep! chah	เป็นเหน็บชา
number	(f)lek	เลข
	buh	เบอร์

(number– –, no.——)	(f)lek (f)tee **no.**	เลขที่ – –
(**no.** day of the month)	wahn! (f)tee **no.**	วันที่——
(address, house no.)	(f)lek (f)tee **no.**	เลขที่——

(**Note**: house numbers are usually of the form
A/B, which is pronounced: A (h)tahp! B   A ทับ B)

(amount, quantity)	jahm!-noo-un	จำนวน
(telephone number)	buh toh-ra-(l)sahp!	เบอร์โทรศัพท์
,,	(r)my (f)lek toh-ra-(l)sahp!	หมายเลขโทรศัพท์
nurse	nahng pa-yah-bahn	นางพยาบาล
nursemaid	kohn! (h)lee-ung (l)dek!	คนเลี้ยงเด็ก
nut (food)	(l)too-uh!	ถั่ว
(of a bolt)	nawt! dtoo-uh mee-uh	น็อตตัวเมีย
observe (to observe, notice)	(r)sahng!-(l)get	สังเกต
occupation (or livelihood, profession)		
	ah-(f)cheep	อาชีพ
occupied (to be occupied, not vacant,		
not free)	(f)my! (f)wahng	ไม่ว่าง
occur (to occur, happen)	(l)gut (f)keun!	เกิดขึ้น
ocean	ma-(r)hah sa-(l)moot!	มหาสมุทร

o'clock (used with the 24-hour clock)

	nah-li-gah	นาฬิกา
October	dtoo!-lah-kohm!	ตุลาคม
octopus	bplah (l)meuk! (h)yahk	ปลาหมึกยักษ์
of (belonging to)	(r)kawng	ของ

off (to take off **something**)

	ow! **something** (l)awk	เอา— —ออก
(to take off clothing)	(l)tawt (f)seu-uh	ถอดเสื้อ
(to turn off **the lights**)	(l)bpit! **fy!**	ปิดไฟ
(to come off, become detached, fall off)		
	(l)loot!	หลุด
office	(h)aw-(h)fit	ออฟฟิศ
(Thai pronunciation of "office")		
	(f)tee tahm! gahn	ที่ทำการ
	(f)tee tahm! ngahn	ที่ทำงาน
	(r)sahm!-(h)nahk! ngahn	สำนักงาน
officer (of the military)	ny ta-(r)hahn	นายทหาร
often	(l)bawy	บ่อย
	(l)bawy (l)bawy	บ่อย ๆ
oil (general term)	(h)nahm!-mahn!	น้ำมัน

(motor oil)	(h)nahm!-mahu! (f)kreu-ung	น้ำมันเครื่อง
(to oil, lubricate)	(l)sy! (h)nahm!-mahn!	ใส่น้ำมัน
(vegetable oil)	(h)nahm!-mahn! (f)peut	น้ำมันพืช
(lard, cooking oil)	(b)nahm!-mahn! (r)moo	น้ำมันหมู
O.K.	O.K.	โอเค
(That's good!)	dee (h)laa-oh	ดีแล้ว
(Agreed!)	(l)dtohk! lohng!	ตกลง
(Correct!)	(l)took (f)dtawng	ถูกต้อง
old (of things)	(l)gow!	เก่า
(of people)	(l)gaa	แก่
(How old are you?)	ah-(h)yoo! (f)tao!-(l)ry!	อายุเท่าไร
(I am **no.** years old.)		
	(r)chahn! ah-(h)yoo! **no.** bpee	ฉันอายุ— —ปี
omelet (egg omelet)	(l)ky! jee-oh	ไข่เจียว
on, upon	bohn!	บน
(to put on top of, overlay, lay one on top		
of another)	(h)tabp!	ทับ
(on some **day** of the week)	ny! **day**	ใน— —
(to go on, continue)	(l)dtaw bpy!	ต่อไป
(to turn on **the lights**)	(l)bput fy!	เปิดไฟ

161

once (one time)	(h)krahng! (l)neung!	ครั้งหนึ่ง
"	(l)neung! (h)krahng!	หนึ่งครั้ง
(at once, immediately)	tahn!-tee	ทันที
(once more)	(l)eek (h)krahng! (l)neung!	อีกครั้งหนึ่ง
one (1)	(l)neung!	หนึ่ง
(one thing or item)	ahn! (l)neung!	อันหนึ่ง
"	ahn! dee-oh	อันเดียว
oneself	dtoo-uh eng	ตัวเอง
	dtohn! eng	คนเอง
one-way (a one-way street)		
	ta-(r)nohn! duhn tahng dee-oh	ถนนเดินทางเดียว
(a one-way ticket)	(r)dtoo-uh bpy!	ตั๋วไป
onion (bulb)	(r)hoo-uh (r)hawm	หัวหอม
(green onion)	(f)dtohn! (r)hawm	ต้นหอม
only (just that)	(f)tao! (h)nahn!	เท่านั้น
(merely, as little as)	(l)sahk!	สัก
open (to open, to be open)	(l)bput	เปิด
"	(l)bput (h)wy!	เปิดไว้
opener (can opener)		
	(f)tee (l)bput gra-(r)bpawng!	ที่เปิดกระป๋อง

(bottle opener)	(f)tee (l)bput (l)koo-ut	ที่เปิดขวด
operate (to operate, perform)	gra-tahm!	กระทำ
(an operator)	(f)poo gra-tahm!	ผู้กระทำ
(to operate surgically)	(l)pah (l)dtaht!	ผ่าตัด
(an operation, surgery)	gahn (l)pah (l)dtaht!	การผ่าตัด
(telephone operator)		
	pa-(h)nahk! ngahn toh-ra-(l)sahp!	พนักงานโทรศัพท์
opium	(l)fihn!	ฝิ่น
opportunity (or chance)	oh-(l)gaht	โอกาส
opposite	dtrohng! (f)kahm	ตรงข้าม
or	(r)reu	หรือ
(either A or B, either one will do)		
	A (r)reu B (f)gaw! (f)dy	—หรือ—ก็ได้
(or not?, as to make a question)		
	(r)reu (l)bplao	หรือเปล่า
orange (to be orange)	(f)sohm!	ส้ม
(the color of)	(r)see (f)sohm!	สีส้ม
(an orange, oranges)	(f)sohm!	ส้ม
(orange juice)	(h)nahm! (f)sohm!	น้ำส้ม
orchestra	wohng! dohn!-dtree	วงดนตรี

orchid (plant)	(f)gloo-ay (h)my	กล้วยไม้
(flower)	(l)dawk (f)gloo-ay (h)my	ดอกกล้วยไม้
order (to order)	(l)sahng!	สั่ง
(in order to)	(f)peu-uh	เพื่อ
(to be orderly, organized)		
	bpen! ra!-(l)bee-up	เป็นระเบียบ
ordinary (to be ordinary, usual, natural)		
	tah-ma-dah	ธรรมดา
(to be usual, routine)	(l)bpo!-ga-(l)dtih!	ปกติ
ore	(r)sin!-(f)raa	สินแร่
organize (to organize)	(l)jaht! ra-(l)bee-up	จัดระเบียบ
organization	ohng-gahn	องค์การ
(club, society, association)	sa-mah-kohm!	สมาคม
other, others	(l)eun	อื่น
(others, other ones)	(l)eun (l)eun	อื่น ๆ
(the other, another)	(l)eek	อีก
ought (ought to, should)	koo-un	ควร
ounce	awn	ออนซ์
our, ours (something of ours)		
something	(r)kawng rao!	——ของเรา

out (l)awk ออก

  (to go out) (l)awk bpy! ออกไป

  (to come out) (l)awk mah ออกมา

  (to take **something** out) ow! **something** (l)awk เอา—ออก

  (to be out, not be home) (f)my! (l)yoo ไม่อยู่

  (to put out a fire) (l)dahp! fy! ดับไฟ

outdoors (in the open air) glahng (f)jaang กลางแจ้ง

  (outside the house) (f)nawk (f)bahn นอกบ้าน

outside (f)nawk นอก

   (f)kahng (f)nawk ข้างนอก

oven dtao! (l)ohp! เตาอบ

over (above, over) (r)neu-uh เหนือ

  (above, on top) (f)kahng bohn! ข้างบน

  (over **no.**, more than **no.**) **no.** (l)gwah ——กว่า

  (too much) gun! bpy! เกินไป

  (to be over, through, to finish, end, quit)

     (f)luhk เลิก

     (f)luhk (h)laa-oh เลิกแล้ว

  (to run over, put on top of, overlay)

     (h)tahp! ทับ

  (to be higher in rank or status, be superior

    to) (r)neu-uh เหนือ

165

owe (to owe)   bpen! (f)nee   เป็นหนี้
    (to owe **someone something**)

       bpen! (f)nee **something someone**   เป็นหนี้——

owing to (because of)   (f)neu-ung (l)jahk   เนื่องจาก

own (**someone** to own **something**)

        something (r)kawng **someone**   ——ของ——
    (to be the owner of **something**)

      bpen! (f)jow! (r)kawng **something**   เป็นเจ้าของ——
    (belonging to oneself) (r)kawng dtohn! eng   ของตนเอง
    (Who owns this?)   (f)nee (r)kawng kry!   นี่ของใคร

owner (or proprietor)   (f)jow! (r)kawng   เจ้าของ
    (owner of **something**)

         (f)jow! (r)kawng **something**   เจ้าของ——

ox   woo-uh   วัว

       woo-uh dtoo-uh (f)poo   วัวตัวผู้
    (ox cart)   gwee-un   เกวียน

oyster   (r)hawy! nahng-rohm!   หอยนางรม

pack (to pack, collect possessions)

         (l)gep! (r)kawng   เก็บของ
    (to pack clothes into a suitcase)

    (l)jaht! gra-(r)bpow! (f)seu-uh (f)pah   จัดกระเป๋าเสื้อผ้า

166

package	(l)haw	ห่อ
	(l)haw (r)kawng	ห่อของ
padlock	goon!-jaa	กุญแจ
	(f)maa goon!-jaa	แม่กุญแจ
page (of a book)	(f)nah nahng!-(r)seu	หน้าหนังสือ
pagoda (stupa, chedi)	jeh-dee	เจดีย์
pail (water pail)	(r)tahng! (h)nahm	ถังน้ำ
pain	kwahm (l)jep! (l)bpoo-ut	ความเจ็บปวด
(to be painful)	(l)jep!	เจ็บ
,,	(l)jep! (l)bpoo-ut	เจ็บปวด
(to relieve the pain)	(f)gaa (l)bpoo-ut	แก้ปวด
paint	(r)see	สี
(to paint)	tah (r)see	ทาสี
(to paint a picture)	ra!-by (r)see	ระบายสี
painter (house painter)	(f)chahng tah (r)see	ช่างทาสี
(artist)	(f)chahng (r)kee-un	ช่างเขียน
painting (a painted picture)	(f)roop (r)kee-un	รูปเขียน
pair	(f)koo	คู่
pajamas	(f)seu-uh gahng-gehng nawn	เสื้อกางเกงนอน
	(f)seu-uh nawn	เสื้อนอน

167

palace	wahng!	วัง
pan (frying pan)	(l)gra!-(h)ta!	กระทะ
pants (trousers)	gahng-gehng	กางเกง
(underpants)	gahng-gehng ny!	กางเกงใน
papaya	ma-la-gaw	มะละกอ
paper	gra-(l)daht	กระดาษ
(newspaper)	nahng!-(r)seu pim!	หนังสือพิมพ์
(typing paper)	gra-(l)daht pim!-(l)deet	กระดาษพิมพ์ดีด
(carbon paper)	gra-(l)daht (h)gawp-(f)pee	กระดาษก๊อปปี้
(toilet paper)	gra-(l)daht chahm!-(h)ra!	กระดาษชำระ
paper clip	(f)loo-ut (l)nep! gra-(l)daht	ลวดเหนี่บกระดาษ
	(f)loo-ut (l)see-up gra-(l)daht	ลวดเสียบกระดาษ
parade	gahn (r)soo-un sa-(r)nahm	การสวนสนาม
parakeet	(h)nohk! gra!-ling	นกกระลิง
parallel (to be parallel, be parallel to)		
	ka-(r)nahn	ขนาน
parcel post	(h)paht!-sa-(l)doo!	พัสดุ
Pardon me! (Excuse me!)	(r)kaw (f)toht	ขอโทษ
,,	(r)kaw ah-py!	ขออภัย

parents—party

(Beg your pardon?, What did you say?)

ah!-ry nah! อะไรนะ

parents (f)paw (f)maa พ่อแม่

(l)bih!-dah mahn-dah บิดามารดา

park (garden) (r)soo-un สวน

(to park) (l)jawt จอด

(to park a car) (l)jawt (h)roht! จอดรถ

(parking lot, parking space)

(f)tee (l)jawt (h)roht! ที่จอดรถ

(No Parking) (f)hahm (l)jawt (h)roht! ห้ามจอดรถ

(public park) (r)soo-un (r)sah-tah-ra!-(h)na! สวนสาธารณ

parrot (h)nohk! (f)gaa-oh นกแก้ว

parsley (l)pahk! chee fa-(l)rahng! ผักชีฝรั่ง

part (or portion, share) (l)soo-un ส่วน

(one part of **something**)

something (l)soo-un (l)neung! ——ส่วนหนึ่ง

(part, section, region, of space or time)

dtawn ตอน

(part or region of a country) (f)pahk ภาค

party (social party) ngahn (h)lee-ung งานเลี้ยง

169

	geen! (h)lee-ung	กินเลี้ยง
pass (to pass)	(l)pahn	ผ่าน
(to pass by)	(l)pahn bpy	ผ่านไป
(to pass, overtake, as when driving)		
	saang	แซง
(admission ticket)		
	(l)baht! (l)pahn bpra-dtoo	บัตรผ่านประตู
(to pass an exam or course)	(l)sawp (f)dy	สอบได้
passenger(s)	(f)poo doy-(r)sahn	ผู้โดยสาร
passport	nahng!-(r)seu duhn tahng	หนังสือเดินทาง
path (way, route)	tahng	ทาง
(footpath, trail)	tahng duhn	ทางเดิน
patient (to be patient, enduring)	(l)oht!-tohn!	อดทน
(patience, perseverance)		
	kwahm (l)oht!-tohn!	ความอดทน
(a patient, sick person)	kohn! (f)ky!	คนไข้
paw (or hoof, foot of animal)	tao	เท้า
	rawy tao	รอยเท้า
pawnshop	rohng (h)rahp! jahm!-nahm!	โรงรับจำนำ
pay (to pay)	(l)jy	จ่าย

170

(to waste **money**)	(r)see-uh ngun!	เสียเงิน
(monthly salary)	ngun! deu-un	เงินเดือน
payment	gahn (h)chy! ngun!	การใช้เงิน
pea (or bean, peanut)	(l)too-uh	ถั่ว
peace (calm, peacefulness)	kwahm sa-(l)ngohp!	ความสงบ
,,	(r)sahn-dtih!-(f)pahp	สันติภาพ
Peace Corps (l)noo-ay (r)sahn-dtih-(f)pahp		หน่วยสันติภาพ
(Peace Corps Volunteer, PCV)		
	ah-(r)sah sa-(l)mahk!	อาสาสมัคร
peak (top, tip)	(f)yawt	ยอด
(mountain top or peak)	(f)yawt (r)kow!	ยอดเขา
peanut	(l)too-uh	ถั่ว
	(l)too-uh lih!-(r)sohng!	ถั่วลิสง
pearl (a pearl, a string of pearls)		
	(l)ky! (h)mook!	ไข่มุก
peasant (farmer)	chow nah	ชาวนา
pedestrian	(f)poo duhn (h)tao	ผู้เดินเท้า
peel (to peel, shell)	(l)bpawk (l)bpleu-uk	ปอกเปลือก
peeling (peel, shell, crust)	(l)bpleu-uk	เปลือก
pen (for writing)	(l)bpahk-gah	ปากกา

(fountain pen) (l)bpahk-gah (l)meuk! seum! ปากกาหมึกซึม

(ball-point pen) (l)bpahk-gah (f)look (f)leun ปากกาลูกลื่น

(enclosure, for pigs) (f)kawk คอก

(for chickens, ducks) (h)lao! เล้า

(cage, for birds, rabbits, etc.) grohng! กรง

pencil din!-(r)saw ดินสอ

people (in general, the public)

kohn! (f)too-uh bpy! คนทั่วไป

(the public, the populace)

bpra-chah-chohn! ประชาชน

(citizens, subjects) (f)raht-sa-dawn ราษฎร

(Thai people) kohn! ty คนไทย

pepper (h)prik! พริก

(h)prik! ty พริกไทย

(pepper sauce) (h)nahm! (h)prik! น้ำพริก

Pepsi (Cola) pep!-see เป๊ปซี่

per (h)la! ละ

(no. times per day)

wahn! (h)la! no. (h)krahng! วันละ——ครั้ง

(cost per item) ahn! (h)la! cost อันละ——

172

(20 baht/dollar)	(l)neung! (r)ree-un (l)dtaw	หนึ่งเหรียญต่อ
	(f)yee-(l)sip! (l)baht	ยี่สิบบาท
(no. km. per hr.)	no. gih!-loh-(h)met!	— —กิโลเมตร
	(l)dtaw (f)choo-uh-mohng	ต่อชั่วโมง
percent	bpuh-sen!	เปอร์เซ็นต์
	(h)rawy (h)la!	ร้อยละ
(no. percent)	(h)rawy (h)la! no.	ร้อยละ— —
perfume	(h)nahm! (r)hawm	น้ำหอม
perhaps (maybe)	bahng tee	บางที
permanent (to be permanent, lasting)		
	(r)tah-wawn	ถาวร
permission	ah!-noo!-(f)yaht	อนุญาต
(to have permission)		
	(f)dy! (h)rahp! ah!-noo!-(f)yaht	ได้รับอนุญาต
permit (to permit, allow)	yawm (f)hy!	ยอมให้
,,	ah!-noo!-(f)yaht	อนุญาต
(a permit, license)	by ah!-noo!-(f)yaht	ใบอนุญาต
person	kohn!	คน
	(f)poo	ผู้

perspire (to perspire, sweat)

       mee (l)ngeu-uh (l)awk   มีเหงื่อออก

  (perspiration, sweat)   (l)ngeu-uh   เหงื่อ

pharmacy (drug store)   (h)rahn (r)ky yah   ร้านขายยา

phonograph   (l)heep (r)see-ung   หีบเสียง

          pik!-ahp!   พิคอั๊บ

  (hi-fi)   hy-fy   ไฮไฟ

photograph (a photo, picture) (f)roop (l)ty   รูปถ่าย

  (to photograph)   (l)ty (f)roop   ถ่ายรูป

    ,,   (l)ty (f)pahp   ถ่ายภาพ

photographer   (f)chahng (l)ty (f)roop   ช่างถ่ายรูป

pick (to pick out, choose)   (f)leu-uk   เลือก

  (to pick **fruit, flowers**)   (l)gep!——   เก็บ——

  (to pick up something with the fingers)

          (l)yip!   หยิบ

  (to pick the teeth)   (f)jim! fahn!   จิ้มฟัน

  (to go pick up **somebody**)

     bpy! (h)rahp! **somebody**   ไปรับ——

pickle (to pickle, be pickled)   dawng   ดอง

174

(pickles, pickled vegetables)

	(l)pahk! dawng	ผักดอง
picture	(f)roop	รูป
	(f)pahp	ภาพ
	(f)roop (f)pahp	รูปภาพ
(a photograph)	(f)roop (l)ty	รูปถ่าย
(a painting)	(f)roop (r)kee-un	รูปเขียน
piece	(h)chin!	ชิ้น
	(f)tawn	ท่อน

(See also section on "Classifiers", in the Appendix.)

pier (or dock, wharf, port, harbor)	(f)tah	ท่า
pig	(r)moo	หมู
pigeon	(h)nohk! (h)pih!-(f)rahp	นกพิราบ
pile (a pile, heap)	gawng	กอง

(to pile **something** up)

	gawng **something** (h)wy!	กอง——ไว้
pill (tablet)	yah (h)met!	ยาเม็ด
	(h)met!	เม็ด
pillow	(r)mawn	หมอน

175

(side pillow, bolster)	(r)mawn (f)kahng	หมอนข้าง
(pillow case, pillowslip)		
	(l)bplawk (r)mawn	ปลอกหมอน
pimple	(r)siw!	สิว
pin (straight pin)	(r)kem! (l)moot!	เข็มหมุด
(safety pin)	(r)kem! (l)glaht!	เข็มกลัด
pinch (to pinch with the fingers)	(l)yik!	หยิก
pineapple	(l)sahp!-bpa-(h)roht!	สับปะรด
pink (to be pink)	chohm!-poo	ชมพู
(color of pink)	(r)see chohm!-poo	สีชมพู
pipe (or tube)	(f)taw	ท่อ
(pipe for smoking tobacco)		
	(f)glawng yah (f)sen!	กล้องยาเส้น
(exhaust pipe)	(f)taw I! (r)see-uh	ท่อไอเสีย
pistol (or revolver)	bpeun (h)pohk!	ปืนพก
pitcher	(l)yeu-uk	เหยือก
pity (to pity)	(r)sohng!-(r)sahn	สงสาร
(What a pity!)	(f)nah (r)sohng!-(r)sahn	น่าสงสาร
„	(f)nah (r)see-uh dy	น่าเสียดาย
place (place, place where)	(f)tee	ที่

(place, location)	(l)haang!	แห่ง
(to place, to lay)	wahng	วาง
plain (to be plain or clear in meaning)		
	(h)chaht!-jen	ชัดเจน
(to be ordinary, simple)	tah-ma-dah	ธรรมดา
plane (carpenter's)	(l)gohp!	กบ
plant (plants, vegetation)	(f)peut	พืช
(to plant)	(l)bplook	ปลูก
(to farm, cultivate)	(h)paw! (l)bplook	เพาะปลูก
(factory)	rohng ngahn	โรงงาน
plantation	(f)ry!	ไร่
plastic	plastic	ปลาสติค
plate (or dish)	jahn	จาน
play (to play)	(f)len!	เล่น
(to play cards)	(f)len! (f)py!	เล่นไพ่
(a play, drama, lakorn)	la-kawn	ละคร
(Thai musical folk drama)	lih!-geh	ลิเก
pleasant (to be pleasant)	sa-(l)nook! sa-by	สนุกสบาย
please (request)	(l)bproht	โปรด
„	ga!-roo!-nah	กรุณา

(invite)	chuhn	เชิญ
(to beg, request)	(r)kaw	ขอ
(please help, do the favor of)	(f)choo-ay	ช่วย
(to please)	tahm! (f)hy! (f)chawp	ทำให้ชอบ
(to satisfy)	tahm! (f)hy! paw jy!	ทำให้พอใจ
pleasure	kwahm yin! dee	ความยินดี
pliers	keem	คีม
plow (a plow, to plow)	(r)ty	ไถ
(to plow the field)	(r)ty nah	ไถนา
plus (to add)	(l)boo-uk	บวก
plywood	(h)my! (l)aht!	ไม้อัด
pocket	gra-(r)bpow!	กระเป๋า
pocketbook (woman's purse)		
	gra-(r)bpow! (r)teu	กระเป๋าถือ
(wallet)	gra-(r)bpow! (l)sy! ngun!	กระเป๋าใส่เงิน
poet	gah-wee	กวี
point (to point, point at)	(h)chee	ชี้
(spot, dot, decimal point)	(l)joot!	จุด
(point of land, peninsula)	(r)laam	แหลม
(to be sharp-pointed)	(r)laam	แหลม

178

(ignition points, platinum)	tawng (r)kow	ทองขาว
poison	yah (h)pit!	ยาพิษ
(to be poisonous)	mee (h)pit!	มีพิษ
pole (or post, pillar)	(r)sow!	เสา
(long slender wooden pole)	(h)my yow	ไม้ยาว
(fishing pole)	kahn! (l)bet!	คันเบ็ด
police (policeman)	dtahm! (l)roo-ut	ตำรวจ
(border police)	dtahm! (l)roo-ut	ตำรวจตระเวน
	dtra-wen chy daan	ชายแดน
polish (to polish, shine)	(l)kaht!	ขัด
(shoe polish)	yah (l)kaht! rawng-(h)tao	ยาขัดรองเท้า
polite (to be polite)	soo!-(f)pahp	สุภาพ
pomelo (like a grapefruit)	(f)sohm!-oh	ส้มโอ
pond	(l)sah!	สระ
(waterhole, well)	(l)baw (h)nahm	บ่อน้ำ
pool (swimming)	(l)sah! (l)ahp-(h)nahm!	สระอาบน้ำ
poor (to be poor, impoverished)	john!	จน
	(rhymes with "bone")	
,,	(f)yahk john!	ยากจน
(to be pitiful)	(f)nah (r)sohng!-(r)sahn	น่าสงสาร

179

population	pohn!-la-meu-ung	พลเมือง
porch (front porch)	(h)mook!	มุข
,,	(f)nah (h)mook!	หน้ามุข
(porch, veranda)	cha-(r)lee-ung	เฉลียง
pork	(h)neu-uh (r)moo	เนื้อหมู
port (harbor, pier, wharf, landing)	(f)tah	ท่า
(harbor, port, seaport)	(f)tah reu-uh	ท่าเรือ
positive (to be positive, sure, certain)		
	(f)naa nawn	แน่นอน
(plus, opposite of negative)	(l)boo-uk	บวก
possible (to be possible)	bpen! bpy! (f)dy	เป็นไปได้
post (or stake)	(l)lahk!	หลัก
postage (cost of postage)		
	(f)kah bpry!-sa-nee-yah-gawn!	ค่าไปรษณียากร
postage stamp	sa-dtaamp	แสตมป์
	doo-ung dtrah bpry!-sa-nee	ดวงตราไปรษณีย์
postcard	bpry!-sa-nee ya!-(l)baht!	ไปรษณีย์บัตร
postman (mailman)	boo!-(l)root!bpry!-sa-nee	บุรุษไปรษณีย์
post office	(f)tee tahm! gahn bpry!-sa-nee	ที่ทำการไปรษณีย์
pot (cooking pot)	(f)maw	หม้อ

potato (yam)	mahn!	มัน
(sweet potato)	mahn! (f)tet	มันเทศ
(Irish potato, not sweet)	mahn! fa-(l)rahng!	มันฝรั่ง
pound (to hammer, nail, pound)	(l)dtawk	ตอก
(to hit with a hammer)	(h)toop!	ทุบ
(to grind, pulverize, crush)	(l)boht!	บด
(unit of weight; pound sterling)	bpawn	ปอนด์
pour (to pour, pour out)	teh	เท
powder	(f)bpaang	แป้ง
	(r)pohng!	ผง
(powdered milk)	nohm! (r)pohng!	นมผง
(face powder)	(f)bpaang (l)paht! (f)nah	แป้งผัดหน้า
power (or energy, strength)	gahm!-lahng!	กำลัง
(influence, authority)	ahm!-(f)naht	อำนาจ
(exponential, mathematical power)		
	gahm!-lahng!	กำลัง
practice (to practice, train, drill)	(l)haht!	หัด
,,	(l)feuk! (l)haht!	ผึกหัด
prawn (or shrimp, lobster)	(f)goong!	กุ้ง

pray (to pray)	(l)soo-ut mohn!	สวดมนต์
pregnant (to be pregnant)	mee (h)tawng	มีท้อง
,,	mee kahn!	มีครรภ์
prepare (to prepare, make ready)	dtree-um	เตรียม
prescription (medical)	by! (l)sahng! yah	ใบสั่งยา
present (or gift)	(r)kawng (r)kwahn!	ของขวัญ
president (or chairman, head, chief)		
	bpra-tahn	ประธาน
(president of a country)		
	bpra-tah-nah (h)tih!-baw!-dee	ประธานาธิบดี
(vice-president)	rawng bpra-tahn	รองประธาน
pressure	kwahm dahn!	ความดัน
pretty (to be pretty)	(r)soo-ay	สวย
(to be beautiful)	ngahm	งาม
,,	(r)soo-ay ngahm	สวยงาม
(to be lovely, cute)	(f)nah (h)rahk!	น่ารัก
price	rah-kah	ราคา
(cost)	(f)kah	ค่า
priest	(h)pra!	พระ

(Bhuddist priest, monk, novice)

(h)pra! (r)sohng! พระสงฆ์

prime minister (or premier)

nah-(h)yohk! (h)raht-ta-mohn!-dtree นายกรัฐมนตรี

prince (f)jow! chy เจ้าชาย

princess (f)jow! (r)yeeng! เจ้าหญิง

print (to print, type) pim! พิมพ์

printing press (f)kreu-ung pim! เครื่องพิมพ์

prison (or jail) (h)kook! คุก

prisoner (or convict) (h)nahk! (f)toht นักโทษ

private (opposite of public)

(l)soo-un (l)book!-kohn! ส่วนบุคคล

,, (l)soo-un dtoo-uh ส่วนตัว

(private first class) ny (l)sip! dtree นายสิบตรี

prize (or award) rahng-wahn! รางวัล

probably (maybe) bahng tee บางที

(most likely, surely, sure to) kohng! คง

problem (or question, riddle, puzzle)

bpahn!-(r)hah ปัญหา

procession ka-boo-un ขบวน

produce (to produce, manufacture) pa-(l)lit! ผลิต

      ,,   tahm! ทำ

profession (or occupation, livelihood)

                    ah-(f)cheep อาชีพ

professor   ah-jahn อาจารย์

          (l)saht-sa!-dtrah-jahn ศาสตราจารย์

profit (gain, to profit, to gain) gahm!-ry! กำไร

  (profit, gain)   (r)pohn! gahm!-ry! ผลกำไร

  (net profit)   gahm!-ry! (l)soot!-tee! กำไรสุทธิ

progress (to progress, advance, develop)

                    ja-run เจริญ

  (progress, advancement, development)

                kwahm ja-run ความเจริญ

prohibit (to prohibit, forbid, stop) (f)hahm ห้าม

  (No ——;—— is prohibited) (f)hahm—— ห้าม ——

  (to not allow, not permit)

              (f)my! yawm (f)hy! ไม่ยอมให้

projector (movie) (f)kreu-ung (r)chy (r)nahng! เครื่องฉายหนัง

  (slide)   (f)kreu-ung (r)chy slide เครื่องฉายสไลด์

promise (a promise, to promise) (r)sahn!-yah สัญญา

promote (to be promoted, to move up)

(f)leu-un (f)keun! เลื่อนขึ้น

(to be promoted to a higher grade or level)

(f)leu-un (h)chahn! เลื่อนชั้น

pronounce (to pronounce) (l)awk (r)see-ung ออกเสียง

propaganda (or advertisement)

gahn (f)ko-sa-nah การโฆษณา

prostitute (r)yeeng! (r)so-peh!-nee หญิงโสเภณี

(whore) ga-(l)ree กะหรี่

protect (to protect, defend) (f)bpawng gahn! ป้องกัน

proud (to be proud of) poom jy! ภูมิใจ

(to feel proud, to have a feeling of

accomplishment) (f)pahk-poom ภาคภูมิ

(to be proud, haughty, vain) (l)ying! หยิ่ง

prove (to prove) (h)pih!-(l)soot พิสูจน์

(proof) (f)kaw (h)pih!-(l)soot ข้อพิสูจน์

province (or township, changwat)

jahng!-(l)waht! จังหวัด

public (the people, public, population)

bpra-chah-chohn! ประชาชน

(public, common)	(r)sah-tah-ra!-(h)na!	สาธารณะ
(opposite of private)	(l)soo-un roo-um	ส่วนรวม
(public health, welfare)		
	(r)sah-tah-ra!-(h)na! bpra-(l)yoht	สาธารณประโยชน์
(public health) (r)sah-tah-ra!-(h)na! (l)sook!		สาธารณสุข
puddle (mud puddle)	(l)baw klohn	บ่อโคลน
pull (to pull, tug)	deung!	ดึง
pulley	(f)rawk	รอก
	(f)look (f)rawk	ลูกรอก
pump (to pump)	(l)soop	สูบ
(a pump)	(f)kreu-ung (l)soop	เครื่องสูบ
pumpkin	(h)fahk! tawng	ฟักทอง
punish (to punish)	tahm! (f)toht	ทำโทษ
(punishment)	gahn tahm! (f)toht	การทำโทษ
puppy	(f)look (r)mah	ลูกหมา
pure (to be pure, unadulterated, virgin,		
innocent)	baw-ri-(l)soot!	บริสุทธิ์
purple	(r)see (f)moo-ung	สีม่วง
purse (woman's pocketbook)		
	gra-(r)bpow! (r)teu	กระเป๋าถือ

(wallet, purse)	gra-(r)bpow! (l)sy! ngun!	กระเป๋าใส่เงิน
push (to push)	dahn!	ดัน
(to shove)	(l)plahk!	ผลัก
put (to put, put in, put on)	(l)sy!	ใส่
(to put, place, lay)	wahng	วาง
(to put out, extinguish)	(l)dahp! fy!	ดับไฟ
(to put on, wear)	(l)sy!	ใส่
,,	(r)soo-um	สวม
quality	koon!-na-(f)pahp	คุณภาพ
quantity	jahm! noo-un	จำนวน
quarter (one-fourth)	(l)neung! ny (l)see	หนึ่งส่วนสี่
,,	(l)seht (l)neung! (l)soo-un (l)see	เศษหนึ่งส่วนสี่
(¼ baht, 25 satang)	sa-(r)leung!	สลึง
quarters (servant's)	(f)bahn kohn! (h)chy!	บ้านคนใช้
,,	reu-un kohn! (h)chy!	เรือนคนใช้
queen	pra!-rah-chih!-nee	พระราชินี
queer (to be queer, strange, unusual)		
	(l)bplaak	แปลก
question (a question)	kahm! (r)tahm	คำถาม
(to ask a question)	(r)tahm	ถาม

quick	reh-oh!	เร็ว
(quickly)	reh-oh! reh-oh!	เร็ว ๆ
quiet (to be silent)	(f)ngee-up	เงียบ
(to be tranquil)	sa-(l)ngohp!	สงบ
(to be still, passive)	chuh-ee chuh-ee	เฉย ๆ
(Quiet!)	(f)ngee-up	เงียบ
quit (to finish, be through, give up)	(f)luhk	เลิก
(to quit a job, resign)	lah (l)awk	ลาออก
rabbit	gra-(l)dty	กระต่าย
rabies (hydrophobia)		
	(f)rohk gloo-uh (h)nahm	โรคกลัวน้ำ
,,	(f)rohk (r)mah (f)bah	โรคหมาบ้า
,,	(f)rohk soo!-(h)nahk! (f)bah	โรคสุนัขบ้า
(a mad dog, rabid dog)	(r)mah (f)bah	หมาบ้า
race (to race)	(f)wing! (l)kaang	วิ่งแข่ง
(race track)	sa-(r)nahm (l)kaang	สนามแข่ง
(horse races)	(l)kaang (h)mah	แข่งม้า
(race, nationality)	(f)chaht	ชาติ
radio	(h)wit!-ta-(h)yoo!	วิทยุ
radish	(f)look daang	ถูกแดง

rag (old cloth)	(f)pah (f)kee (b)riw!	ผ้าขี้ริ้ว
rai (See "ry".)		
railroad, railway	tahng (h)roht! fy!	ทางรถไฟ
rain	(r)fohn!	ฝน
(to rain)	(r)fohn! (l)dtohk!	ฝนตก
(to be rainy)	mee (r)fohn! (l)dtohk!	มีฝนตก
rainbow	(h)roong!	รุ้ง
raincoat	(f)seu-uh (r) fohn!	เสื้อฝน
raise (to raise, lift up)	(h)yohk! (f)keun!	ยกขึ้น
rake (a rake, to rake)	(f)kraht	คราด
rank	(h)yoht!	ยศ
(level, class, grade)	(h)chahn!	ชั้น
rape (to rape)	(l)kohm! (r)keun	ข่มขืน
rare (to be rare, hard to find)	(r)hah (f)yahk	หายาก
(to cook rare, not be well-done)		
	(l)sook! (l)sook! (l)dip! (l)dip!	สุก ๆ ดิบ ๆ
rat	(r)noo	หนู
rattan (wicker)	(r)wy	หวาย
raw (to be raw, uncooked)	(l)dip!	ดิบ
razor	(f)meed gohn	มีดโกน

(razor blades)	by (f)meed gohn	ใบมีดโกน
reach (to arrive, get to)	(r)teung!	ถึง
(to reach out with one's hand)	(f)eu-um	เอื้อม
,,	(f)yeun	ยื่น
read (to read)	(l)ahn	อ่าน
ready (to be ready, set, completed)	(h)prawm	พร้อม
(to be all set, neat, tidy, in good order)		
	(f)ree-up (h)rawy	เรียบร้อย
real (to be real, true)	jing!	จริง
(to be genuine, authentic, pure)	(h)taa	แท้
really? (Is that true?)	jing! jing! (r)reu	จริงๆหรือ
reason (or cause)	(l)het	เหตุ
(reason for doing something)		
	(l)het (r)pohn!	เหตุผล
receipt	by! (h)rahp! ngun!	ใบรับเงิน
	by! (l)set!	ใบเสร็จ
receive (to receive, accept)	(h)rahp!	รับ
(to get, obtain, to have received)		
	(f)dy! (h)rahp!	ได้รับ
recently (just recently)		
(f)meu-uh reh-oh reh-oh (h)nee		เมื่อเร็วๆนี้

190

recipe   dtahm! (l)rahp!   คำรับ

recommend (to recommend) (h)naa! nahm!   แนะนำ

record (or note, report) n.   bahn!-(h)teuk!   บันทึก

   (to note, report, record)   bahn!-(h)teuk!   บันทึก

   (to record sound) bahn!-(h)teuk! (r)see-ung   บันทึกเสียง

   (phonograph record) (l)paan (r)see-ung   แผ่นเสียง

recover (to recover from sickness)   (r)hy   หาย

red (to be red)   daang   แดง

   (the color red)   (r)see daang   สีแดง

Red Cross   sa-pah gah-(f)chaht   สภากาชาด

reduce (to reduce, decrease, lower **something**)

          (h)loht! **something** lohng!   ลด——ลง

   (reduced price, be on sale) (h)loht! rah-kah   ลดราคา

refrigerator   (f)dtoo yen!   ตู้เย็น

regarding (concerning) (l)gee-oh (l)gahp!   เกี่ยวกับ

register (to register, to register mail)

           (l)joht! ta!-bee-un   จดทะเบียน

   (registered mail)

        (l)joht!-(r)my lohng! ta!-bee-un   จดหมายลงทะเบียน

registration (for a vehicle)

          ta!-bee-un (h)roht!   ทะเบียนรถ

regular (to be regular, usual, natural)

tah-ma-dah ธรรมดา

(to be usual, regular, routine)

(l)bpo!-ga-(l)dtih! ปกติ

(regularly, regularly scheduled, steady, constantly) bpra-jahm! ประจำ

relative (kin) (f)yaht ญาติ

relax (to relax, be relaxed, be at leisure)

(l)yawn jy! หย่อนใจ

release (to release, let go, let loose) (l)bplawy ปล่อย

religion (l)sah-sa-(r)nah ศาสนา

remember (to remember) jahm! (f)dy จำได้

remind dteu-un jy! เตือนใจ

remove (to take **something** out)

ow! **something** (l)awk เอา——ออก

(to take **something** off)

(l)tawt **something** (l)awk ถอด——ออก

(to remove clothes) (l) tawt (f)seu-uh ถอดเสื้อ

rent (to rent) (f)chow! เช่า

(to rent someone, to lease) (f)hy! (f)chow! ให้เช่า

(rental price, the rent) (f)kah (f)chow! ค่าเช่า

repair (to repair, fix, mend)	(f)gaa	แก้
,,	(f)sawm	ซ่อม
repeat (to repeat)	(h)sahm!	ซ้ำ

(Please repeat, say again.)

                (f)poot (h)sahm! (l)eek tee   พูดซ้ำอีกที

(Please repeat, say again.)

(f)poot (h)sahm! (l)eek (h)krahng! (l)neung!   พูดซ้ำอีกครั้งหนึ่ง

replace (to replace)	taan (f)tee	แทนที่
report (a report, to report)	ry ngahn	รายงาน

(to report, give information)

                      (f)jaang kwahm   แจ้งความ

representative	(f)poo taan	ผู้แทน
request (to request, ask for, beg)	(r)kaw	ขอ
require (to require, want, need)		
	(f)dtawng gahn	ต้องการ
requirement	kwahm (f)dtawng gahn	ความต้องการ
reserve (to reserve, book)	(h)book!	บุ๊ค
(to make a reservation)	jawng	จอง
(to reserve a seat)	jawng (f)tee (f)nahng!	จองที่นั่ง
(Please reserve two seats.)	(f)choo-ay	

jawng (f)tee (f)nahng! (r)sawng (f)tee   ช่วยจองที่นั่งสองที่

resign (to resign, quit)   lah (l)awk   ลาออก

respect (to respect, to have respect for)

                      (h)nahp!-(r)teu   นับถือ

  (to show respect, pay reverence)

                      kow!-(h)rohp!   เคารพ

responsible (to be responsible for)

                (h)rahp! (l)pit!-(f)chawp   รับผิดชอบ

  (responsibility)

         kwahm (h)rahp! (l)pit!-(f)chawp   ความรับผิดชอบ

rest (to rest)   (h)pahk!   พัก

  (the rest, remains, that which is left)

                      (f)tee (r)leu-uh   ที่เหลือ

restaurant   (h)rahn (r)ky ah-(r)hahn   ร้านขายอาหาร

  (large restaurant)   (h)paht!-dtah-kahn   ภัตตาคาร

retire (to retire from one's occupation)

                  (l)bploht! ga-(r)see-un   ปลดเกษียณ

return (to go back)   (l)glahp!   กลับ

        ,,   (l)glahp! bpy!   กลับไป

  (to come back)   (l)glahp! mah   กลับมา

194

(to give back)	keun	คืน
,,	keun (f)hy!	คืนให้
,,	(l)sohng! keun	ส่งคืน
(a return trip ticket)		
	(r)dtoo-uh bpy! (l)glahp!	ตั๋วไปกลับ
reward	rahng-wahn!	รางวัล
rhythm (or timing, beat)	jahng!-(l)wa!	จังหวะ
ribbon	(h)rih!-(f)bihn!	ริบบิ้น
(typewriter ribbon)		
	(f)pah (l)meuk! pim! (l)deet	ผ้าหมึกพิมพ์ติด
rice	(f)kow	ข้าว
(rice field, paddy)	nah	นา
(fried rice)	(f)kow (l)paht!	ข้าวผัด
(glutinous rice)	(f)kow (r)nee-oh	ข้าวเหนียว
rich (to be rich, wealthy)	roo-ay	รวย
ride (to ride **on** an animal or cycle)	(l)kee	ขี่
(to ride **in** a vehicle)	(f)nahng!	นั่ง
,,	bpy!	ไป
rifle	bpeun yow	ปืนยาว

right (to be right, correct)	(l)took	ถูก
"	(l)took (f)dtawng	ถูกต้อง
(opposite of left)	(r)kwah	ขวา
(on the right-hand side)		
	tahng (r)kwah meu	ทางขวามือ
(right here)	dtrohng! (f)nee	ตรงนี่
(a right angle)	moom! (l)chahk	มุมฉาก
ring (finger ring)	(r)waan	แหวน
(to ring a bell)	(l)sahn!——	สั่น——
"	dtee——	ตี——
ripe (to be ripe)	(l)sook!	สุก
rise (to rise, rise up, grow)	(f)keun!	ขึ้น
river	(f)maa-(h)nahm!	แม่น้ำ
road (street, roadway)	ta-(r)nohn!	ถนน
(route, path, way)	tahng	ทาง
(highway)	ta-(r)nohn! (r)loo-ung	ถนนหลวง
(the main road)	ta-(r)nohn! (l)yai!	ถนนใหญ่
roast (to roast, bake in an oven)	(l)ohp!	อบ
(to cook over an open fire, barbecue, broil)		
	(f)yahng	ย่าง

(to toast, bake, barbecue, roast) (f)bping!		บิ้ง
rob (to rob, steal)	(l)ka!-moy	ขโมย
robber	(l)ka!-moy	ขโมย
rock (or stone, stones)	(r)hin!	หิน
roll (to roll, wind, coil)	(h)moo-un	ม้วน
(a roll or reel of **something**)		
	(h)moo-un **something**	ม้วน——
(to roll along)	(f)gling!	กลิ้ง
(a bread roll) ka-(r)nohm!bpahng! glohm!		ขนมปังกลม
roof	(r)lahng!-kah	หลังคา
room	(f)hawng!	ห้อง
(bedroom)	(f)hawng! nawn	ห้องนอน
(dining room)	(f)hawng! ah-(r)hahn	ห้องอาหาร
,,	(f)hawng! (h)rahp!-(l)bpra-tahn	ห้องรับประทาน
	ah-(r)hahn	อาหาร
(living room)	(f)hawng! (h)rahp! (l)kaak	ห้องรับแขก
(pantry, food storeroom)		
	(f)hawng! (h)pabk! ah-(r)hahn	ห้องพักอาหาร
(storeroom)	(f)hawng! (l)gep! (r)kawng	ห้องเก็บของ
(single room, a single)	(f)hawng! dee-oh	ห้องเดี่ยว

197

(double room, a double)	(f)hawng! (f)koo	ห้องคู่
(space, place)	(f)tee	ที่
(Ex: no room to put **something**)		
	(f)my! mee (f)tee (l)sy!— —	ไม่มีที่ใส่— —
rooster	(l)gy! dtoo-uh (f)poo	ไก่ตัวผู้
root (of a plant)	(f)rahk	ราก
rope (or string, cord)	cheu-uk	เชือก
rose (flower)	(l)dawk goo!-(l)lahp	ดอกกุหลาบ
rot (to be rotten, decayed)	(f)now!	เน่า
rough (to be rough, bumpy, uneven)		
	(l)kroo!-(l)kra!	ขรุขระ
(a rough surface)	(h)peun (l)kroo!-(l)kra!	พื้นขรุขระ
(a bumpy road)	ta-(r)nohn! (l)kroo!-(l)kra!	ถนนขรุขระ
round (to be round, circular)	glohm!	กลม
row (or line)	(r)taa-oh	แถว
(to row a boat)	jaa-oh reu-uh	แจวเรือ
rubber	yahng	ยาง
(rubber band)	yahng wohng! wohng!	ยางวง ๆ
rug (or carpet)	prohm!	พรม
(foot rug, scatter rug)		
	prohm! (h)chet! (h)tao	พรมเช็ดเท้า

(mat, woven floor mat) (l)seu-uh เสื่อ

ruin (to ruin, destroy, demolish) tahm!-ly ทำลาย

ruler (for measuring) (h)my bahn-(h)taht! ไม้บรรทัด

run (to run) (f)wing! วิ่ง

 (to flow) (r)ly! ไหล

 (to run away) (r)nee bpy! หนีไป

  ,, (f)wing! (r)nee วิ่งหนี

 (to run over, be run over) (h)tahp! ทับ

 (to run, as a motor or clock) duhn เดิน

rust sa-(r)nim! สนิม

 (to rust, get rusty) (f)keun! sa-(r)nim! ขึ้นสนิม

 (to be rusty) bpen! sa-(r)nim! เป็นสนิม

ry (unit of land measure) (also written as "rai")

A square area equal to 1600 square meters, ไร่
or 40m × 40m, or 131ft. × 131ft.

One ry equals 0.396 acres.

One acre equals 2.53 ry.

One ry equals 400 square wa.

sack (or bag, pouch) (r)toong! ถุง

 (gunny sack) gra-(l)sawp กระสอบ

sad (to be sad)	(f)sow!	เศร้า
,,	(f)sow! (l)sohk	เศร้าโศก
safe (to be safe)	(l)bplawt-py!	ปลอดภัย
safety	kwahm (l)bplawt-py!	ความปลอดภัย
(welfare)	sa-(l)waht! dih!-(f)pahp	สวัสดิภาพ
(safety pin)	(r)kem! (l)glaht!	เข็มกลัด
sailboat	reu-uh by	เรือใบ
sailor	ga-lah-(r)see	กะลาสี
	ta-(r)hahn reu-uh	ทหารเรือ
salad	sa-(l)laht!	สลัด
	yahm!	ยำ
(mixed green salad)	yahm! (l)yai!	ยำใหญ่
salary (monthly pay)	ngun! deu-un	เงินเดือน
sale (to have a sale, reduced price, discount)		
	(h)loht! rah-kah	ลดราคา
(for sale, will sell)	(l)ja! (r)ky	จะขาย
salesman	kohn! (r)ky (r)kawng	คนขายของ
salt	gleu-uh	เกลือ
(to salt, put on salt)	(l)sy! gleu-uh	ใส่เกลือ
(salt water)	(h)nahm! kem!	น้ำเค็ม

salty (to be salty)   kem! เค็ม

salute (to salute, to bow, pay respect to)

                        kahm!-(h)nahp! คำนับ

  (a military salute with the hand)

                        wahn!-(h)ta-(h)ya-(l)haht! วันทยหัตถ์

  (the customary Thai salute of respect)

                        (f)wy ไหว้

same (to be the same, be similar) (r)meu-un เหมือน

  (to be the same as, be similar to)

                      (r)meu-un (l)gahp! เหมือนกับ

  (to be alike, the same together)

                      (r)meu-un gahn! เหมือนกัน

  (to be equal to or equal with something

   else, in size or some dimensional quality)

                      (f)tao (l)gahp! เท่ากับ

  (to be the same or be equal together, in

   size or some dimensional quantity)

                      (f)tao! gahn! เท่ากัน

  (to be identical to, be identical with)

                      dee-oh gahp! เดียวกับ

(to be identically the same) dee-oh gahn! เดียวกัน
(the same thing, identical thing)

        ahn! dee-oh gahn! อันเดียวกัน

(the same person)   kohn! dee-oh gahn! คนเดียวกัน
(at the same time, simultaneously)

        (h)prawm gahn! พร้อมกัน

      ,,   weh-lah dee-oh gahn! เวลาเดียวกัน

sample (a sample, example) dtoo-uh (l)yahng ตัวอย่าง

sand   sy ทราย

sandpaper   gra-(l)daht sy กระดาษทราย

sanitary (to be sanitary)

      (l)soo!-(r)kah (h)pih!-bahn สุขาภิบาล
(sanitation)

     gahn (l)soo!-(r)kah (h)pih!-bahn การสุขาภิบาล

satisfactory (to be satisfactory)

      bpen! (f)tee paw jy! เป็นที่พอใจ

satisfy (to be satisfied)   paw jy! พอใจ

(to satisfy)   tahm! (f)hy! paw jy! ทำให้พอใจ

Saturday   wahn! (r)sow! วันเสาร์

satang (1/100 baht)   sa-dtahng สตางค์

(25 satang, $\frac{1}{4}$ baht)   sa-(r)leung! สลึง

saucer	jahn rawng (f)too-ay	จานรองถ้วย
saucy (in taste)	mee (h)roht!(f)chaht	มีรสชาติ
sausage	(f)sy! (l)grawk	ไส้กรอก
save (to save, keep)	(l)bpra-(l)yaht!	ประหยัด
(to rescue someone)	(f)choo-ay chee-(h)wit!	ช่วยชีวิต
(to save money)	(l)gep! ngun! (h)wy!	เก็บเงินไว้
(savings bank)	ta-nah-kahn awm-(r)sin!	ธนาคารออมสิน
saw (a saw, to saw)	(f)leu-ay	เลื่อย
(hacksaw, metal saw)	(f)leu-ay (l)lek!	เลื่อยเหล็ก
say (to say; said, says)	(l)bawk	บอก
„	(f)wah	ว่า
(to say that . . ., says that . . ., said that . . .)		
	bawk (f)wah	บอกว่า
(to speak, talk)	(f)poot	พูด
scale, scales (balance scales, machine for weighing)	(f)kreu-ung (f)chahng!	เครื่องชั่ง
scare (to scare, frighten)		
	tahm! (f)hy! (l)dtohk! jy!	ทำให้ตกใจ
(to be scared, frightened)	(l)dtohk! jy!	ตกใจ
(to fear, be afraid of)	gloo-uh	กลัว

school	rohng ree-un	โรงเรียน
(college)	(h)wit!-ta-yah-ly	วิทยาลัย
(university)	ma-(r)hah (h)wit!-ta-yah-ly	มหาวิทยาลัย
science	(h)wit!-ta-yah-(l)saht	วิทยาศาสตร์
(scientist)	(h)nahk! (h)wit!-ta-yah-(l)saht	นักวิทยาศาสตร์
scissors	gahn!-gry	กรรไกร
score (of a game or contest)	(f)dtaam	แต้ม
(tie score)	(l)sa!-(r)muh gahn!	เสมอกัน
scorpion	ma-laang (l)bpawng!	แมลงป่อง
scour (to scour, scrub, polish)	(l)kaht!	ขัด
scouring powder	yah (l)kaht!	ยาขัด
	yah (l)kaht! (f)hawng! (h)nahm	ยาขัดห้องน้ำ
scout (a boy scout)	(f)look (r)seu-uh	ลูกเสือ
scratch (to scratch oneself with the fingers)		
	gow!	เกา
(to scratch or be scratched with fingernails, claws, thorns, barbs, etc., as to inflict injury)	(l)koo-un	ข่วน
(to scratch a line on the surface)	(l)keet	ขีด
scream (to scream, cry out)	(h)rawng	ร้อง

204

screen (wire screen for mosquitos)

        (h)moong! (f)loo-ut   มุ้งลวด

  (screen for dividing rooms, partition)

        (l)chahk   ฉาก

  (movie screen)   jaw (r)nahng!   จอหนัง

screw   sa-groo   สกรุ

        dta-bpoo koo-ung   ตะปูควง

screwdriver   (r)ky! koo-ung   ไขควง

        sah-goo!-ry   ซากุไร

scrub (to scrub)   (r)too   ถู

  (to scour)   (l)kaht!   ขัด

sea   ta!-leh   ทะเล

seacoast, seashore, seaside   chy ta!-leh   ชายทะเล

        (l)fahng! ta!-leh   ฝั่งทะเล

seal (to seal, as an envelope)

        (l)bpit! pa-(l)neuk!   ปิดผนึก

  (sealing wax)   (f)krahng!   ครั่ง

  (seal, brand, trademark)   dtrah   ตรา

seasick (to be seasick)   mao! (f)kleun   เมาคลื่น

season   (h)reu!-doo   ฤดู

(rainy season)	(h)reu!-doo (r)fohn!	ฤดูฝน
(summer, hot season)	(h)reu!-doo (h)rawn	ฤดูร้อน
(dry season)	(h)reu!-doo (h)laang	ฤดูแล้ง
(winter, cold season)	(h)reu!doo (r)now	ฤดูหนาว
(spring)	(h)reu!-doo by! (h)my (l)plih!	ฤดูใบไม้ผลิ
(autumn, fall)		
	(h)reu!-doo by! (h)my (f)roo-ung	ฤดูใบไม้ร่วง
(to season food)	bproong! (h)roht!	ปรุงรส
seat (a seat, place to sit)	(f)tee (f)nahng!	ที่นั่ง
(to sit down)	(f)nahng! lohng!	นั่งลง
(Please be seated.)	chun (f)nahng!	เชิญนั่ง
second (2nd)	(f)tee (r)sawng	ที่สอง
(unit of time)	(h)wih!-nah-tee	วินาที
secret (to be secret, hidden)	(h)lahp!	ลับ
(a secret)	kwahm (h)lahp!	ความลับ
secretary	leh-(r)kah-(h)noo!-gahn	เลขานุการ
section (or part, region, of space or time)		
	dtawn	ตอน
(department, division, subdivision)		
	pa-(l)naak	แผนก

206

see (to see)	(r)hen!	เห็น
(to look, to look at)	doo	ดู
(to look at intently, to stare)	mawng	มอง
(to look carefully and see something)		
	mawng (r)hen! **something**	มองเห็น— —
(to look carefully but cannot find or see)		
	mawng (f)my! (r)hen!	มองไม่เห็น
(to go see **someone**)	bpy! (r)hah **someone**	ไปหา— —
(to go see **something**)	bpy! doo **something**	ไปดู— —
(to go see a movie)	bpy! doo (r)nahng!	ไปดูหนัง
seed, seeds	(h)met!	เม็ด
	ma-(h)let! (f)peut	เมล็ดพืช
seem (seems as though, seems like)		
	doo (r)meu-un	ดูเหมือน
seldom (not often)	(f)my! (l)bawy	ไม่บ่อย
self (oneself, myself, himself, etc.)	eng	เอง
„	dtoo-uh eng	ตัวเอง
selfish (to think only of oneself)		
	(r)hen! (l)gaa dtoo-uh	เห็นแก่ตัว
(to be selfish, merciless, mean) jy! dahm!		ใจดำ

sell (to sell)	(r)ky	ขาย
(for sale, will sell)	(l)ja! (r)ky	จะขาย
send (to send, ship)	(l)sohng!	ส่ง
sentence (grammatical)	bpra-(l)yohk	ประโยค
September	gahn!-yah yohn!	กันยายน
sergeant	(l)sip! (l)ek	สิบเอก
servant	kohn! (h)chy!	คนใช้
(servant's quarters)	(f)bahn kohn! (h)chy!	บ้านคนใช้
,,	reu-un kohn! (h)chy!	เรือนคนใช้
serve (to serve someone)	(h)rahp! (h)chy!	รับใช้
(to wait on a table)	(h)suhf!	เซิฟ
,,	duhn (h)dtoh!	เดินโต๊ะ
(to serve the food)		
	(h)yohk! ah-(r)hahn (f)hy!	ยกอาหารให้
(to serve drinks)		
	(l)jaak (f)kreu-ung (f)deum	แจกเครื่องดื่ม
service	baw-ri-gahn	บริการ
set (to set **something** down)		
	wahng **something** (h)wy!	วาง——ไว้
(to set the table)	(l)jaht! (h)dto! ah-(r)hahn	จัดโต๊ะอาหาร

(to set a clock)	(f)dtahng! nah-li-gah	ตั้งนาฬิกา
(a set, a complete set, as furniture, glasses, books, etc.)	(h)choot!	ชุด
seven (7)	(l)jet!	เจ็ด
several (many)	(r)ly	หลาย
(two or three)	(r)sawng—(r)sahm	สอง—สาม
sew (to sew)	(h)yep!	เย็บ
(to sew clothes)	(h)yep! (f)pah	เย็บผ้า
sewage	(h)nahm! (r)soh-(f)krohk	น้ำโสโครก
sewing machine	(l)jahk! (h)yep! (f)pah	จักรเย็บผ้า
shade (a shade, to be shaded)	(f)rohm!	ร่ม
(in the shade; indoors)	ny! (f)rohm!	ในร่ม
shadow	ngow!	เงา
(shadow play)	(r)nahng! dta-loong!	หนังตลุง
shake (to shake something)	ka-(l)yow! **something**	เขย่า——
(to shake, tremble, vibrate)	(l)sahn!	สั่น
(to shake hands)	(l)jahp! meu	จับมือ
shall, will	(l)ja!	จะ
shampoo	shampoo	แชมพู

209

(to wash the hair)   (l)sa! (r)pohm!   สระผม

shape (or appearance, form, figure)

            (f)roop (f)rahng   รูปร่าง

shark   bplah cha-(r)lahm   ปลาฉลาม

sharp (to be sharp, a sharp edge)   kohm!   คม

   (to be sharp pointed)   (r)laam   แหลม

   (at **noon** sharp)   (f)tee-ung dtrohng!   เที่ยงตรง

sharpen (to sharpen, make sharp, as a pencil

   or stick)   (r)lao!   เหลา

   (to sharpen a knife)   (h)lahp! (f)meed   ลับมีด

shave (to shave)   gohn   โกน

      ,,   gohn (l)noo-ut   โกนหนวด

shaving cream   kreem! gohn (l)noo-ut   ครีมโกนหนวด

she, her   (r)kow!   เขา

           (r)kow! (f)poo-(r)ying   เขาผู้หญิง

sheep   (l)gaa!   แกะ

sheet (bedsheet)   (f)pah bpoo (f)tee nawn   ผ้าปูที่นอน

   (one sheet of **something**)

           something (l)neung! (l)paan   ——หนึ่งแผ่น

shelf (a shelf)	(f)hing!	หิ้ง
(a shelf of a cabinet or case)	(h)chahn!	ชั้น
shell, seashell, shellfish	(r)hawy!	หอย
sheriff (district officer)	ny ahm!-puh	นายอำเภอ
shine (to shine light, shine light on)	(l)sawng!	ส่อง
(to shine, emit light)	(l)sawng! (r)saang	ส่องแสง
(to shine a light)	(l)sawng! fy!	ส่องไฟ
(to polish)	(l)kaht!	ขัด
(to be shiny)	bpen! mahn!	เป็นมัน
ship (or boat)	reu-uh	เรือ
(to ship, send)	(l)sohng!	ส่ง
shirt	(f)seu-uh (h)chuht	เสื้อเช็ต
(undershirt)	(f)seu-uh (h)chahn! ny!	เสื้อชั้นใน
shoe	rawng-(h)tao	รองเท้า
(shoe repairman, cobbler)		
(f)chahng (f)sawm rawng-(h)tao		ช่างซ่อมรองเท้า
shoelace	(f)cheu-uk (l)pook rawng-(h)tao	เชือกผูกรองเท้า
shoot (to shoot)	ying!	ยิง
(to shoot a gun)	ying! bpeun	ยิงปืน
shop (or store)	(h)rahn	ร้าน

211

(workshop)	rohng ngahn	โรงงาน
shore (or seashore, seacoast)	(l)fahng! ta!-leh	ฝั่งทะเล
,,	chy ta!-leh	ชายทะเล
(river bank)	(l)fahng! (h)nahm	ฝั่งน้ำ
short (to be short in length)	(f)sahn!	สั้น
(to be short in height, of people)		
	(f)dtee-uh	เตี้ย
(to be short in height, of things)	(l)dtahm!	ต่ำ
(a short time)	weh-lah (f)sahn!	เวลาสั้น
(not a long time)	(f)my! nahn	ไม่นาน
shorthand	cha-wa-(f)lek	ชวเลข
(a stenographer)	(h)nahk! cha-wa-(f)lek	นักชวเลข
shorts (short pants)		
	gahng gehng (r)kah (f)sahn!	กางเกงขาสั้น
(undershorts)	gahng gehng ny!	กางเกงใน
should (ought to)	koo-un	ควร
(probably should, had better)		
	(r)hen! ja! (f)dtawng!	เห็นจะต้อง
shout (to shout, yell)	dta-gohn	ตะโกน
(to cry out)	(h)rawng	ร้อง

shovel	(f)ploo-uh	พลั่ว
(small narrow spade)	(r)see-um	เสียม
show (to show, display, be shown)		
	(l)sa-(r)daang	แสดง
(I will show you.)	(r)chahn! (l)ja!	ฉันจะ
	(l)sa-(r)daang (f)hy koon! doo	แสดงให้คุณดู
(Show me. Let me see.)	(r)kaw doo	ขอดู
(You show me, by demonstration.)		
koon! (l)sa-(r)daang (f)hy! (r)chahn! doo		คุณแสดงให้ฉันดู
(Show me, by pointing it out.)		
	(h)chee (f)hy! (r)chahn! doo	ชี้ให้ฉันดู
(to show, project on a screen, as a movie)		
	(r)chy	ฉาย
shower (to shower, bathe)	(l)ahb-(h)nahm	อาบน้ำ
(rain showers)	(r)fohn! bprawy	ฝนปรอย
shrimp (or prawn, lobster)	(f)goong!	กุ้ง
(mantis-shrimp)	(f)gahng!	กั้ง
shrink (to shrink)	(l)hoht!	หด
shut (to close, shut, shut off)	(l)bpit!	ปิด
shy (to be shy, bashful) I (same as "eye")		อาย

213

sick (to be sick, ill, to get sick) (f)my! sa-by		ไม่สบาย
(to be sick of **something**)		
(l)beu-uh **something**		เบื่อ— —
(to be homesick) (h)keet! (r)teung! (f)bahn		คิดถึงบ้าน
(to be airsick)	mao! reu-uh bin!	เมาเรือบิน
(to be carsick)	mao! (h)roht!	เมารถ
(to be seasick)	mao! (f)kleun	เมาคลื่น
side	(f)kahng	ข้าง
(This side up) (f)dahn (h)nee (f)keun!		ด้านนี้ขึ้น
sidewalk	tahng (h)tao	ทางเท้า
sieve (or strainer)	dta-graang	ตะแกรง
sightseeing (to go sightseeing)		
bpy! (f)tee-oh chohm!		ไปเที่ยวชม
sign (or poster, placard, label, tag) (f)bpy		ป้าย
(to sign one's name)	sen! (f)cheu	เซ็นชื่อ
,,	lohng! (f)cheu	ลงชื่อ
,,	lohng! nahm	ลงนาม
signature	ly sen!	ลายเซ็น
silent (to be quiet, still, silent) (f)ngee-up		เงียบ
silk	(r)my!	ไหม

(silk cloth)	(f)pah (r)my!	ผ้าไหม
(silk cloth, smooth, of lesser quality than above)	praa	แพร
silver (the metal)	ngun!	เงิน
(the color)	(r)see ngun!	สีเงิน
silverware, tableware	(f)kreu-ung ngun!	เครื่องเงิน
(spoons and forks etc.)	(h)chawn (f)sawm	ช้อนซ่อม
similar (see "same")		
simultaneously (at the same time, all together)		
	(h)prawm gahn!	พร้อมกัน
since (from a certain time or point)		
	(f)dtahng! (l)dtaa	ตั้งแต่
(because)	(h)praw! (f)wah	เพราะว่า
sing (to sing)	(h)rawng pleng	ร้องเพลง
singer	(h)nahk! (h)rawng	นักร้อง
single (one)	dee-oh	เดี่ยว
(one item or thing)	ahn! dee-oh	อันเดียว
(one person)	kohn! dee-oh	คนเดียว
(a single room)	(f)hawng! dee-oh	ห้องเดียว
(to be unmarried)	bpen! (l)soht	เป็นโสด

sink (or bowl, basin)	(l)ahng	อ่าง
(wash basin)	(l)ahng (h)lahng (f)nah	อ่างล้างหน้า
(to sink, not float)	johm!	จม
(to sink in water)	johm! (h)nahm	จมน้ำ
sir, ma'am (spoken by females)	ka!	คะ
(spoken by males)	(h)krahp!	ครับ
(*Note,* The "r" in "(h)krahp!" is often omitted in speaking.)		
sister (younger sister)	(h)nawng (r)sow	น้องสาว
(older sister)	(f)pee (r)sow	พี่สาว
sister-in-law	sa-(h)py!	สะใภ้
(wife of one's younger brother)		
	(h)nawng sa-(h)py!	น้องสะใภ้
(wife of one's older brother)		
	(f)pee sa-(h)py!	พี่สะใภ้
sit (to sit)	(f)nahng!	นั่ง
(to sit down)	(f)nahng! lohng!	นั่งลง
(Please sit down.)	chuhn (f)nahng!	เชิญนั่ง
six (6)	(l)hohk!	หก
size	ka-(l)naht	ขนาด

216

skill (manual skill, craftsmanship)

(r)fee meu ฝีมือ

(a skilled craftsman of some **trade**)

(f)chahng **trade** ช่าง——

skilled   mee kwahm chahm!-nahn มีความชำนาญ

skin (of a person or animal)

(r)pyoo! (r)nahng! ผิวหนัง

(peeling, rind)   (l)bpleu-uk เปลือก

skirt (clothing)   gra-bprohng กระโปรง

sky   (h)fah ฟ้า

(h)tawng (h)fah ท้องฟ้า

slap (to slap)   (l)dtohp! ตบ

sleep (to sleep, to be asleep)   (l)lahp! หลับ

(to lie down and sleep)   nawn (l)lahp! นอนหลับ

(to be numb, asleep, as an arm or leg)

(h)roo-(l)seuk! chah รู้สึกชา

(to be numb, asleep, as an arm or leg)

bpen! (l)nep! chah เป็นเหน็บชา

sleepy (to be sleepy)   (f)ngoo-ung nawn ง่วงนอน

sleeve (of a coat, shirt)   (r)kaan (f)seu-uh แขนเสื้อ

217

slice (to slice, cut into pieces)	(l)hahn!	หั่น
slide (to slide, shift, move along)	(f)leu-un	เลื่อน
slim (to be slim, thin) (of people)	(r)pawm	ผอม
slingshot	(r)nahng! sa-dtik!	หนังสติ๊ก
slippers (shower) rawng-(h)tao	(l)dtaa	รองเท้าแตะ
slippery (to be slippery)	(f)leun	ลื่น
slow	(h)chah	ช้า
(slowly)	(h)chah (h)chah	ช้าๆ
small (to be little in size)	(h)lek!	เล็ก
„	(h)lek! (h)lek!	เล็กๆ
(a little, a little bit)	(l)nawy!	หน่อย
(a little bit)	(h)nit! (l)nawy	นิดหน่อย
(to be little, minor, inferior)	(h)nawy!	น้อย
small pox	(r)fee-(l)daht	ฝีดาษ
smart (to be smart, intelligent)	sa-mart	สมาร์ท
(to be clever, intelligent)	cha-(l)laht	ฉลาด
(to be intelligent)	(r)wy!-(h)prip! dee	ไหวพริบดี
smell (odor, scent)	(l)glin!	กลิ่น
(to smell with the nose)	(f)dy! (l)glin!	ได้กลิ่น
(to sniff)	dohm!	ดม

(to have a nice smell)	(r)hawm	หอม
(to have a bad smell)	(r)men!	เหม็น
smile (to smile)	(h)yim!	ยิ้ม
smoke n.	kwabn!	ควัน
(to smoke a **cigarette**)	(l)soop boo!-(l)ree	สูบบุหรี่
smooth (to be smooth, even)	(f)ree-up	เรียบ
(to be smooth and level)	(f)rahp (f)ree-up	ราบเรียบ
snake	ngoo	งู
(cobra)	ngoo (l)how!	งูเห่า
(king cobra)	ngoo johng!-ahng	งูจงอาง
(banded krait)	ngoo (r)sahm (l)lee-um	งูสามเหลี่ยม
sneeze (to sneeze)	jahm	จาม
snow n.	hih!-(h)ma!	หิมะ
(to snow)	hih!-(h)ma! (l)dtohk!	หิมะตก
so (in order to)	(f)peu-uh	เพื่อ
(in order to, so that, for)	(f)peu-uh (f)hy!	เพื่อให้
,,	(f)peu-uh (f)wah	เพื่อว่า
(so, thus, hence)	dahng! (h)nahn!	ดังนั้น
(therefore)	(h)praw!-cha-(h)nahn!	เพราะฉะนั้น
(so, then, therefore)	jeung!	จึง

219

soak (to soak, immerse)	(f)chaa	แช่
soap	sa-(l)boo	สบู่
social, society	(r)sahng!-kohm!	สังคม
sock, socks	(r)toong! (f)tao	ถุงเท้า
	(r)toong! (f)tao (f)sahn!	ถุงเท้าสั้น
(stockings, hose)	(r)toong! (f)tao yow	ถุงเท้ายาว
sofa	(f)gow!-(f)ee yow	เก้าอี้ยาว
soft (to be soft, tender, flexible)	(l)awn	อ่อน
(to be soft, yielding, as a pillow or mattress)		
	(l)awn (f)noom!	อ่อนนุ่ม
(to be soft, delicate, flexible, fuzzy, fluffy)		
	(f)nim!	นิ่ม
softly (or lightly, gently)	bao! bao!	เบา ๆ
soft drink (bottled beverage)		
	(f)kreu-ung (f)deum	เครื่องดื่ม
(Coca-cola)	koh!-(h)lah	โคล่า
(Pepsi-cola)	pep!-(f)see	เป๊ปซี่
solder n.	dta-(l)goo-uh (l)baht!-gree	ตะกั่วบัดกรี
(to solder)	(l)baht!-gree	บัดกรี
(soldering iron)	(r)hoo-uh (h)raang	หัวแร้ง

220

soldier	ta-(r)hahn	ทหาร
(of the army)	ta-(r)hahn (l)bohk!	ทหารบก
(of the navy)	ta-(r)hahn reu-uh	ทหารเรือ
(of the air-force)	ta-(r)hahn ah-(l)gaht	ทหารอากาศ
(of the marines)		
	ta-(r)hahn nah-(h)wik!-ga-yoh-tin!	ทหารนาวิกโยธิน
some (some––, a certain amount of––)		
	––bahng (**classifier**)	––บาง
(some, any)	(f)bahng	บ้าง
(use at end of sentence)		
(––any?,––some?)	(f)bahng (r)my	บ้างไหม
somebody, someone	bahng kohn!	บางคน
(someone, anyone, who?)	kry!	ใคร
(someone)	kry! kohn! (l)neung!	ใครคนหนึ่ง
someplace (in some places)	bahng (l)haang!	บางแห่ง
(see "somewhere")		
something	bahng (l)sing!	บางสิ่ง
	bahng (l)yahng	บางอย่าง
sometime	bahng weh-lah	บางเวลา
sometimes (at times, perhaps)	bahng tee	บางที

221

somewhere   (l)sahk! (l)haang! (l)neung!   สักแห่งหนึ่ง
(to not know where something is located,
it is somewhere)

    something (l)yoo (f)tee(r)ny! (f)my! (h)roo —อยู่ที่ไหนไม่รู้

son   (f)look chy   ลูกชาย

song   pleng   เพลง

soon (to be fast, early)   reh-oh!   เร็ว
   (in the near future) reh-oh! reh-oh! (h)nee   เร็ว ๆ นี้
   (shortly, in a short time) (f)my! (h)chah   ไม่ช้า
       ,,   (f)my! nahn   ไม่นาน
   (in a moment, in a minute) bpra-(r)dee-oh   ประเดี๋ยว

sore (to be sore, painful, to hurt)   (l)jep!   เจ็บ
   (to ache, pain)   (l)bpoo-ut   ปวด
   (to smart, sting)   (l)saap   แสบ

sorry (to be sorry, to regret)   (r)see-uh (l)jy!   เสียใจ
   (I am sorry.)   (r)chahn! (r)see-uh (l)jy!   ฉันเสียใจ
   (Sorry about that!)

        (r)see-uh (l)jy! (f)doo-ay   เสียใจด้วย

sound (or noise, tone) n.   (r)see-ung   เสียง

soup   (h)soop!   ซุป

222

(mildly seasoned soup)	gaang (l)jeut	แกงจืด
sour (to be sour, taste sour)	(f)bpree-oh	เปรี้ยว
south, southern	(f)dty	ใต้
(the direction of south)	(h)tit! (f)dty	ทิศใต้
(the southern part of the country)		
	(l)bpahk! (f)dty	ปักษ์ใต้
sow (to sow)	(l)wahn	หว่าน
spank (to spank, hit)	dtee	ตี
spark plug	(r)hoo-uh tee-un	หัวเทียน
sparrow	(h)nohk! gra-(l)jawk	นกกระจอก
speak (to speak, talk, say)	(f)poot	พูด
special	(h)pee!-(l)set	พิเศษ
(to send by Special Delivery)		
	(l)sohng! (h)pee!-(l)set	ส่งพิเศษ
speed n.	kwahm reh-oh!	ความเร็ว
(speed limit)		
	kwahm reh-oh! dtahm (l)goht!	ความเร็วตามกฎ
spell (to speell a word)	sa-(l)goht!	สะกด
,,	sa-(l)goht! dtoo-uh	สะกดตัว
spend (to spend, expend, use)	(h)chy!	ใช้

223

(to spend, pay)	(l)jy	จ่าย
(to spend or pay money)	(l)jy ngun!	จ่ายเงิน
(to spend money wastefully)	(r)see-uh ngun!	เสียเงิน
spider	maang moom!	แมงมุม
	ma-laang moom!	แมงมุม
(spider web, cobweb)	yai ma-laang moom!	ใยแมงมุม
spill (to spill)	(l)hohk!	หก
(to spill **something**)		
	tahm! **something** (l)hohk!	ทำ——หก
spinach	(l)pahk! (r)kohm!	ผักขม
spit (to spit, spit out)	(f)boo-un	บ้วน
,,	(l)tohm!	ถ่ม
(to spit saliva)	(l)tohm! (h)nahm!-ly	ถ่มน้ำลาย
(saliva)	(h)nahm!-ly	น้ำลาย
sponge, sponge rubber	fawng (h)nahm	ฟองน้ำ
spool (a spool of thread)	(f)dy (l)lawt	ด้ายหลอด
spoon	(h)chawn	ช้อน
(teaspoon)	(h)chawn chah	ช้อนชา
(tablespoon)	(h)chawn (h)dto!	ช้อนโต๊ะ
sport, sports, athletics	gee-lah	กีฬา

224

spot, spots (or speck, dot, point)   (l)joot!   จุด

spray (to spray)   (l)cheet   ฉีด

  (spray can)   gra-(r)bpawng (l)cheet   กระป๋องฉีด

spring (coiled spring, as of a watch)   lahn   ลาน

  (a natural spring, fountain)

                    (h)nahm! (h)poo!   น้ำพุ

  (spring season)

          (h)reu!-doo by! (h)my (l)plih!   ฤดูใบไม้ผลิ

square (geometric figure)   (l)see (l)lee-um   สี่เหลี่ยม

  (square measure)   dta-rahng   ตาราง

(Ex: **no.** square feet) no. dta-rahng (h)foot   — ตาราง —

  (squared, to the second power)

            gahm!-lahng! (r)sawng   กำลังสอง

  (to square, to raise to the second power)

        (h)yohk! gahm!-lahng! (r)sawng   ยกกำลังสอง

  (square root)   (f)rahk (f)tee (r)sawng   รากที่สอง

squash (vegetable)   (h)fahk!   ฟัก

squeeze (to squeeze, press, compress) (l)beep   บีบ

  (to squeeze out with pressure, to press,

    as to extract juices)   (h)kahn!   คั้น

225

(to press, to iron, to force out, to lengthen by squeezing)	(f)reet	รีด
squid	bplah (l)meuk!	ปลาหมึก
squirrel	gra-(f)rawk	กระรอก
stain (to get stained, dirty, soiled)	(f)bpeu-un	เปื้อน
stairs	bahn!-dy!	บันได
(upstairs)	(h)chahn! bohn!	ชั้นบน
,,	(f)kahng bohn!	ข้างบน
(downstairs)	(h)chahn! (f)lahng	ชั้นล่าง
,,	(f)kahng (f)lahng	ข้างล่าง
stake (or post)	(l)lahk!	หลัก
stamp (postage stamp)	sa-dtaamp	แสตมป์
,,	doo-ung dtrah bpry!-sa-nee	ดวงตราไปรษณี
(to stamp, mark)	bpra-(h)tahp! dtrah	ประทับตรา
stamp-colleeting	gahn(l)sa-(r)sohm! sa-dtaam	การสะสมแสตม
stand (to stand, stand erect)	yeun	ยืน
(to stand up)	yeun (f)keun!	ยืนขึ้น
,,	(h)look! (f)keun!	ลุกขึ้น

staple, staples (for fastening papers)

      (f)loo-ut (r)sahm!-(l)rahp!   ลวดสำหรับเย็บ

      (h)yep! gra-(l)daht   กระดาษ

 (stapler, stapling machine)

      (f)kreu-ung (h)yep! gra-(l)daht   เครื่องเย็บกระดาษ

star (or planet, or movie star)   dow   ดาว

 (movie star)   dah-rah (r)nahng!   ดาราหนัง

   ,,   dah-rah (f)pahp-pa-yohn!   ดาราภาพยนตร์

starch n.   (f)bpaang   แป้ง

 (to starch, use starch)   lohng! (f)bpaang   ลงแป้ง

stare (to stare, to look at intently)   mawng   มอง

 (to stare)   mawng doo   มองดู

   ,,   (f)jawng! doo   จ้องดู

start (to start, begin)   (f)ruhm   เริ่ม

   ,,   (f)ruhm (f)dtohn!   เริ่มต้น

   ,,   (f)dtahng! (f)dtohn!   ตั้งต้น

 (since, starting from some time or point)

      (f)dtahng! (l)dtaa   ตั้งแต่

 (to start a car or motor) (l)dtit! (f)kreu-ung   ติดเครื่อง

starve (to starve, be starved)   oht!   อด

(to go without food)	oht! ah-(r)hahn	อดอาหาร
(to starve to death)	oht! dty	อดตาย
state (or territory)	(h)raht!	รัฐ
(United States of America)		
	sa-(l)ha-(h)raht! ah-meh-rih!-gah	สหรัฐอเมริกา
station	sa-(r)tah-nee	สถานี
(railway station)	sa-(r)tah-nee (f)roht!fy!	สถานีรถไฟ
(bus station)	sa-(r)tah-nee (h)roht!-meh	สถานีรถเมล์
(radio station)	sa-(r)tah-nee (h)wit-ta-yoo	สถานีวิทยุ
(gas station)		
	sa-(r)tah-nee dtum (h)nahm!mahn!	สถานีเติมน้ำมัน
stationery (writing materials)		
	(f)kreu-ung (r)kee-un	เครื่องเขียน
statue	(f)roop sa-(l)lahk!	รูปสลัก
stay (to stay, be at some location)	(l)yoo	อยู่
(to stay over, to rest, as at a hotel or		
someone's home)	(h)pahk! (l)yoo	พักอยู่
(to stay and wait, to remain for a while)		
	kawy (l)yoo	คอยอยู่
steak	(h)neu-uh sa-(h)dtek	เนื้อสะเต็ก

228

steal (to steal, rob)	(l)ka-moy	ขโมย
steam n.	I! (h)nahm	ไอน้ำ
(to steam, cook)	(f)neung!	นึ่ง
(steamed eggs)	(l)ky! (r)dtoon!	ไข่ตุ๋น
steel	(l)lek! (f)glah	เหล็กกล้า
stenographer	(h)nahk! cha-wa-(f)lek	นักชวเลข
step (a step, pace, to step, take a step)	(f)gow	ก้าว
stepfather	(f)paw (h)lee-ung	พ่อเลี้ยง
stepmother	(f)maa (h)lee-ung	แม่เลี้ยง
stick (of wood) (in general)	(b)my	ไม้
(walking stick)	(h)my (h)tao	ไม้เท้า
(to stick, attach)	(l)dtit!	ติด
sticky (to be sticky)	(r)nee-oh	เหนียว
stiff (to be stiff, hard, firm, strong)	(r)kaang!	แข็ง
still (or yet)	yahng!	ยัง
sting (an insect to sting)	(l)dtawy	ต่อย
(to smart, sting)	(l)saap	แสบ
stingy (to be stingy, tight with one's money)		
	(f)kee (r)nee-oh	ขี้เหนียว
stink (to stink, have a bad smell)	(r)men!	เหม็น

stir (to stir)   kohn!   คน

stockings (long stockings, hose)

       (r)toong! (f)tao yow   ถุงเท้ายาว

   (see "socks")

stomach (abdomen)   (h)tawng   ท้อง

   (the stomach)   gra-(h)paw!   กระเพาะ

stomachache   (l)bpoo-ut (h)tawng   ปวดท้อง

   (to have a stomachache)

       (l)boo-ut (h)tawng   ปวดท้อง

stone, stones (or rock)   (r)hin!   หิน

   (a rock of any size)   (f)gawn (r)hin!   ก้อนหิน

   (gravel, pebbles)   (l)groo-ut   กรวด

       ,,   (f)gawn (l)groo-ut   ก้อนกรวด

stool (or bench)   (h)mah (f)nahng!   ม้านั่ง

stop (to stop, cease, halt)   (l)yoot!   หยุด

   (to turn **something** off)   (l)bpit! **something**   ปิด——

   (traffic stop sign)   (f)bpy (l)yoot! (h)roht!   ป้ายหยุดรถ

   (bus-stop sign)   (f)bpy (l)jawt! (h)roht!   ป้ายจอดรถ

stopper (for a bottle)   (l)jook!   จุก

       ,,   (l)jook! (l)koo-ut   จุกขวด

(a cork)	(l)jook! (h)my! (h)kawk!	จุกไม้ก๊อก
store (or shop)	(h)rahn	ร้าน
(store, commercial establishment, firm)		
	(f)hahng (h)rahn	ห้างร้าน
(to store or keep **something**)		
	(l)gep! **something** (h)wy	เก็บ——ไว้
storeroom	(f)hawng! (l)gep! (r)kawng	ห้องเก็บของ
(pantry, food storeroom)		
	(f)hawng! (h)pahk! ah-(r)hahn	ห้องพักอาหาร
storm	pah-(h)yoo!	พายุ
(rainstorm)	pah-(h)yoo! (r)fohn!	พายุฝน
(windstorm)	lohm! pah-(h)yoo!	ลมพายุ
story (or tale, subject matter)	(f)reu-ung	เรื่อง
(account, matter, case)	(f)reu-ung rao	เรื่องราว
(news)	(l)kow	ข่าว
(story or floor of a building)	(h)chahn!	ชั้น
stove	dtao! (rhymes with "cow")	เตา
(stove for cooking)	dtao! fy!	เตาไฟ
(gas stove)	dtao! (h)gaas	เตาแก๊ส
(electric stove)	dtao! fy! (h)fah	เตาไฟฟ้า

231

straight (to be straight, direct)	dtrohng!	ตรง
(to go straight ahead)	dtrohng! bpy!	ตรงไป
strain (to strain, filter)	grawng	กรอง
(a strainer, filter)	(f)kreu-ung grawng	เครื่องกรอง
strange (to be strange, unusual, queer)		
	(l)bplaak	แปลก
straw (drinking straw, soda straw)		
	(l)lawt gra-(l)daht	หลอดกระดาษ
	(l)lawt (l)doot	หลอดดูด
(straw, rice straw)	fahng	ฟาง
stream (or small river)	lahm!-tahn	ลำธาร
street	ta-(r)nohn!	ถนน
(lane, soi)	sawy	ซอย
streetcar, trolley	(h)roht! rahng	รถราง
stretch (to stretch, extend, lengthen)	(f)yeut	ยืด
string (or rope, cord)	(f)cheu-uk	เชือก
stripe (a line, stripe, streak)	(h)riw!	ริ้ว
(a line, lines)	(f)sen!	เส้น
strong (strength, power, force)	raang	แรง

232

(to be powerful, have strength)

(r)kaang! raang แข็งแรง

(to be strong in taste, be concentrated)

(l)gaa แก่

stuck (to get stuck, get stuck in) (l)dtit! ติด

(to get stuck in mud) (l)dtit! (l)lohm! ติดหล่ม

student (or pupil) (h)nahk! ree-un นักเรียน

(a student of higher institutions)

(h)nahk! (l)seuk!-(r)sah นักศึกษา

study (to study, learn) ree-un เรียน

(to study higher education) (l)seuk!-(r)sah ศึกษา

(to study from books) doo nahng!-(r)seu ดูหนังสือ

stupid (to be stupid, foolish) (f)ngoh โง่

(to be crazy) (f)bah บ้า

(to be crazy, half-wit) bah bah baw baw บ้า ๆ บอ ๆ

style (or model, type) (l)baap แบบ

(kind, type, variety) cha-(h)nit! ชนิด

submarine reu-uh dahm! (h)nahm เรือดำน้ำ

subtract (to subtract) (h)lohp! ลบ

(A minus B is C) B (h)lohp! A (r)leu-uh C – ลบ–เหลือ–

233

success (to be successful, to finish, to have
    finished, completed)   (r)sahm!-(l)ret!   สำเร็จ
    (success, accomplishment, completion)
                kwahm (r)sahm!-(l)ret!   ความสำเร็จ
    (success, prosperity)
    kwahm (r)sohm!-boon (f)roong! reu-ung   ความสมบูรณ์
                             รุ่งเรือง

such (such as, like)   (f)chen!   เช่น
    (such as that, like that) (f)chen! (h)nahn!   เช่นนั้น
    (such as this, like this)   (f)chen! (h)nee   เช่นนี้
suck (to suck)   (l)doot   ดูด
suddenly   tahn! dy!   ทันใด
sugar   (h)nahm! dtahn   น้ำตาล
    (brown sugar)   (h)nahm! dtahn daang   น้ำตาลแดง
    (sugar cane)   (f)awy   อ้อย
suggest (to suggest, advise)   (h)naa!-nahm!   แนะนำ
suicide (to commit suicide)

                (f)kah dtoo-uh dty   ฆ่าตัวตาย
    (a suicide)   gahn (f)kah dtoo-uh dty   การฆ่าตัวตาย
suit (of clothes)   (f)seu-uh gahng gehng   เสื้อกางเกง
234

(classifier for suits of clothing)	(h)choot!	ชุด
suitcase	gra-(r)pow!	กระเป๋า
	gra-(r)pow! duhn tahng	กระเป๋าเดินทาง
(travel bag, handbag)	gra-(r)pow! (f)hue!	กระเป๋าหิ้ว
summer	(h)reu!-doo (h)rawn	ฤดูร้อน
sun	(h)pra-ah-(h)tit!	พระอาทิตย์
	dta-wahn!	ตะวัน
	doo-ung ah-(h)tit!	ดวงอาทิตย์
(to be sunny, the sun is out)		
	(r)saang (l)daat	แสงแดด
"	(l)daat (l)awk	แดดออก
Sunday	wahn! ah-(h)tit!	วันอาทิตย์
(Sunday Market)	dta-(l)laht (h)naht!	ตลาดนัด
sunlight, sunshine	(l)daat	แดด
	(r)saang (l)daat	แสงแดด
	(r)saang ah-(h)tit!	แสงอาทิตย์
sunrise	(h)pra-ah-(h)tit! (f)keun!	พระอาทิตย์ขึ้น
	dta-wahn! (f)keun!	ตะวันขึ้น
	dta-wahn! (l)awk	ตะวันออก
sunset	(h)pra-ah-(h)tit! (l)dtohk!	พระอาทิตย์ตก
	dta-wahn! (l)dtohk!	ตะวันตก

235

superstitious (to be superstitious)

	(r)teu lahng	ถือลาง
	(r)teu (f)chohk (r)teu lahng	ถือโชคถือลาง
supervise (to look after, tend)	doo laa	ดูแล
(to control, place under supervision)		
	(f)koo-up koom	ควบคุม
supervisor	(f)poo (f)koo-up koom	ผู้ควบคุม
supper (or dinner)	ah-(r)hahn yen!	อาหารเย็น
(dinner, the evening meal)		
	ah-(r)hahn (f)kahm!	อาหารค่ำ
sure (to be sure, certain)	(f)naa	แน่
,,	(f)naa jy!	แน่ใจ
(to be certain, definite)	(f)naa nawn	แน่นอน
(surely, sure to, most likely, probably will)		
	kohng! (l)ja!	คงจะ
surgery	gahn (l)pa-(l)dtaht!	การผ่าตัด
surname (family name, last name)		
	nahm sa-goon!	นามสกุล
surprise (to be surprised, astonished)		
	bpra-(l)laht jy!	ประหลาดใจ

(to be amazed, surprised)	(l)bplaak jy!	แปลกใจ
suspect (to suspect)	(r)sohng!-(r)sy!	สงสัย
swallow (to swallow)	gleun	กลืน
swamp	beung!	บึ่ง
(a marsh)	(r)nawng	หนอง
swear (to speak obscenely)	(f)poot (l)sa-(l)boht!	พูดสบมา
(to speak vulgar, crude, taboo words)	(f)poot (l)yahp	พูดหยาบ
(swear words, vulgar words)	kahm! (l)yahp	คำหยาบ
sweat (perspiration)	(l)ngeu-uh	เหงื่อ
(to sweat, perspire)	mee (l)ngeu-uh (l)awk	มีเหงื่อออก
sweater	(f)seu-uh gahn! (r)now	เสื้อกันหนาว
sweep (to sweep)	(l)gwaht	กวาด
sweet (to taste sweet)	(r)wahn	หวาน
(sweets, dessert)	(r)kawng (r)wahn	ของหวาน
(candies, pastries)	ka-(r)nohm!	ขนม
(to be sweet in manner, gentle)	(l)awn (r)wahn	อ่อนหวาน
sweetheart (or lover, lovers)	(f)koo (h)rahk!	คู่รัก

(dear)	(f)tee (h)rahk!	ที่รัก
swell (to be swollen)	boo-um	บวม
swim (to swim)	(f)wy (h)nahm	ว่ายน้ำ
(to play in the water)	(f)len! (h)nahm	เล่นน้ำ
swimming suit	(h)choot! (l)ahb-(h)nahm	ชุดอาบน้ำ
	(f)seu-uh (l)ahb-(h)nahm	เสื้ออาบน้ำ
swing (a swing)	ching!-(b)chah	ชิงช้า
(to swing)	(l)gwaang	แกว่ง
switch (electric switch)	sa-wit!	สวิตช์
swollen (to be swollen)	boo-um	บวม
sword (or sabre)	(l)dahp	ดาบ
(sword and sheath, worn with a uniform)		
	gra-(l)bee	กระบี่
symbol (or mark, sign)	(f)kreu-ung (r)my	เครื่องหมาย
	(r)sahn!-ya-(h)lahk!	สัญญลักษณ์
sympathy	kwahm (r)hen! jy	ความเห็นใจ
(to sympathize with)	(r)hen! jy!	เห็นใจ
syphilis	gahm-ma (f)rohk	กามโรค
system (or form, custom, manner)		
	ra-(l)bohp!	ระบบ

(system, form, as of government)

	ra-(l)bee-up	ระเบียบ

(electrical system) ra-(l)bohp! fy! (h)fah ระบบไฟฟ้า

table	(h)dto!	โต๊ะ
(coffee table)	(h)dto! glahng	โต๊ะกลาง
(dining table)	(h)dto! ah-(r)hahn	โต๊ะอาหาร
tablecloth	(f)pah bpoo (h)dto!	ผ้าปูโต๊ะ
tablespoon	(h)chawn (h)dto!	ช้อนโต๊ะ
tail	(r)hahng	หาง
tailor	(f)chahng (l)dtaht! (f)seu-uh	ช่างตัดเสื้อ
(tailor shop)	(h)rahn (l)dtaht! (f)seu-uh	ร้านตัดเสื้อ
take (to take)	ow!	เอา

(to take **something** to **some place**)

ow! **something** bpy! **some place** เอา--ไป--

(to take **something** to **someone**)

ow! **something** bpy! (f)hy! **someone** เอา–ไปให้–

(to take **someone** to **some place**)

pah **someone** bpy! **some place** พา–ไป–

(to lead **someone** to **some place**)

nahm! **someone** bpy! **some place** นำ–ไป–

(to take **something** away)

ow! **something** bpy! เอา——ไป

(to take **something** out)

ow! **something** (l)awk เอา——ออก

(to take off clothing, to undress)

(l)tawt (f)seu-uh ถอดเสื้อ

(to take medicine) geen! yah กินยา

(to take off, as an airplane) (l)awk ออก

(to take off and fly) (l)awk bin! ออกบิน

talk (to talk, speak, say) (f)poot พูด

(to chat, gossip) kooy! คุย

(to talk disparagingly to or about someone)

(f)wah ว่า

tall (to be tall, high) (r)soong สูง

tambon (subdiv. of ampur) dtahm!-bohn! ตำบล

(kamnan, headman of a tambon)

gahm!-nahn! กำนัน

tame (to be tame, domesticated) (f)cheu-ung เชื่อง

tangerine (f)sohm! (r)kee-oh (r)wahn ส้มเขียวหวาน

tank (r)tahng! ถัง

(water tank)	(r)tahng! (h)nahm	ถังน้ำ
(gasoline tank)	(r)tahng! (b)nahm!-mahn!	ถังน้ำมัน
(military tank)	(h)roht! (r)tahng!	รถถัง
tape (Scotch tape)	Scawt tape	สกอตเทป
,,	tape (l)dtit! gra-(l)daht	เทปติดกระดาษ
(adhesive tape)	plaas-tuh	ปลาสเต้อร์
(measuring tape)	(r)sy (h)waht!	สายวัด
(recording tape)		
	tape bahn!-(h)teuk! (r)see-ung	เทปบันทึกเสียง
tape recorder		
	(f)kreu-ung bahn!-(h)teuk! (r)see-ung	เครื่องบันทึกเสียง
taste n.	(h)roht!	รส
(to taste)	chim!	ชิม
(to be tasteless)	(f)my! mee (h)roht!	ไม่มีรส
,,	(l)jeut	จืด
(to taste delicious)	ah!-(l)rawy	อร่อย
(Does it taste good?)	ah!-(l)rawy (r)my!	อร่อยไหม
tax (or duty, tariff)	pah-(r)see	ภาษี
taxi	(h)taak-(f)see	แท็กซี่
	(h)roht! (h)taak-(f)see	รถแท็กซี่

(a rented car, rental car)	(h)roht! (f)chow!	รถเช่า
tea	chah	ชา
(tea to drink)	(h)nahm! chah	น้ำชา
(tea leaves)	by chah	ใบชา
(tea pot)	gah (h)nahm! chah	กาน้ำชา
(tea kettle)	gah (f)dtohm! (h)nahm	กาต้มน้ำ
teach (to teach, instruct, educate, train)		
	(r)sawn	สอน
teacher	kroo	ครู
	(f)poo (r)sawn	ผู้สอน
(teacher who has a degree, professor)		
	ah-jahn	อาจารย์
(professor)	(l)saht-sa-dtrah-jahn	ศาสตราจารย์
teak (teakwood)	(h)my! (l)sahk!	ไม้สัก
team	(h)choot!	ชุด
(a group, party)	(f)poo-uk	พวก
tear (to tear up, rip, get torn)	(l)cheek	ฉีก
(to be torn, worn out)	(l)kaht	ขาด
(tears, teardrops)	(h)nahm! dtah	น้ำตา
tease (to tease, mock)	(h)law	ล้อ

(to tease, kid, joke)	(h)law (f)len!	ล้อเล่น
(to annoy by teasing)	(f)glaang	แกล้ง
teaspoon	(h)chawn chah	ช้อนชา
teeth, tooth	fahn!	ฟัน
telegram	toh-ra-(f)lek	โทรเลข
(to send a telegram)	(l)sohng! toh-ra-(f)lek	ส่งโทรเลข
telephone	toh-ra-(l)sahp!	โทรศัพท์

(to telephone **someone**)

toh-ra-(l)sahp! bpy! (r)teung! **someone**   โทรศัพท์ไปถึง--

toh bpy! **someone**   โทรไป--

(to talk on the phone)

(f)poot toh-ra-(l)sahp!   พูดโทรศัพท์

| (telephone number) | buh toh-ra-(l)sahp! | เบอร์โทรศัพท์ |
| ,, | (r)my (f)lek | หมายเลข |

(telephone operator)

pa-(h)nahk!-ngahn toh-ra-(l)sahp!   พนักงานโทรศัพท์

(telephone directory)

sa-(l)moot! toh-ra-(l)sahp!   สมุดโทรศัพท์

| **telescope** | (f)glawng ka-(r)yai | กล้องขยาย |
| **television** | toh-ra-(f)pahp | โทรภาพ |

243

	toh-ra-(h)taht!	โทรทัศน์
tell (to tell, say)	(l)bawk	บอก
(to tell a story, narrate)	(f)lao	เล่า
temperature	kwahm (h)rawn	ความร้อน
	bpa-(l)rawt	ปรอท
(degrees)	ohng!-(r)sah	องศา
temple (wat)	(h)waht!	วัด
temporary, temporarily	(f)choo-uh krao	ชั่วคราว
ten (10)	(l)sip!	สิบ
tenant	(f)poo (f)chow!	ผู้เช่า
tennis	ten-nis!	เทนนิส
tent	gra-johm	กระโจม
termite (or white ant)	(l)bploo-uk	ปลวก
terrorist (or revolutionist)	(f)poo (l)gaw gahn	ผู้ก่อการ
(communist terrorist)	(f)poo (l)gaw	ผู้ก่อการ
	gahn (h)ry kawm-miw!-(h)nis!	ร้ายคอมมิวนิสต์
test (to test, try out, experiment)		
	(h)toht! lawng	ทดลอง
(to take a test, examination)	(l)sawp	สอบ
(a test, an examination)	gahn (l)sawp	การสอบ

Thailand, Thai	ty	ไทย
(the country of)	bpra-(f)tet ty	ประเทศไทย
„	meu-ung ty	เมืองไทย
(the Thai nation, Thai nationality)		
	(f)chaht ty	ชาติไทย
(a Thai person)	kohn! ty	คนไทย
(a Thai, the Thais)	chow ty	ชาวไทย
(the Thai language)	pah-(r)sah ty	ภาษาไทย
than	(l)gwah	กว่า
(to be less than **something**)		
	(h)nawy (l)gwah **something**	น้อยกว่า—
(to be more than **something**)		
	(f)mahk (l)gwah **something**	มากกว่า—
thank you (very polite)	(l)kawp koon!	ขอบคุณ
(informal)	(l)kawp jy!	ขอบใจ
Thank you, Sir. (said by males)		
	(l)kawp koon! (b)krahp!	ขอบคุณครับ
(said by females)	(l)kawp koon! (h)ka!	ขอบคุณคะ
that (that **something**)	something (h)nahn!	—นั้น
(that one, nearby)	(f)nahn!	นั้น
„	ahn! (h)nahn!	อันนั้น

245

(that one over there, yonder, more distant)

| | (f)nohn | โน้น |
| ,, | ahn! (h)nohn | อันโน้น |

(that, that which)	(f)tee	ที่
(that way, that direction)	tahng (h)nahn!	ทางนั้น
(that way, like that)	(l)yahng (h)nahn!	อย่างนั้น
,,	(f)chen! (h)nahn!	เช่นนั้น
(that, as a conjunction)	(f)wah	ว่า

the (No direct translation.)

theater (the building)   rohng la-kawn   โรงละคร

(the theater, drama, play, performance)

la-kawn   ละคร

(Thai musical folk drama)   lih!-geh   ลิเก

(a comedy, farce)   la-kawn dta-(l)lok!   ละครตลก

their (their——, ——belonging to them)

(people only)   ——(r)kawng (r)kow!   — ของเขา

(——belonging to two people)

——(r)kawng (r)kow! (h)tahng!(r)sawng   — ของเขาทั้งสอง

(——belonging to two or more people)

——(r)kawng (r)kow! (h)tahng! (r)ly   — ของเขาทั้งหลาย

(their——,——belonging to them)

(not people)   ——(r)kawng mahn! ——ของมัน

theirs (No direct translation. Translate the equivalent: "their——")

them (people only)   (r)kow! เขา

(two people) (r)kow! (h)tahng! (r)sawng เขาทั้งสอง

(two or more people)

    (r)kow! (h)tahng! (r)ly เขาทั้งหลาย

(animals or things only)   mahn! มัน

themselves   dtoo-uh (r)kawng (r)kow! ตัวของเขา

dtoo-uh (r)kawng (r)kow! (h)tahng! (r)ly ตัวของเขาทั้งหลาย

then (at that time)   weh-lah (h)nahn! เวลานั้น

(consequently)   (l)cha!-(b)nahn! ฉะนั้น

(then, so, therefore)   jeung! จึง

(and then)   (h)laa-oh (f)gaw! แล้วก็

there (nearby)   (f)tee (f)nahn! ที่นั่น

(over there, over yonder, more distant)

    (f)tee (f)nohn ที่โน่น

(there is, there are)   mee มี

therefore   (h)praw!-cha-(h)nahn! เพราะฉะนั้น

(so, thus, hence)	dahng! (h)nahn!	ดังนั้น
(so, then therefore)	jeung!	จึง
thermometer	bpa-(l)rawt	ปรอท
thermos (bottle)	gra-(l)dtik! (h)nahm	กระติกน้ำ
these (these——)	——(h)nee	——นี้
(these things)	(l)sing! (h)nee	สิ่งนี้
„	ahn! (h)nee	อันนี้
(these, this group)	(l)lao! (h)nee	เหล่านี้
(these people)	kohn! (h)nee	คนนี้
they (people only)	(r)kow!	เขา
(two people)	(r)kow! (h)tahng!(r)sawng	เขาทั้งสอง
(two or more people)		
	(r)kow! (h)tahng! (r)ly	เขาทั้งหลาย
(animals or things)	mahn!	มัน
(two things)	mahn! (h)tahng! (r)sawng	มันทั้งสอง
(two or more things)		
	mahn! (h)tahng! (r)ly	มันทั้งหลาย
thick (to be thick, in dimension)	(r)nah	หนา
(to be concentrated)	(f)kohn!	ข้น
(to be thick, strong, of coffee or tea)	(l)gaa	แก่

thief (or burglar)	ka-moy	ขโมย
thin (to be thin, in dimension)	bahng	บาง
(to be lean, of people, animals)	(r)pawm	ผอม
thing, things	(l)sing!	สิ่ง
	(r)kawng	ของ
(things)	(l)sing! (r)kawng	สิ่งของ
(small thing or things)	ahn!	อัน
think (to think)	(h)keet!	คิด
(to think that . . . .)	(h)keet! (f)wah	คิดว่า
(to think of, to miss)	(h)keet! (r)teung!	คิดถึง
(I think so.)		
(r)chahn! (h)keet! (f)chen! (h)nahn!		ฉันคิดเช่นนั้น
(I think so.)		
(r)chahn! (h)keet! (l)yahng! (h)nahn!		ฉันคิดอย่างนั้น
(I don't think so.)		
(r)chahn! (f)my! (h)keet! (f)chen! (h)nahn!		ฉันไม่คิดเช่นนั้น
third (3rd)	(f)tee (r)sahm	ที่สาม
(one-third, 1/3)		
(l)set (l)neung! (l)soo-un (r)sahm		เศษหนึ่งส่วนสาม

(two-thirds, 2/3)

	(l)set (r)sawng (l)soo-un (r)sahm	เศษสองส่วนสาม
thirsty (to be thirsty)	(r)hue! (h)nahm	หิวน้ำ
,,	gra-(r)hy (h)nahm	กระหายน้ำ
this (this **something**)	**something** (h)nee	——นี้
(this one)	(f)nee	นี่
,,	ahn! (h)nee	อันนี้
,,	(l)sing! (h)nee	สิ่งนี้
(this person)	kohn! (h)nee	คนนี้
(this way, this direction)	tahng (h)nee	ทางนี้
(this way, like this)	(l)yahng (h)nee	อย่างนี้
,,	(f)chen! (h)nee	เช่นนี้
thorn (or barb)	(r)nahm	หนาม
those (those **something**)	**something** (h)nahn!	——นั้น
(those things)	ahn! (h)nahn!	อันนั้น
,,	(l)sing! (h)nahn!	สิ่งนั้น
(that group)	(l)lao! (h)nahn!	เหล่านั้น
(those people)	kohn! (h)nahn!	คนนั้น
thousand (1,000)	pahn!	พัน
	(l)neung! pahn!	หนึ่งพัน

	pahn! (l)neung!	พันหนึ่ง
(ten thousand, 10,000)	(l)meun	หมื่น
(hundred thousand, 100,000)	(r)saan	แสน
thread n.	(f)dy	ด้าย
three (3)	(r)sahm	สาม
throat	kaw (r)hawy	คอหอย
	lahm! kaw	ลำคอ
(a sore throat)	kaw (l)jep!	คอเจ็บ
„	(l)jep! kaw	เจ็บคอ
through (to pass through)	(l)pahn	ผ่าน
(to walk through)	duhn (l)pahn	เดินผ่าน
(to pass through, come in and go out)		
	(l)pahn (f)kow! (l)awk	ผ่านเข้าออก
(to send or pass **something** through)		
	ow! **something** (l)sohng! (l)pahn	เอา– – ส่งผ่าน
(in, through)	tahng	ทาง
(to be through, to be over, to finish, end, quit)	(f)luhk	เลิก
throughout (all– –,all during– –)		
	dta-(l)lawt– –	ตลอด

throw (to throw, cast, fling)	(f)kwahng	ขว้าง
(to toss, throw, cast)	yohn	โยน
(to throw away, discard)	(h)ting!	ทิ้ง
(to throw **something** away)		
	(h)ting! **something** bpy!	ทิ้ง――ไป
thumb	(h)nue! (r)hoo-uh (f)maa meu	นิ้วหัวแม่มือ
	(h)nue! (f)bpohng	นิ้วโป้ง
thumbtack	(h)bpek! (l)dtit! gra-(l)dabt	เป๊กติดกระดาษ
thunder	(h)fah (h)rawng	ฟ้าร้อง
Thursday	wahn! (h)preu!-(l)haht!	วันพฤหัส
thus (so, thus, hence)	dahng! (h)nahn!	ดังนั้น
(therefore)	(h)praw!-cha-(h)nahn!	เพราะฉะนั้น
tical (same as "baht")		――
tick (woodtick)	(l)hep!	เห็บ
ticket	(r)dtoo-uh	ตั๋ว
(or ballot, coupon, card)	(l)baht!	บัตร
(admission ticket)		
	(l)baht! (l)pahn bpra-dtoo	บัตรผ่านประตู
(classifier for tickets)	(f)tee	ที่
tickle (to tickle)	(f)jee	จี้

(to be ticklish)	(h)jahk!-(l)ga!-(f)jee	จั๊กจี้
tidy (to be tidy, neat, be in good order)		
	(f)ree-up (h)rawy	เรียบร้อย
	(l)moht! (l)joht	หมดจด
tie (to tie, bind, fasten)	(l)pook	ผูก
(a necktie)	(h)nek!-ty!	เน็คไท
"	(f)pah (l)pook kaw	ผ้าผูกคอ
tiger	(r)seu-uh	เสือ
tight (to be tight-fitting, packed, crowded)		
	(f)naan!	แน่น
"	(h)kahp!	คับ
(to be tight, taut, tense, strained)	dteung!	ตึง
tighten (to tighten **something**)		
	(l)pook **something** (f)hy! (f)naan	ผูก——ให้แน่น
tile (roof tile, floor tile, etc.)	gra-(f)beu-ung	กระเบื้อง
till (see "until")		
time	weh-lah	เวลา
(occurrence, time, times)	(h)krahng!	ครั้ง
"	(r)hohn!	หน
(occasion)	krao	คราว

253

(to be on time)	dtrohng! weh-lah	ตรงเวลา
(at the same time, simultaneously)		
	(h)prawm gahn!	พร้อมกัน
(all the time)	dta-(l)lawt weh-lah	ตลอดเวลา
(What time is it?)	weh-lah (f)tao!-(r)ry!	เวลาเท่าไร
„	(l)gee mohng	กี่โมง
timetable	dtah-rahng weh-lah	ตารางเวลา
timing (or rhythm, beat, timing interval)		
	jahng!-(l)wa!	จังหวะ
tin (the metal)	dee-(l)book!	ดีบุก
(tin can)	gra-(r)bpawng!	กระป๋อง
(tin foil)	gra-(l)daht dee-(l)book!	กระดาษดีบุก
tiny	(h)nit!	นิด
(tiny, a tiny bit)	(h)nit! dee-oh	นิดเดียว
(tiny, wee, small, tiny bit)	(h)nit! (l)nawy	นิดหน่อย
(to be tiny)	(h)lek! (h)nit! dee-oh	เล็กนิดเดียว
(to be small, tiny)	(h)bpee-uk	เปี๊ยก
tip (or end)	bply	ปลาย
(money)	ngun! tip!	เงินทิป
„	ngun! rahng-wahn!	เงินรางวัล

tire (for a vehicle)	yahng (h)roht!	ยางรถ
(the outer tire, casing)	yahng (f)nawk	ยางนอก
(the inner tire, inner tube)	yahng ny!	ยางใน
tired (to be tired, fatigued)	(l)neu-ay	เหนื่อย
(to be tired out, worn out)	plee-uh	เพลีย
(to feel stiff and sore)	(f)meu-ay	เมื่อย
(to be tired of something, be bored)		
	(l)beu-uh	เบื่อ
to (to or for **someone**)	(l)gaa **someone**	แก่ - —
(to **some place**)	(r)teung **some place**	ถึง — —
(in order to)	(f)peu-uh	เพื่อ
toad	kahng-(h)kohk!	คางคก
toast (toasted bread)		
	ka-(r)nohm! bpahng! (f)bping!	ขนมปังปิ้ง
(to toast, cook by toasting)	(f)bping!	ปิ้ง
tobacco	yah (l)soop	ยาสูบ
(prepared tobacco, pipe tobacco)		
	yeh (f)sen!	ยาเส้น
today	wahn!-(h)nee	วันนี้
toe	(h)nue! (h)tao	นิ้วเท้า
("nue" rhymes with "few")		

together	gahn!	กัน
	(f)doo-ay gahn!	ด้วยกัน
(all together, at the same time,		
simultaneously)	(h)prawm gahn!	พร้อมกัน
(to put together, combine)	roo-um gahn!	รวมกัน
toilet	(f)soo-um	ส้วม
(bathroom, restroom, etc.)		
	(f)hawng! (h)nahm	ห้องน้ำ
,,	(f)hawng! (f)soo-um	ห้องส้วม
,,	(f)hawng! soo!-(r)kah	ห้องสุขา
(toilet paper)	gra-(l)daht! chahm!-(h)ra!	กระดาษชำระ
tomato	ma-(r)keu-uh-(f)tet	มะเขือเทศ
tomorrow	(f)proong!-(h)nee	พรุ่งนี้
(the day after tomorrow)	ma!-reun (h)nee	มะรืนนี้
tongue	(h)leen!	ลิ้น
tonight	keun (h)nee	คืนนี้
too (or also)	doo-ay	ด้วย
(to be excessive)	gun bpy!	เกินไป
(too much of **something**)		
something (f)mahk bpy!		——มากไป

(too much of **something**)

	something (f)mahk gun bpy!	——มากเกินไป
(Me, too!)	(r)chahn! (f)doo-ay	ฉันด้วย
tool (handtool of any kind)	(f)kreu-ung meu	เครื่องมือ
tooth, teeth	fahn!	ฟัน
toothache	(l)bpoo-ut fahn!	ปวดฟัน
toothbrush	bpraang (r)see fahn!	แปรงสีฟัน
toothpaste	yah (r)see fahn!	ยาสีฟัน
toothpick	(h)my (f)jim! fahn!	ไม้จิ้มฟัน
toothpowder	yah (r)see fahn! (r)pohng!	ยาสีฟันผง
top (on top, upper part)	(f)kahng! bohn!	ข้างบน
(peak, tip)	(f)yawt	ยอด
(lid, cover, top)	(r)fah	ฝา
,,	(r)fah (l)bpit!	ฝาปิด
(a toy top)	(f)look (l)kahng	ลูกข่าง
torn (to be torn, worn out) (of clothing)		
	(l)kaht	ขาด
(to be ripped)	(l)cheek	ฉีก
tortoise, turtle	(l)dtao!	เต่า
toss (to toss, throw, cast)	yohn	โยน

257

total (or quantity, number, amount)

	jahm! noo-un	จำนวน
(the total number) (f)yawt jahm! noo-un	ยอดจำนวน
touch (to touch, take hold of, catch) (l)jahp!	จับ
(Don't touch!) (l)yah (l)jahp!	อย่าจับ

tough (to be tough, chewy, as of meat)

	(r)nee-oh	เหนียว
tour (to tour, sightsee) (f)tawng (f)tee-oh	ท่องเที่ยว
,, (f)tee-oh bpy!	เที่ยวไป
,, bpy! (f)tee-oh chohm!	ไปเที่ยวชม
(a tour guide, person)	
(f)poo nahm! (f)tee-oh	ผู้นำเที่ยว

tourist (or traveller)

	(h)nahk! (f)tawng (f)tee-oh	นักท่องเที่ยว
towel (bath towel) (f)pah (h)chet! dtoo-uh	ผ้าเช็ดตัว
(face towel) (f)pah (h)chet! (f)nah	ผ้าเช็ดหน้า
(hand towel) (f)pah (h)chet! meu	ผ้าเช็ดมือ
(dish towel) (f)pah (h)chet! chahm	ผ้าเช็ดชาม
(paper towel) gra-daht (h)chet! meu	กระดาษเช็ดมือ
tower (r)haw	หอ

(water tower)

    (r)haw (r)tahng! (l)gep! (h)nam   หอถังเก็บน้ำ

(radio tower)   (r)haw (h)wit!-ta-(h)yoo!   หอวิทยุ

town   meu-ung   เมือง

toy   (f)kreu-ung (f)len!   เครื่องเล่น

track (railroad tracks)   rahng (h)roht! fy!   รางรถไฟ

tractor   (h)roht! tractor   รถแทร็คเค้อร์

(Caterpillar tractor)

    (h)roht! dteen dta-(l)kahp   รถตีนตะขาบ

trade (to trade, swap, exchange)

    (f)laak (l)bplee-un   แลกเปลี่ยน

(to exchange A for B)

    (f)laak (l)bplee-un A bpen! B   แลกเปลี่ยน—เป็น

traffic (road traffic)   ja-rah-jawn   จราจร

    ,,   gahn ja-rah-jawn   การจราจร

(bad traffic, to be crowded with autos)

    (h)roht! (f)naan!   รถแน่น

trail (or way, path, route)   tahng   ทาง

(footpath)   tahng duhn   ทางเดิน

trailer (of a vehicle)   (h)roht! (f)poo-ung   รถพ่วง

train (railroad train)	(h)roht! fy!	รถไฟ
(to train, practice, drill)	(l)haht!	หัด
,,	(l)feuk!	ฝึก
,,	(l)feuk! (l)haht!	ฝึกหัด
transformer	(f)kreu-ung bplaang fy!	เครื่องแปลงไฟ
	(f)maw bplaang fy!	หม้อแปลงไฟ
(stepdown)	step-down	สเตปดาว
(step-up)	step-up	สเตปอัพ
translate (to translate)	bplaa	แปล
translation	gahn bplaa	การแปล
translator, interpreter	kohn! bplaa	คนแปล
	pa-nahk!-ngahn bplaa	พนักงานแปล
transparent (to be transparent)		
	(l)bprohng (r)sy!	โปร่งใส
trap (to trap, snare, catch)	(l)dahk!	ดัก
(a trap)	(l)gahp! (l)dahk!	กับดัก
(a mousetrap, rat trap)		
	(l)gahp! (l)dahk! (r)noo	กับดักหนู
trash	(l)set (r)kawng	เศษของ
(garbage)	(l)set ah-(r)hahn	เศษอาหาร

(waste, refuse, garbage)	ka-(l)ya!	ขยะ
,,	moon (r)fawy	มูลฝอย
(a trash can, waste basket)		
	(r)tahng! (r)pohng!	ถังผง
,,	(r)tahng! ka-(l)ya!	ถังขยะ
travel (to travel, take a trip)	duhn tahng	เดินทาง
(to travel for pleasure)	bpy! (f)tee-oh	ไปเที่ยว
(travel, travelling)	gahn duhn tahng	การเดินทาง
tray	(l)taht	ถาด
tree	(f)dtohn! (h)my	ต้นไม้
(classifier for trees)	(f)dtohn!	ต้น
tresspass (to tresspass)	(l)book! (h)rook!	บุกรุก
(No Tresspassing, Do not enter.)		
	(f)hahm (f)kow!	ห้ามเข้า
triangle	(f)roop (r)sahm (l)lee-um	รูปสามเหลี่ยม
tricycle	(h)roht! (r)sahm (h)law	รถสามล้อ
trip (to trip and fall)	(l)hohk! (h)lohm!	หกล้ม
(to take a trip, to travel)	duhn tahng	เดินทาง
(to take a pleasure trip)	bpy! (f)tee-oh	ไปเที่ยว
(a trip)	gahn duhn tahng	การเดินท่าง

trolley (or streetcar)   (h)roht! rahng   รถราง

trouble (to be troublesome)   lahm!-(l)bahk   ลำบาก

   (trouble, difficulty) kwahm lahm!-(l)bahk   ความลำบาก

   (to be in trouble, to worry, be upset)

                   (l)deu-ut (h)rawn   เดือดร้อน

trousers (pants)   gahng-gehng   กางเกง

trowel (garden hand trowel) (f)ploo-uh meu   พลั่วมือ

truck   (h)roht! goo!-dahng!   รถกุดัง

           (h)roht! bahn-(h)took!   รถบรรทุก

true (to be true, real)   jing!   จริง

   (Is it true?, Really?)   jing! jing! (r)reu   จริง ๆ หรือ

   (That's not true!)

              (f)my! bpen! kwahm jing!   ไม่เป็นความจริง

   (to be faithful, true, loyal) (f)seu-(l)saht!   ซื่อสัตย์

trunk (for storage, shipment)

        gra-(r)bpow! duhn tahng   กระเป๋าเดินทาง

   (of an automobile)   gra-bprohng (h)ty   กระโปรงท้าย

      ,,   gra-bprohng (r)lahng!   กระโปรงหลัง

   (of an elephant)   ngoo-ung (h)chahng   งวงช้าง

trust (to trust, have faith in)	(h)wy! jy!	ไว้ใจ
,,	(f)cheu-uh jy!	เชื่อใจ
(to trust, believe in)	(f)cheu-uh (r)teu	เชื่อถือ
truth	kwahm jing!	ความจริง
try (to try, try out, try on)	lawng	ลอง
(to experiment, test, try out)		
	(h)toht! lawng	ทดลอง
(to try and see what something is like)		
	lawng doo	ลองดู
(to attempt, endeavor, persevere, keep		
trying)	pa-yah-yahm	พยายาม
tub (washtub, washbowl)	(l)ahng	อ่าง
(bucket, pail, barrel, tank)	(r)tahng!	ถัง
(bathtub)	(l)ahng (l)ahb-(h)nahm	อ่างอาบน้ำ
tube	(l)lawt	หลอด
(pipe, hose, tube)	(f)taw	ท่อ
(inner tube for a tire)	yahng ny!	ยางใน
(a radio tube, electron tube)		
	(l)lawt (h)wit!-ta-(h)yoo!	หลอดวิทยุ
tuberculosis (T.B.)	tee bee	ที.บี.

263

	wan-na-(f)rohk	วัณโรค
Tuesday	wahn! ahng!-kahn	วันอังคาร
tunnel	oo!-mohng!	อุโมงค์
(cave)	(f)tahm!	ถ้ำ
turkey	(l)gy! ngoo-ung	ไก่งวง
turn (to turn, rotate, spin)	(r)moon!	หมุน
(to turn, as when driving a car)	(h)lee-oh	เลี้ยว
(to turn left)	(h)lee-oh (h)sy	เลี้ยวซ้าย
(to turn right)	(h)lee-oh (r)kwah	เลี้ยวขวา
(to turn back, return)	(l)glahp!	กลับ
(to turn a car around)	(l)glahp! (h)roht	กลับรถ
(to turn oneself around)	(r)hahn! dtoo-uh	หันตัว
(to turn over, turn upside down)	(f)kwahm!	คว่ำ
(to turn on **something**)	(l)bpuht **something**	เปิด—
(to turn off **something**)	(l)bpit! **something**	ปิด—
(to turn on a light)	(l)bpuht fy!	เปิดไฟ
(to turn off a light)	(l)bpit! fy!	ปิดไฟ
(to turn, as a page)	(h)plik!	พลิก
turnip	(r)hoo-uh (l)pahk! (l)gaht	หัวผักกาด
turtle, tortoise	(l)dtao!	เต่า

tusk (elephant tusk)	ngah (h)chahng	งาช้าง
twenty (20)	(f)yee-(l)sip!	ยี่สิบ
twice (two occurrences)	(r)sawng (h)krahng!	สองครั้ง
(twice as **much**, long, high, etc.)		
	(f)**mahk** (r)sawng (f)tao!	มากสองเท่า
twins	(f)look (l)faat	ลูกแฝด
twist (to twist)	(l)bit!	บิด
two (2)	(r)sawng	สอง
(in a telephone number)	toh	โท
type (or model, style)	(l)baap	แบบ
(kind, species)	cha-(h)nit!	ชนิด
(to type, typewrite)	pim! (l)deet	พิมพ์ดีด
typewriter	(f)kreu-ung pim! (l)deet	เครื่องพิมพ์ดีด
(typewriter ribbon)		
	(f)pah (l)meuk! pim! (l)deet	ผ้าหมึกพิมพ์ดีด
typist	pa-(h)nahk! ngahn pim! (l)deet	พนักงานพิมพ์ดีด
tyre (for a vehicle)	yahng (h)roht!	ยางรถ
(the outer tyre, casing)	yahng (f)nawk	ยางนอก
(the inner tyre, inner tube)	yahng ny!	ยางใน
ugly (to be ugly)	(f)nah (l)glee-ut	น่าเกลียด

umbrella—underwear

umbrella	(f)rohm!	ร่ม
unbutton (to unbutton)	(l)bploht! gra-doom!	ปลดกระดุม
uncle (older brother of father or mother)		
	loong!	ลุง
(younger brother of father)	ah	อา
(younger brother of mother)	(h)nah	น้า
,,	(h)nah chy	น้าชาย
uncover (to uncover, to take the cover off)		
	(l)bpuht (l)awk	เปิดออก
,,	ow! (r)fah (l)awk	เอาฝาออก
under (under, below, underneath)	(f)dty	ใต้
(below, down below)	(f)kahng (f)lahng	ข้างล่าง
(underside)	(f)kahng (f)dty	ข้างใต้
underpants	gahng-gehng ny!	กางเกงใน
undershirt	(f)seu-uh (h)chahn! ny!	เสื้อชั้นใน
understand (to understand)	(f)kow!-jy!	เข้าใจ
(I do not understand.)		
	(r)chahn! (f)my! (f)kow!-jy!	ฉันไม่เข้าใจ
(to misunderstand)	(f)kow!-jy! (l)peet!	เข้าใจผิด
underwear	(f)seu-uh (f)pah (h)chahn! ny!	เสื้อผ้าชั้นใน

266

undo (to undo, unfasten, untie) (f)gaa แก้

undress (to undress) (l)tawt (f)seu-uh ถอดเสื้อ

   ,,   (f)gaa (f)pah แก้ผ้า

unemployed (to be unemployed, unoccupied)

        (f)wahng ngahn ว่างงาน

 (an unemployed person)

      kohn! (f)wahng ngahn คนว่างงาน

unfasten (to unfasten, untie, undo) (f)gaa แก้

   ,,   (f)gaa (l)awk แก้ออก

unfriendly (to be unfriendly)

     (f)my! bpen! (f)peu-un ไม่เป็นเพื่อน

   ,, (f)my! bpen! (h)mit! ไม่เป็นมิตร

unhappy (to be unhappy)

     (f)my mee kwahm (l)sook! ไม่มีความสุข

uniform (any kind) (f)kreu-ung (l)baap เครื่องแบบ

 (military uniform)

     (f)kreu-ung (l)baap ta-(r)hahn เครื่องแบบทหาร

united   sa-(l)ha— — สห— —

 (United States of America)

    sa-(l)ha-(h)raht! ah-meh-rih!-gah สหรัฐอเมริกา

267

(United Nations)

	sa-(l)ha-bpra-chah-(f)chaht	สหประชาชาติ
university	ma-(r)hah (h)wit!-ta-yah-ly	มหาวิทยาลัย

unlock (to unlock, unlock with a key)

	(r)ky! goon!-jaa	ไขกุญแจ

unlucky (to be unlucky)

	(f)chohk! (f)my! dee	โชคไม่ดี
(to have bad luck)	soo-ay	ซวย

unmarried (to be unmarried, be single)

	bpen! (l)soht	เป็นโสด
unpack (to unpack)	ow! (r)kawng (l)awk	เอาของออก
untie (to untie, unfasten, undo)	(f)gaa	แก้
,,	(f)gaa (l)awk	แก้ออก
until, till	john! (rhymes with "bone")	จน
(right up until——)	john! (l)gwah——	จนกว่า——
(until reaching——)	john (r)teung!——	จนถึง
unwrap (to unwrap, untie, undo)	(f)gaa	แก้
,,	(f)gaa (l)awk	แก้ออก

up (or upwards, increase, rise, grow, etc.)

	(f)keun!	ขึ้น

(to go up)	(f)keun! bpy!	ขึ้นไป
(to come up)	(f)keun! mah	ขึ้นมา
upon, on	bohn!	บน
(on top of)	(f)kahng bohn!	ข้างบน
upside down (to be upside down, turn upside down)	(f)kwahm!	คว่ำ
(to turn upside down)	(l)glahp!	กลับ
upstairs	(f)kahng bohn!	ข้างบน
	(h)chahn! bohn!	ชั้นบน
urine(urine,tourinate)	(l)bpat!-(r)sah-(h)wa!	ปัสสาวะ
,,	(f)yee-oh	เยี่ยว
(to have the urge to urinate)		
	(l)bpoo-ut (f)yee-oh	ปวดเยี่ยว
us, we	rao! (rhymes with "cow")	เรา
use (to use)	(h)chy!	ใช้
(use, the use of)	gahn (h)chy!	การใช้
(usefulness, benefit)	bpra-(l)yoht	ประโยชน์
(to use up; use all up completely)		
	(h)chy! (l)moht!	ใช้หมด

(to be used up, to be all gone)

(l)moht! (h)laa-oh หมดแล้ว

used (to be all used up, be all gone)

(l)moht! (h)laa-oh หมดแล้ว

used to (ever) kuh-ee เคย

(to be accustomed to) tahm! john! kuh-ee ทำจนเคย

useful (to be useful) mee bpra-(l)yoht มีประโยชน์

useless (to be useless)

(f)my! mee bpra-(l)yoht ไม่มีประโยชน์

usual (usually, as usual) dtahm tah-ma-dah ตามธรรมดา

,, (f)chen! kuh-ee เช่นเคย

(usual, normal, routine)

(l)bpohk!-ga-(l)dtih! ปกติ

vacant (to be vacant, free, unoccupied)

(f)wahng ว่าง

vacation weh-lah (l)yoot! (h)pahk เวลาหยุดพัก

(a holiday) wahn! (l)yoot! วันหยุด

(to take a vacation) (l)yoot! ngahn หยุดงาน

(school vacation)

weh-lah (l)yoot! (f)pahk ree-un เวลาหยุดภาคเรียน

vaccinate (to vaccinate)　　(l)bplook (r)fee　ปลูกฝี

　(vaccination)　　gahn (l)bplook (r)fee　การปลูกฝี

　(to get a shot)　　(l)cheet yah　ฉีดยา

valley　　(l)hoop! (r)kow!　หุบเขา

valuable (to be valuable, precious)

　　　　　　mee rah-kah　มีราคา

value (cost, price)　　(f)kah　ค่า

　(price)　　rah-kah　ราคา

　(value, worth)　　koon! (f)kah　คุณค่า

various (or different)　　(l)dtahng (l)dtahng　ต่าง ๆ

varnish　　(h)nahm!-mahn! (h)chahk! ngow　น้ำมันชักเงา

vase (for flowers)　　jaa-gahn!　แจกัน

veal　　(h)neu-uh (f)look woo-uh　เนื้อลูกวัว

vegetable　　(l)pahk!　ผัก

　(vegetable oil)　　(h)nahm!-mahn! (l)pahk!　น้ำมันผัก

　(vegetation, plants)　　(f)peut　พืช

vehicle (any kind)　　(h)roht!　รถ

　(classifier for vehicles)　　kahn!　คัน

velocity (or speed)　　kwahm reh-oh　ความเร็ว

271

---

venereal disease, VD (gonorrhea, the clap)

| | (f)rohk (r)nawng-ny | โรคหนองใน |

  (syphillis)   gahm-ma (f)rohk   กามโรค

  (VD, contracted by a man)

                        (f)rohk (f)poo-(r)ying!   โรคผู้หญิง

  (VD, contracted by a woman)

                        (f)rohk boo!-(l)root!   โรคบุรุษ

very (or very much, very many)   (f)mahk   มาก

  (so much, so very)   (h)nahk!   นัก

  (exactly, quite, very)   tee dee-oh   ทีเดียว

  (really, truly, very, very much)   (h)taa   แท้

  (not very, not quite, hardly)

                        (f)my! (f)kawy   ไม่ค่อย

veterinarian   (l)saht! (f)paat   สัตวแพทย์

via (by means of)   doy   โดย

  (by way of)   tahng   ทาง

  (by way of, by means of)   doy tahng   โดยทาง

vicinity (or region, environs, zone)

                        baw-ri-wen   บริเวณ

Vietnam, Vietnamese   (f)wee-ut nahm   เวียตนาม

	yoo-un	ญวน
(a Vietnamese person)	chow yoo-un	ชาวญวน
(the country of)	bpra-(f)tet yoo-un	ประเทศญวน
view (scenic view)	view	วิว
	(pronounced "wiew")	

village (a hamlet, a group of houses)

| | (l)moo (f)bahn | หมู่บ้าน |
| (a villager, commoner) | chow (f)bahn | ชาวบ้าน |

(puyaiban, headman of village)

	(f)poo (l)yai! (f)bahn	ผู้ใหญ่บ้าน
vine (small vines, creepers)	kreu-uh	เครือ
(large vines)	(r)tao! wahn!	เถาวัลย์
vinegar	(h)nahm! (f)sohm!	น้ำส้ม
	(h)nahm! (f)sohm! (r)sy choo	น้ำส้มสายชู
violet (the color of)	(r)see (h)met! ma-bprahng	สีเม็ดมะปราง
visa	visa (pronounced "wee-sah")	วีซ่า
	bpra-(h)tahp! dtrah (r)kawng	ประทับตราของ
	sa-(r)tahn-(f)toot	สถานทูต
visit (to visit)	(f)yee-um	เยี่ยม

(to go visit)	bpy! (f)yee-um	ไปเยี่ยม
„	bpy! (r)hah	ไปหา
(to come to visit)	mah (r)hah	มาหา
(visiting hours)	weh-lah (f)yee-um	เวลาเยี่ยม
visitor	(f)poo mah (r)hah	ผู้มาหา
vitamin	wih!-dtah-min!	วิตามิน
voice (or sound, noise, tone)	(r)see-ung	เสียง
voltage	raang fy! (h)fah	แรงไฟฟ้า
volunteer (to volunteer)	ah-(r)sah	อาสา
„	sa-(l)mahk!	สมัคร
vomit (to vomit)	ah-jee-un	อาเจียน
„	(f)oo-uk	อ้วก
vote (to vote with a ballot)	lohng! ka-naan	ลงคะแนน
(to vote orally)	(l)awk (r)see-ung	ออกเสียง
vowel	sa!-(l)ra!	สระ
(Ex: the vowel sound "ah")	sa!-(l)ra! ah	สระอา
wa (unit of linear measure equal to 2 meters or 2.1782 yards)	wah	วา
wage, wages (monthly pay)	ngun deu-un	เงินเดือน
wagon (or cart)	(h)roht!	รถ

(ox-cart)	gwee-un	เกวียน
waist (of the body)	eho!	เอว
,,	(f)bahn! eho!	บั้นเอว
wait (to wait, wait for)	kawy	คอย
,,	raw	รอ
(wait a moment)	(r)dee-oh dee-oh	เดี๋ยวเดียว
,,	(r)dee-oh (l)gawn	เดี๋ยวก่อน
,,	raw (l)sahk! (f)kroo	รอสักครู่
waiter, waitress	kohn! duhn (h)dto!	คนเดินโต๊ะ
wake (to wake up, awaken)	(l)dteun	ตื่น
(to arouse or waken someone)	(l)bplook!	ปลุก
(to call)	(f)ree-uk	เรียก
(to get up, arise)	(h)look! (f)keun!	ลุกขึ้น
walk (to walk)	duhn	เดิน
(a walk, path, trail)	tahng duhn	ทางเดิน
wall (or partition)	(r)fah	ฝา
(interior wall)	(r)fah pa-(r)nahng!	ฝาผนัง
(stone wall)	gahm!-paang	กำแพง
wallet	gra-(r)bpow!	กระเป๋า
	gra-(r)bpow! ngun!	กระเป๋าเงิน

275

	gra-(r)bpow! (l)sy! ngun!	กระเป๋าใส่เงิน
want (to want, need, require)		
	(f)dtawng gahn	ต้องการ
(to want, to take)	ow!	เอา
(Do you want it? Do you want some?)		
	ow! (r)my!	เอาไหม
(would like to— —)	(l)yahk	อยาก
,,	(l)yahk (l)ja!	อยากจะ
war	(r)sohng!-krahm	สงคราม
wardrobe (clothes cabinet)	(f)dtoo (f)seu-uh	ตู้เสื้อ
warehouse	rohng (r)sin! (h)kah	โรงสินค้า
(godown)	goo!-dahng!	กุดัง
warm (to be warm, to warm something up)		
	(l)oon!	อุ่น
(to be warm, of weather)	(l)ohp! (l)oon!	อบอุ่น
warrant officer	ny dahp	นายดาบ
was (see "be")		
wash (to wash, wash off, things other than		
hair or clothes)	(h)lahng	ล้าง
(to launder)	(h)sahk!	ซัก

276

(to wash clothes)	(h)sahk! (f)pah	ซักผ้า
(to wash and iron)	(h)sahk! (f)reet	ซักรีด
(to wash the hair, to shampoo)		
	(l)sa! (r)pohm!	สระผม

washerman, washerwoman

	kohn! (h)sahk! (f)pah	คนซักผ้า
waste (to waste, use up wastefully)	(r)see-uh	เสีย
,,	bpleu-ung	เปลือง
(to use up, lose, waste)	(l)moht! bpleu-ung	หมดเปลือง
(to waste money)	(r)see-uh ngun!	เสียเงิน
(to waste time)	(r)see-uh weh-lah	เสียเวลา
(waste material, rubbish)	(l)set (r)kawng	เศษของ
,,	ka-(l)ya!	ขยะ
,,	moon (r)fawy	มูลฝอย
(waste paper)	(l)set gra-(l)daht	เศษกระดาษ
(waste basket, trash can)		
	(r)tahng! (r)pohng!	ถังผง
(garbage can)	(r)tahng! ka-(l)ya!	ถังขยะ
wat (temple)	(h)waht!	วัด
watch (to look at)	doo	ดู

(to take care of, as with a baby) doo laa		ดูแล
(to watch someone who is demonstrating something)	mawng doo	มองดู
,,	(f)fow! doo	เฝ้าดู
(to be watching for someone or something)	(f)fow! kawy	เฝ้าคอย
(to be on watch, be on guard)	(l)yoo yahm	อยู่ยาม
(Watch out!)	ra-wahng!	ระวัง
(wristwatch) nah-li-gah (f)kaw meu		นาฬิกาข้อมือ
watchman (or guard)	kohn! yahm	คนยาม
water	(h)nahm	น้ำ
(boiled water)	(h)nahm! (f)dtohm!	น้ำต้ม
(city water)	(h)nahm! bpra!-bpah	น้ำประปา
(city water supply)	bpra!-bpah	ประปา
(cold water)	(h)nahm! yen!	น้ำเย็น
(distilled water)	(h)nahm! (l)glahn!	น้ำกลั่น
(drinking water)	(h)nahm! geen!	น้ำกิน
,,	(h)nahm! (l)deum	น้ำดื่ม
(fresh water)	(h)nahm! (l)jeut	น้ำจืด
(hot water)	(h)nahm! (h)rawn	น้ำร้อน

(ice water)

(h)nahm! (l)sy! (h)nahm! (r)kaang น้ำใส่น้ำแข็ง

(rain water) (h)nahm! (r)fohn! น้ำฝน

(salt water) (h)nahm! kem! น้ำเค็ม

(well water) (h)nahm! (l)baw น้ำบ่อ

(to water, pour water on) (h)roht! (h)nahm รดน้ำ

water buffalo kwy ควาย

waterfall (h)nahm! (l)dtohk! น้ำตก

watermelon dtaang moh แตงโม

wave, waves (as of water, radio, etc.)

(f)kleun คลื่น

(to wave **something**) (l)bohk **something** โบก——

(to wave the hand) (l)bohk meu โบกมือ

wax n. (f)kee (f)peung! ขี้ผึ้ง

(to wax, to polish, shine) (l)kaht! ขัด

way (or path, road, route) tahng ทาง

(method, means) tahng ทาง

,, (h)wih!-tee วิธี

(the way or method of doing something)

(h)wih!-tee tahm! วิธีทำ

279

    (this way, like this)   (l)yahng (h)nee   อย่างนี้

    (that way, like that)   (l)yahng (h)nahn!   อย่างนั้น

    (to be in the way, obstruct)

                        (l)kaht! (r)kwahng   ขัดขวาง

we, us   rao! (rhymes with "cow")   เรา

weak (to be weak, frail, feeble)   (l)awn-aa   อ่อนแอ

    (to not be strong)   (f)my! (r)kaang! raang   ไม่แข็งแรง

    (to be tired out, worn out)   plee-uh   เพลีย

wealthy (to be wealthy, rich)   roo-ay   รวย

wear (to wear, to put on)   (l)sy!   ใส่

         ,,   (r)soo-um   สวม

    (to wear out, become worn out, of clothing)

                        (l)kaht   ขาด

    (to get out of order, become worn, as a

    machine)   (r)see-uh   เสีย

    (to become defective)   chahm!-(h)root!   ชำรุด

weather (or climate)   ah-(l)gaht   อากาศ

weave (to weave cloth)   taw (f)pah   ทอผ้า

web (spider web, cobweb)

              yai! ma-laang moom!   ใยแมลงมุม

wed (to wed, marry)	(l)dtaang ngahn	แต่งงาน
,,	(r)sohm!-(h)roht!	สมรส
wedding	gahn (l)dtaang ngahn	การแต่งงาน
	gahn (r)sohm!-(h)roht!	การสมรส
Wednesday	wahn! (h)poot!	วันพุธ
weed (weeds, grass)	(f)yah	หญ้า
(to weed, pull out weeds)		
	ow! (f)yah (l)awk	เอาหญ้าออก
week	ah-(h)tit!	อาทิตย์
	(l)sahp!-dah	สัปดาห์
(next week)	ah-(h)tit! (f)nah	อาทิตย์หน้า
(last week)	ah-(b)tit! (f)tee (h)laa-oh	อาทิตย์ที่แล้ว
(weekly, each week)	(h)took! ah-(h)tit!	ทุกอาทิตย์
weekend	wahn! (r)sow! ah-(h)tit!	วันเสาร์อาทิตย์
	wahn! (l)soot (l)sahp!-dah	วันสุดสัปดาห์
weigh (to weigh)	(f)chahng!	ชั่ง
(to weigh **something** or **somebody**)		
	(f)chahng! (h)nahm! (l)nahk!——	ชั่งน้ำหนัก——
(How much do you weigh?)		
	koon! (l)nahk! (f)tao!-(l)ry	คุณหนักเท่าไร

(I weigh **no.** pounds.)

(r)chahn! (l)nahk! **no.** pawn.　ฉันหนัก—ปอนด์

weight　　　　　(h)nahm! (l)nahk!　น้ำหนัก

welcome (to welcome, to receive guests)

(f)dtawn (h)rahp!　ต้อนรับ

(You're welcome.)　　(f)my! bpen! ry!　ไม่เป็นไร

weld (to weld, vulcanize, join metals)

(f)cheu-um　เชื่อม

(to solder)　　　(l)baht!-gree　บัดกรี

welfare (public)

(r)sah-tah-ra-(h)na! bpra-(l)yoht　สาธารณประโยชน์

well (to be well, happy, comfortable,

healthy)　　　　　　　sa-by dee　สบายดี

(to do something well, skillfully) (l)gehng!　เก่ง

,,　　　tahm! (l)gehng!　ทำเก่ง

(to get well, recover from sickness) (r)hy　หาย

(a well, water hole, pond) (l)baw (h)nahm　บ่อน้ำ

(an oil well)　　(l)baw (h)nahm!-mahn!　บ่อน้ำมัน

well-done (to be cooked thoroughly) (l)sook!　สุก

(to cook well-done) tahm! (f)hy! (l)sook!　ทำให้สุก

282

(to be well-done, of food)	(l)sook! dee	สุกดี
,,	(l)sook! (l)sook!	สุก ๆ
were (see "be")		
west	dta-wahn! (l)dtohk!	ตะวันตก
(the direction of west)		
	(h)tit! dta-wahn! (l)dtohk!	ทิศตะวันตก
wet (to be wet, soaked)	(l)bpee-uk	เปียก
what, what?	ah!-ry!	อะไร
(What?, What did you say?)	ah!-ry!nah!	อะไรนะ
(at what time?)	weh-lah (f)tao!-(l)ry!	เวลาเท่าไร
wheat	(r)sah-lee	สาลี
	(f)kow (r)sah-lee	ข้าวสาลี
wheel	(h)law	ล้อ
when	(f)meu-uh	เมื่อ
(when?, in a question)	(f)meu-uh (l)ry!	เมื่อไร
(at what time? or hour?)		
	weh-lah (f)tao!-(l)ry	เวลาเท่าไร
(just as, as soon as)	paw	พอ
where	(f)tee (r)ny!	ที่ไหน
(Where are you going?)	bpy! (r)ny!	ไปไหน

(Where have you been?)	bpy! (r)ny mah	ไปไหนมา
(Where do you come from?)		
	koon! mah (l)jahk (r)ny	คุณมาจากไหน
which (or who, that)	(f)tee	ที่
(which?, in a question)	(r)ny!	ไหน
(which one?)	ahn! (r)ny!	อันไหน
while (during the time)	ka-(l)na! (f)tee	ขณะที่
(for a while)	(f)choo-uh (f)kroo	ชั่วครู่
(in a while, after a while)		
	(l)eek (f)choo-uh (f)kroo	อีกชั่วครู่
whip (to whip, beat, hit)	dtee	ตี
(a whip)	(f)saa	แส้
whiskey	(h)wit!-sa-(f)gee	วิสกี้
	(f)lao!	เหล้า
(Mekong, a popular Thai brand)		
	(f)maa-(r)kohng	แม่โขง
(Kwang Thong, a popular Thai brand)		
	gwahng tawng	กวางทอง
whisper (to whisper)	gra-(h)sip!	กระซิบ

whistle (a whistle, a toy whistle)

                    (h)nohk! (l)weet   นกหวีด

  (to whistle, to blow a whistle)

                    (r)pue (l)bpahk   ผิวปาก

        ("pue" rhymes with "few")

      (the sound of a whistle)

          (r)see-ung (r)pue (l)bpahk   เสียงผิวปาก

  (a steam whistle, train whistle) (l)woot   หวูด

white (white, to be white)   (r)kow   ขาว

         ,,   (r)kow (r)kow   ขาว ๆ

  (the color of white)   (r)see (r)kow   สีขาว

white ant (termite)   (l)bploo-uk   ปลวก

who, whom   kry!   ใคร

  (who, that)   (f)tee   ที่

  (the person who)   (f)poo (f)tee   ผู้ที่

whole (all, entire)   (l)moht!   หมด

  (all of it, the whole lot) (h)tahng! (l)moht!   ทั้งหมด

whose (whose?, in a question) (r)kawng kry!   ของใคร

  (Whose is this?)   (f)nee (r)kawng kry!   นี่ของใคร

  (who, that)   (f)tee   ที่

why (why?, in a question)	tahm! my!	ทำไม
wicker (rattan)	(r)wy	หวาย
wide (to be wide, broad)	(f)gwahng	กว้าง
width	kwahm (f)gwahng	ความกว้าง
wife	pahn!-ra-yah	ภรรยา
	(h)pa-(h)rih!-yah	ภริยา
(colloquial form)	mee-uh	เมีย
(a minor wife)	mee-uh (h)nawy	เมียน้อย
wild (to be wild, savage, untamed)		
	(l)bpah (l)teu-un	ป่าเถื่อน
will (legal document)	pih!-ny!-gahm!	พินัยกรรม
will (or shall, indicating future tense)	(l)ja!	จะ
win (to win, win out, to conquer)	cha-(h)na!	ชนะ
(winner)	(f)poo cha-(h)na!	ผู้ชนะ
(to win in a lottery)		
	(l)took (h)lawt-dtuh-(f)ree	ถูกล็อตเตอรี่
wind (or breeze, air)	lohm!	ลม
(The wind is blowing.)	lohm! (h)paht!	ลมพัด
(to be windy, a strong wind)		
	lohm! (l)jaht!	ลมจัด

(a strong wind)	lohm! raang	ลมแรง
(to wind, wind up, coil up, roll up)		
	(h)moo-un	ม้วน
window	(f)nah-(l)dtahng	หน้าต่าง
(window pane, glass)	gra-(l)johk!	กระจก
windshield	(f)tee gahn! lohm!	ที่กันลม
	gra-(l)johk! (f)nah	กระจกหน้า
wine	(f)lao! ah!-(l)ngoon!	เหล้าองุ่น
wing	(l)bpeek	ปีก
winter	(h)reu!-doo (r)now	ฤดูหนาว
wipe (to wipe, wipe up)	(h)chet!	เช็ด
wire	(f)loo-ut	ลวด
(a piece of wire)	(f)sen! (f)loo-ut	เส้นลวด
(a roll of wire)	(l)koht! (f)loo-ut	ขดลวด
(electric wire)	(f)loo-ut fy! (h)fah	ลวดไฟฟ้า
(electric wire, power line)	(r)sy fy! (h)fah	สายไฟฟ้า
(barbed wire)	(f)loo-ut (r)nahm	ลวดหนาม
wish (to wish, desire, want)	(f)dtawng! gahn	ต้องการ
(to dream of, desire)	(l)bpraht-ta-(r)nah	ปรารถนา
(a wish, desire)	kwahm (l)bpraht-ta-(r)nah	ความปรารถนา

(to wish to, would like to)	(l)yahk (l)ja!	อยากจะ
with	(l)gahp!	กับ
(by, by means of)	doy	โดย
withdraw (to withdraw from an account)		
	(r)tawn	ถอน
,,	(r)tawn ngun!	ถอนเงิน
,,	(l)buk ngun!	เบิกเงิน
without (to be without, to be free from)		
	(l)bpraht-sa-(l)jahk	ปราศจาก
witness (a witness)	pa-yahn	พยาน
woman, women	(f)poo-(r)ying!	ผู้หญิง
	(l)sa-dtree	สตรี
wonderful (to be wonderful, strange, unusual)		
	(l)bplaak bpra-(l)laht	แปลกประหลาด
wood	(h)my	ไม้
woods (or forest, jungle)	(l)bpah	ป่า
wool (lamb's wool)	(r)kohn! (l)gaa!	ขนแกะ
word, words	kahm!	คำ
work (a job, work)	ngahn	งาน
,,	gahn ngahn	การงาน

(to work, to do work)   tahm! ngahn ทำงาน

worker (or workman, laborer) kohn! ngahn คนงาน

workshop (or factory, plant)   rohng ngahn โรงงาน

world (the world, the earth)   (f)lohk โลก

worm   (r)nawn หนอน

  (to be wormy, to have worms)

               bpen! (r)nawn เป็นหนอน

          „   mee (r)nawn มีหนอน

  (earthworm)   (f)syi deu-un ไส้เดือน

worn (to be worn out, of clothing) (l)kaht ขาด

  (to break down, get out of order) (r)see-uh เสีย

  (to become damaged, be defective)

          chahm!-(h)root! ชำรุด

worry (to be worried, concerned about)

         (l)hoo-ung ห่วง

     „ bpen! (l)hoo-ung เป็นห่วง

  (to worry, be depressed) (f)gloom! jy! กลุ้มใจ

worse (to be worse than——)

      leh-oh (l)gwah—— เลวกว่า

  (to get worse, to worsen) leh-oh lohng! เลวลง

289

(worst, to be the worst)

leh-oh (f)tee (l)soot!   เลวที่สุด

worship (to worship)   boo-chah   บูชา

(to respect, revere, believe in)

(h)nahp!-(r)teu   นับถือ

worst (to be the worst) leh-oh (f)tee (l)soot!   เลวที่สุด

worth (or value)   koon! (f)kah   คุณค่า

would like to   (l)yahk   อยาก

(l)yahk (l)ja!   อยากจะ

wound (an injury, wound, to be injured,
wounded)   (l)baht (l)jep!   บาดเจ็บ

(a wound, cut)   (l)baht (r)plaa   บาดแผล

wrap (to wrap, to package)   (l)haw   ห่อ

(to wrap all around)   (l)haw (f)hoom!   ห่อหุ้ม

wreck (to wreck, to smash)   (l)dtaak   แตก

(to break, break apart)   (l)hahk!   หัก

(an auto wreck, collision) (h)roht! chohn!   รถชน

wrench (hand wrench, any kind) goon!-jaa   กุญแจ

(crescent wrench, adjustable wrench)

goon!-jaa (f)leu-un   กุญแจเลื่อน

(open-end wrench) goon!-jaa (l)bpahk dty   กุญแจปากตาย

290

wrestling	moo-ay (f)bplahm!	มวยปล้ำ
wrinkle (to be wrinkled, folded)	(f)yohn!	ย่น
wrist	(f)kaw meu	ข้อมือ
wristwatch	nah-li-gah (f)kaw meu	นาฬิกาข้อมือ
write (to write, draw)	(r)kee-un	เขียน
(to write)	(r)kee-un nahng-(r)seu	เขียนหนังสือ
(a writer)	(h)nahk! (r)kee-un	นักเขียน
wrong (to be wrong, incorrect, to miss)		
	(l)peet!	ผิด
(not correct, not right)	(f)my! (l)took	ไม่ถูก
(Excuse me, I have the wrong number.)		
	(r)kaw (f)toht (h)krahp! (or "ka!")	ขอโทษครับ(คะ)
	(l)dtaw toh-ra-(l)sahp! (l)peet!	ต่อโทรศัพท์ผิด
X-ray	X-ray (same pronunciation)	เอ็กซเรย์
yard (or lawn, field)	sa-(r)nahm	สนาม
(lawn, yard of a house)	sa-(r)nahm (f)yah	สนามหญ้า
(measure, 3 feet)	(r)lah	หลา
yawn (to yawn)	(r)how	หาว
year	bpee	ปี
(yearly, annually)	bpra-jahm! bpee	ประจำปี
„	ry bpee	รายปี

(each year, every year)	(h)took! bpee	ทุกปี
(next year)	bpee (f)nah	ปีหน้า
(New Year)	bpee (l)my!	ปีใหม่
(year, when used with children's age		
below 12-13 years)	(l)koo-up	ขวบ
yell (to yell, shout)	dta-gohn	ตะโกน
yellow (to be yellow)	(r)leu-ung	เหลือง
(the color of yellow)	(r)see (r)leu-ung	สีเหลือง
yes (Yes, Sir.) (spoken by males)	(h)krahp!	ครับ
(spoken by females)	ka!	คะ
(Yes!, to be so, that's it!)	(f)chy!	ใช่
(Yes, correct.)	(f)chy! (h)laa-oh	ใช่แล้ว
yesterday	(f)meu-uh wahn	เมื่อวาน
	(f)meu-uh wahn (h)nee	เมื่อวานนี้
(the day before yesterday)	wahn seun (h)nee	วานซืนนี้
,,	(f)meu-uh wahn seun (h)nee	เมื่อวานซืนนี้
yet (or still)	yahng!	ยัง
(not yet, in answer to a yes-or-no question)		
	yahng!	ยัง
(He hasn't come yet.)	yahng! (f)my! mah	ยังไม่มา
you (polite, informal)	koon!	คุณ

(very respectfully)	(f)tahn	ท่าน
(used by adults when addressing a child)		
	(r)noo	หนู
young (to be young)	(l)awn	อ่อน
(to be young, adolescent, of men and boys)		
	(l)noom!	หนุ่ม
(to be young, adolescent, of women)		
	(r)sow	สาว
your (your **something, something** belonging		
to you) **something**	(r)kawng koon!	——ของคุณ
,, **something**	(r)kawng (f)tahn	——ของท่าน
yours (No direct translation. Translate the		
equivalent : "your **something**" or "belong-		
ing to you.")		
yourself	dtoo-uh (f)tahn eng	ตัวท่านเอง
zero (0)	(r)soon	ศูนย์
zinc (or galvanized iron)	(r)sahng!-ga-(r)see	สังกะสี
zipper	sip!	ซิป
zoo	(r)soo-un (l)saht!	สวนสัตว์

293

APPENDIX

Numbers

0	(r)soon	๐	ศูนย์
1	(l)neung!	๑	หนึ่ง
2	(r)sawng	๒	สอง
	toh (used in telephone numbers)	๒	โท
3	(r)sahm	๓	สาม
4	(l)see	๔	สี่
5	(f)hah	๕	ห้า
6	(l)hohk!	๖	หก
7	(l)jet!	๗	เจ็ด
8	(l)bpaat	๘	แปด
9	(f)gow	๙	เก้า
10	(l)sip!	๑๐	สิบ
11	(l)sip!-eht!	๑๑	สิบเอ็ด
12	(l)sip!-(r)sawng	๑๒	สิบสอง
13	(l)sip!-(r)sahm	๑๓	สิบสาม
14	(l)sip!-(l)see	๑๔	สิบสี่
15	(l)sip!-(f)hah	๑๕	สิบห้า

295

Numbers

16	(l)sip!-(l)hohk!	๑๖	สิบหก
17	(l)sip!-(l)jet!	๑๗	สิบเจ็ด
18	(l)sip!-(l)bpaat	๑๘	สิบแปด
19	(l)sip!-(f)gow	๑๙	สิบเก้า
20	(f)yee-(l)sip!	๒๐	ยี่สิบ

21	(f)yee-(l)sip!-(l)eht!	๒๑	ยี่สิบเอ็ด
	yeep-(l)eht! (colloquial)	๒๑	— —
22	(f)yee-(l)sip!-(r)sawng	๒๒	ยี่สิบสอง
	yeep-(r)sawng (colloquial)	๒๒	— —
etc.			

30	(r)sahm-(l)sip!	๓๐	สามสิบ
40	(l)see-(l)sip!	๔๐	สี่สิบ
50	(f)hah-(l)sip!	๕๐	ห้าสิบ
60	(l)hohk!-(l)sip!	๖๐	หกสิบ
70	(l)jet!-(l)sip!	๗๐	เจ็ดสิบ
80	(l)bpaat-(l)sip!	๘๐	แปดสิบ
90	(f)gow-(l)sip!	๙๐	เก้าสิบ
<u>100</u>	(l)neung! (h)rawy	๑๐๐	หนึ่งร้อย
	(h)rawy (l)neung! (colloquial)	๑๐๐	ร้อยหนึ่ง

296

101	(l)neung! (h)rawy (l)neung!		
	(colloquial)	๑๐๑	หนึ่งร้อยหนึ่ง
	(l)neung! (h)rawy eht!	๑๐๑	หนึ่งร้อยเอ็ด
200	(r)sawng (h)rawy	๒๐๐	สองร้อย
250	(r)sawng (h)rawy (f)hah (l)sip!	๒๕๐	สองร้อยห้าสิบ
1,000	(l)neung! pahn!	๑,๐๐๐	หนึ่งพัน
	pahn! (l)neung! (colloquial)	๑,๐๐๐	พันหนึ่ง
1,100	(l)neung! pahn! (l)neung! (h)rawy		
		๑,๑๐๐	หนึ่งพันหนึ่งร้อย
	pahn! (h)rawy	๑,๑๐๐	พันร้อย
1,500	(l)neung! pahn! (f)hah (h)rawy	๑,๕๐๐	หนึ่งพันห้าร้อย
	pahn! (f)hah (h)rawy	๑,๕๐๐	พันห้าร้อย
	pahn! (f)hah	๑,๕๐๐	พันห้า
10,000	(l)neung! (l)meun	๑๐,๐๐๐	หนึ่งหมื่น
	(l)meun (l)neung! (colloquial)	๑๐,๐๐๐	หมื่นหนึ่ง
15,000	(l)neung! (l)meun (f)hah pahn!	๑๕,๐๐๐	หนึ่งหมื่นห้าพัน
	(l)meun (f)hah	๑๕,๐๐๐	หมื่นห้า
20,000	(r)sawng (l)meun	๒๐,๐๐๐	สองหมื่น
100,000	(l)neung! (r)saan	๑๐๐,๐๐๐	หนึ่งแสน
	(r)saan (l)neung! (colloquial)	๑๐๐,๐๐๐	แสนหนึ่ง

297

Numbers—Telling Time

1,000,000 (1 million)	(l)neung! (b)lahn	๑,๐๐๐,๐๐๐ หนึ่งล้าน
	(h)lahn (l)neung! (colloquial)	๑,๐๐๐,๐๐๐ ล้านหนึ่ง
10 million	(l)sip! (h)lahn	๑๐,๐๐๐,๐๐๐ สิบล้าน
100 million	(h)rawy (h)lahn	๑๐๐,๐๐๐,๐๐๐ ร้อยล้าน
1,000 million (1 billion)	pahn! (h)lahn	๑,๐๐๐,๐๐๐,๐๐๐ พันล้าน

decimal point	(l)joot!	จุด
positive, plus	(l)boo-uk	บวก
negative, minus	(h)lohp!	ลบ
house address: no./no.	**no.** (h)tahp! **no.**	—ทับ—

Telling Time—Colloquial System

HOURS

1 a.m.	dtee (l)neung!	ตีหนึ่ง
2 a.m.	dtee (r)sawng	ตีสอง
3 a.m.	dtee (r)sahm	ตีสาม
4 a.m.	dtee (l)see	ตีสี่
5 a.m.	dtee (f)hah	ตีห้า
6 a.m.	(l)hohk! mohng (h)chow	หกโมงเช้า
,,	(f)yahm! (f)roong!	ย่ำรุ่ง

298

7 a.m.	(l)jet! mohng (h)chow	เจ็ดโมงเช้า
,,	mohng (h)chow	โมงเช้า
8 a.m.	(l)bpaat mohng (h)chow	แปดโมงเช้า
,,	(r)sawng mohng (h)chow	สองโมงเช้า
9 a.m.	(f)gow mohng (h)chow	เก้าโมงเช้า
,,	(r)sahm mohng (h)chow	สามโมงเช้า
10 a.m.	(l)sip! mohng (h)chow	สิบโมงเช้า
,,	(l)see mohng (h)chow	สี่โมงเช้า
11 a.m.	(l)sip! eht! mohng (h)chow	สิบเอ็ดโมงเช้า
,,	(f)hah mohng (h)chow	ห้าโมงเช้า
12 a.m. (noon)	(l)sip! (r)sawng mohng	สิบสองโมง
,,	(f)tee-ung	เที่ยง
1 p.m.	(l)by mohng	บ่ายโมง
2 p.m.	(l)by (r)sawng mohng	บ่ายสองโมง
3 p.m.	(l)by (r)sahm mohng	บ่ายสามโมง
4 p.m.	(l)by (l)see mohng	บ่ายสี่โมง
,,	(l)see mohng yen!	สี่โมงเย็น
5 p.m.	(f)hah mohng	ห้าโมง
,,	(f)hah mohng yen!	ห้าโมงเย็น

Telling Time

6 p.m.	(l)hohk! mohng yen!	หกโมงเย็น
,,	(f)yahm! (f)kahm!	ย่ำค่ำ

7 p.m.	(l)neung! (f)toom!	หนึ่งทุ่ม
,,	(f)toom! (l)neung!	ทุ่มหนึ่ง
,,	(f)toom!	ทุ่ม
8 p.m.	(r)sawng (f)toom!	สองทุ่ม
9 p.m.	(r)sahm (f)toom!	สามทุ่ม
10 p.m.	(l)see (f)toom!	สี่ทุ่ม
11 p.m.	(f)hah (f)toom!	ห้าทุ่ม

12 p.m. (midnight)	(f)tee-ung keun	เที่ยงคืน
,,	(r)sawng yahm	สองยาม

MINUTES — Colloquial or Official System

2 : 05 p.m.	(l)by (r)sawng mohng	บ่ายสองโมง
	(f)hah nah-tee	ห้านาที
2 : 12 p.m.	(l)by (r)sawng mohng	บ่ายสองโมง
	(l)sip! (r)sawng nah-tee	สิบสองนาที
2 : 15 p.m.	(l)by (r)sawng mohng	บ่ายสองโมง
	(l)sip! (f)hah nah-tee	สิบห้านาที

300

2 : 20 p.m.	(l)by (r)sawng mohng	บ่ายสองโมง
	(f)yee (l)sip! nah-tee	ยี่สิบนาที
2 : 30 p.m.	(l)by (r)sawng mohng	บ่ายสองโมง
	(r)sahm (l)sip! nah-tee	สามสิบนาที
	(l)by (r)sawng mohng (f)kreung!	บ่ายสองโมงครึ่ง
2 : 40 p.m.	(l)by (r)sawng mohng	บ่ายสองโมง
	(l)see (l)sip! nah-tee	สี่สิบนาที
	(l)eek (f)yee (l)sip! nah-tee	อีกยี่สิบนาที
	(l)by (r)sahm mohng	บ่ายสามโมง
2 : 45 p.m.	(l)by (r)sawng mohng	บ่ายสองโมง
	(l)see (l)sip! (f)hah nah-tee	สี่สิบห้านาที
	(l)eek (l)sip! (f)hah nah-tee	อีกสิบห้านาที
	(l)by (r)sahm mohng	บ่ายสามโมง
2 : 55 p.m.	(l)by (r)sawng mohng	บ่ายสองโมง
	(f)hah (l)sip! (f)hah nah-tee	ห้าสิบห้านาที
	(l)eek (f)hah nah-tee	อีกห้านาที
	(l)by (r)sahm mohng	บ่ายสามโมง

Telling Time—Months of the Year

Official System

The official system uses the 24-hour clock. The number of hours is followed by "nah-li-gah." Example:

10 a.m. (1000) (l)sip! nah-li-gah   สิบนาฬิกา

10 p.m. (2200) (f)yee (l)sip! (r)sawng nah-li-gah   ยี่สิบสองนาฬิกา

Minutes in the official system are expressed as the number of minutes after the hour, as in the colloquial sytem.

Days of the Week

Monday	wahn! jahn!	วันจันทร์
Tuesday	wahn! ahng!-kahn	วันอังคาร
Wednesday	wahn! (h)poot!	วันพุธ
Thursday	wahn! (h)pa!-(h)reu!-(l)haht!	วันพฤหัส ๆ
Friday	wahn! (l)sook!	วันศุกร์
Saturday	wahn! (r)sow!	วันเสาร์
Sunday	wahn! ah-(h)tit!	วันอาทิตย์

Months of the Year

January	(h)mok!-ga!-rah kohm!	มกราคม
February	goom!-pah pahn!	กุมภาพันธ์

March	mee-nah kohm!	มีนาคม
April	meh-(r)sah yohn!	เมษายน
May	(h)preut!-sa-pah kohm!	พฤษภาคม
June	(h)mit!-too!-nah yohn!	มิถุนายน
July	ga!-(h)rahk!-ga!-dah kohm!	กรกฎาคม
August	(r)sing!-(r)hah kohm!	สิงหาคม
September	gahn!-yah yohn!	กันยายน
October	dtoo!-lah kohm!	ตุลาคม
November	(h)preut!-sa!-(l)jih!-gah yohn!	พฤศจิกายน
December	tahn!-wah kohm!	ธันวาคม

CLASSIFIERS

In the Thai language each noun (that is, a word representing an object, a thing, or a person) can be classified into one or more certain groups or classes of objects having similar characteristics. Each such group is represented by a word called a classifying noun or a **classifier,** which often accompanies the noun whenever the noun is counted, modified, or referred to. The Thai language contains many classifiers; however, some of

303

Classifiers

the most useful and commonly-used classifiers are listed below.   Examples of their use follow.

Kind of objects, or classification	Classifier	
1. person, persons	kohn!	คน
2. animals, fish, insects, tables, chairs, desks, playing cards, cigarettes, shirts, coats, dresses, trousers, parts, letters of the alphabet	dtoo-uh	ตัว
3. automobiles, vehicles other than carts, spoons, forks, umbrellas, things with handles	kahn!	คัน
4. books, carts, candles, knives, axes, pins, needles	(f)lem!	เล่ม
5. houses, mosquito nets	(r)lahng	หลัง
6. buildings	rohng	โรง
7. lumps or cubes of sugar, pieces of charcoal, bricks, cakes of soap, rocks, clouds	(f)gawn	ก้อน
8. pairs of things, shoes, earrings, pairs of animals	(f)koo	คู่

Kind of objects, or classification	Classifier
9. a piece or pieces of anything, pieces of meat, bread, cloth, furniture, bones	(h)chin! ชิ้น
10. suit of clothing, set of furniture, dishes, books, deck of cards, set of plays, games	(h)choot! ชุด
11. documents, letters, newspapers, banknotes, lottery tickets, papers with writing or printing on them	cha-(l)bahp! ฉบับ
12. trees, plants, posts, columns, pillars	(f)dtohn! ต้น
13. round and hollow objects, fruit, eggs, containers, boxes, cups, bags, buckets, tin-cans, leaves, certificates, tickets	by! ใบ
14. thin, flat objects, sheets of paper, boards, phonograph records, plates of glass, slabs of stone, slices of bread, slices of bacon	(l)paan แผ่น

Classifiers

Kind of objects, or classification	Classifier
15. seeds, pills, gems, fruit pits, buttons (h)met!	เม็ด
16. fruit (any kind), mountains, certain round or small objects, balls (f)look	ลูก
17. fruit (any kind) (r)pohn!	ผล
18. loaves of bread 1. bpawn	ปอนด์
2. (r)taa-oh	แถว
19. boats, ships, airplanes, long round objects, bamboo, sugar-cane lahm!	ลำ
20. rope, string or wire strung in the air, kite string, bracelets, necklaces, belts (r)sy	สาย
21. lines, strands of hair, thread, string, ropes, wire (f)sen!	เส้น
22. packages, bundles, things wrapped (l)haw	ห่อ
23. seats, toilet bowls, ashtrays (f)tee	ที่
24. small objects, toothpicks, erasers, fragments, pieces of iron, things in general, a substitute for almost any other classifier. ahn!	อัน

Examples showing use of classifiers.

(Classifier is in bold letters.)

1. two girls (f)poo-(r)ying! (r)sawng **kohn!** ผู้หญิงสองคน
2. this book nahng!-(r)seu (f)**lem!** (h)nee หนังสือเล่มนี้
3. five oranges   (f)sohm! (f)hah **by!** ส้มห้าใบ
                       (f)sohm! (f)hah (f)**look** ส้มห้าลูก
                       (f)sohm! (f)hah (r)**pohn!** ส้มห้าผล
4. one spoon   (h)chawn **kahn!** (l)neung! ช้อนคันหนึ่ง
                (h)chawn **ahn!** (l)neung! ช้อนอันหนึ่ง
5. small dog   (r)mah **dtoo-uh** (h)lek! หมาตัวเล็ก

YES and NO

"Yes-or-no" questions can be answered several ways in Thai, each way depending upon the words used in forming the questions. Outlined below are the most common types of yes-or-no questions followed by the manner in which they may be answered "yes" or "no".

1. *QUESTION*: ____(verb)____ (r)my!

        YES: Repeat the (verb).

         NO: (f)my!____(verb)____

     Example: mee (r)my! (Do you have it?)

        YES: mee   **NO**: (f)my! mee

Yes and No

---

2. *QUESTION*: <u>(adj. or adv.)</u> (r)my!

    YES: Repeat the (adj or adv.)

     NO: (f)my! <u>(adj. or adv.)</u>

  Example: (l)yai! (r)my! (Is it big?)

    YES: (l)yai!   **NO**: (f)my! (l)yai!

---

3. *QUESTION*: bpen! <u>(adj.)</u> (r)my!

    YES: bpen! <u>(adj.)</u> (or) (f)chy!

     NO: (f)my! bpen! <u>(adj.)</u> (or) (f)my (f)chy!

  Example: bpen! (h)by! (r)my! (Is he deaf?)

    YES: bpen! (h)by!   (or) (f)chy! (or) bpen!

     NO: (f)my! bpen! (h)by! (or) (f)my! (f)chy!
               (r)my! bpen!

---

4. *QUESTION*: _____(r)reu

    YES: Answer same as with 1., 2., and 3. above.

     NO: ,,   ,,   ,,

---

5. *QUESTION*: <u>(verb) or (adj., adv.)</u> (r)reu (l)bplao

    YES: Repeat the (verb) or (adj., adv.)

     NO: (l)bplao

  Example: koon! (l)ja! bpy! (r)reu (l)bplao

        (Are you going to go or not?)

    YES: bpy!   **NO**: (l)bplao

---

6. *QUESTION*: _____(verb)_____ (r)reu yahng
   YES : Repeat the (verb) (or) (verb) (h)laa-oh
   NO : yahng (or) yahng (f)my! (verb)
   Example : (r)kow mah (r)reu yahng
   (Has he come yet?)
   YES : mah (h)laa-oh   **NO** : yahng (f)my! mah

7. *QUESTION*: _____(statement)_____ (f)chy! (r)my!
   YES : (f)chy!   **NO** : (f)my! chy!
   Example : bpy! tahng (h)nee (f)chy! (r)my!
   (Go this way, is that right?)
   YES : (f)chy!   **NO** : (f)my! chy!

8. *Questions of the type* : " _____(r)my!" or " _____(r)reu"
   can also be answered simply by YES—
   by men   : "(h)krahp!"
   by women : "ka!"
   particularly if the question is leading to a "yes" answer.
   Example : koon! (yoo) (h)bahn (h)nee (r)reu
   (You live in this house?)
   Answer : (h)krahp!
   (Yes, I do.)
   The words "(h)krahp!" and "ka!" mean "Yes, sir (ma'am)"
   or "Yes, sir (ma'am), I understand."

───────

309

NOTES

NOTES

NOTES

NOTES

NOTES

NOTES

NOTES

NOTES

PHONETIC SYSTEM

Consonant	*Examples of Phonetic Sound*
b	as in "ball"
bp	no English equivalent; a hard sound similar to both b and p
ch	as in "child"
d	as in "dare"
dt	no English equivalent; a hard sound similar to both d and t
f	as in "fool"
g	as in "go", **NOT** as in "gentle"
h	as in "hit"
j	as in "jump"
k	as in "kit"
l	as in "late"
m	as in "mother"
n	as in "not"

Consonant	Examples of Phonetic Sound
ng	as in "ring", but also used at the beginning of words and syllables
p	as in "pot"
r	as in "red" (but often mispronounced as "l")
s	as in "set"
t	as in "tell"
w	as in "well"
y	as in "yell" when at the beginning of a syllable, or as in "my" when at the end

Vowel (single)	Examples of Phonetic Sound
a, ah	a as in father ("–a" is equal to "–ah!")
aa	a as in cat, sad, man
ai, I, y	y as in my, or ie as in pie
ao, ow	ow as in cow
aw	aw as in paw, saw

Vowel (single)	*Examples of Phonetic Sound*
awy	—**awi**— as in drawing
e, eh	e as in bed, pet ("e" is equal to "eh!")
ee	ee as in bleed
eu	no English equivalent, similar to the English "oo" in "good"
i, ih	i as in tip, with ("i" is equal to "ih!")
I, ai, y	same as I or eye
o, oh	o as in bone, same as oh ("—o" is equal to "—oh!")
oo	oo as in food, cool
ooy	—**oo ea**— as in too easy
ow, ao	ow as in cow
oy	oy as in boy, toy
u, uh	u as in drum, but ("u" is equal to "uh!")
ue	ue as in hue, cue; or ew as in few
y, I, ai	y as in my

Vowel (double) *Examples of Phonetic Sound*
  (diphthong)

  aa-oh phonetic "aa" + "oh"

  ee-oh —eo as in Reo, or —io as in Rio de Janiero

  ee-uh, ee-u— —ia as in India

  eh-oh phonetic "eh" + "oh"

  eu-ay phonetic "eu" + "ay" as in day

  eu-uh, eu-u— phonetic "eu" + "uh"

  oo-ay —o way as in two way

  oo-uh, oo-u -o u- as in two up

  uh-ee phonetic "uh" + "ee"

Symbols

  (l) low tone

  (h) high tone

  (r) rising tone

  (f) falling tone

  Hyphen (-) separates syllables within a word

  Exclamation mark (!) Pronounce syllable quickly.

  n. noun

  v. verb